"Claudyne Wilder is one of the finest presenters in the business. This is an excellent book—read it!"

Dorothy Jongeward, Co-author of Born To Win

"An important book for anyone who requires effective communication for success. As a clinical psychologist, I'm enthusiastic about beginning to apply these clear and precise presentation skills with clients and professional colleagues."

Marion London, Ed.D., Psychologist, Southeastern Counseling Associates

"Studded with nuggets of wisdom drawn from her rich background, Wilder's book transcends the ordinarily limited terrain of presentation skills."

Linda Peterson, Lotus Development Corporation

"Claudyne Wilder has written an outstanding primer for giving presentations. This entertaining book is very well organized and easy to use. Moreover, the author's advice is excellent—the sound, seasoned counsel of someone who *knows* what she is talking about. Anyone using this book is sure to profit from it. This book has already earned a permanent place near my desk—I'm certain I'll be referring to it years from now before I make that next important presentation."

Bill Hodgetts, Fidelity Investments

"A great guide for beginners or old pros: comprehensive, clear, creative, and very useful. It is rich with ideas on how to communicate effectively in all kinds of situations."

Stuart Langton, Ph.D., President, Stuart Langton & Associates, Development Services

"A practical book for a practical art. Wilder's step-by-step approach will help anyone with an idea to sell."

Michael L. Woodnick, Northeastern University

"Whether you make presentations to one person or to thousands, *The Presentations Kit* is a most comprehensive, crisply rendered, and accessible handbook you will find invaluable in maximizing your effectiveness."

Chris Roden, Certified Financial Planner

"As business becomes more service-oriented and technology decentralizes decision-making down the management ladder, effective communication and presentation become more crucial to your success. Wilder's *The Presentations Kit* gives you the tools you need to succeed—and a good read, too!"

Joanna Tamer, CEO, S.O.S., Inc.

"This book has good ideas and suggestions for anyone who wants to improve the ability to provide information."

Windsor H. Hunter, Founder, Teradyne Connection Systems, Inc.

"Well organized, rich in content—something for anybody who has to make speeches or presentations."

Walter Wells, Manager of Corporate Training & Development, The Gillette Company

"Claudyne Wilder has done a first-rate job of providing a solid conceptual framework and a treasury of practical suggestions for making effective presentations."

Peter G. Smith, Vice President & Director, Communications & Entertainment, Canadian Imperial Bank of Commerce

"I thought there was nothing left to say about presentation skills; Claudyne Wilder has written an imaginative and refreshing book on the subject. Her style is energetic, and her message offers creative approaches even the seasoned presenter will appreciate.

Judith Cassel, Motivation Speaker & Seminar Leader

"This book, in my judgment, is a valuable tool in mastering the art of persuasion whether you are presenting before a trial judge, a panel of appellate judges, or even an insurance adjuster."

Stanley E. Sacks, Attorney, Sacks & Sacks

"This book is a must for every outplacement counselor and job seeker. Networking and interviewing steps and hints are in every section of this valuable and practical presentation kit."

Beverly H. Robsham, Robsham & Associates

"This book is destined to become the 'Presenters Bible.' It has it all! Every supervisor in our organization must have a copy."

D'amian & Bridget Rose, Matol Botanical Field Advisory Supervisors

"I have found Ms. Wilder's book to be invaluable in helping me to prepare for presentations. Her use of visuals combined with her no-nonsense approach has made her book an easy-to-use management tool."

Nancy Vescuso, Vice President, Systems Engineering, Inc.

"An excellent tool for improving one's abilities in making presentations. It is practical and insightful, and the methods described are easy to implement."

Nelly Sepulveda Rathmill, National Sales Director, Princess House Inc.
(A Colgate-Palmolive Company)

"This book contains a wealth of information for the reader. Claudyne Wilder has produced an excellent resource for anyone who gives presentations."

Kenneth R. Robinson, HRD/OD Consultant, Digital Equipment Corporation

"The only way to learn to make effective presentations is to practice making effective presentations. Claudyne Wilder's book holds your hand through the process and gives you the support you need to train yourself to be effective."

Bill Barnes, Vice President of Human Resources, Interleaf

"This book is rich with wisdom, humor, and unforgettable techniques to provide a fresh way of thinking about giving presentations."

Cynthia Hargrove, Training Specialist, Management Consulting Service,
United Way of Massachusetts Bay

"Claudyne Wilder demystifies the presentation skill learning process. Her approach is flexible, fun, and effective—as a presentation should be."

Tan D. Nguyen, IBM Corporation

"A most thorough and thoughtful work on the subject of communicating ideas and presenting—filled with common sense and practical ideas."

Martin R. Strasmore, Senior Consultant, Robert H. Schaffer & Associates

THE
PRESENTATIONS
KIT

THE PRESENTATIONS KIT

10 Steps for Selling Your Ideas

Revised and Updated Edition

Claudyne Wilder

JOHN WILEY & SONS, INC.
New York • Chichester • Brisbane • Toronto • Singapore

Copyright © 1994 by Claudyne Wilder.
Published by John Wiley & Sons, Inc.

Excerpt from *The King and I,* page 8, © 1951 by Richard Rodgers
and Oscar Hammerstein II. Copyright renewed. Williamson Music Co., owner of
publication and allied rights throughout the world. Used by permission. All
rights reserved. Excerpt from *Negotiate to Close* on p. 233 by Gary Karrass,
copyright 1985, Fireside Books, St. Louis, MO, used with permission. Excerpt
from *My Voice Will Go with You,* p. 249, by Milton Erickson, copyright 1982,
W. W. Norton, New York, used with permission.

Library of Congress Cataloging-in-Publication Data:

ISBN 0-471-31092-1 (cloth)
ISBN 0-471-31089-1 (paperback)

Printed in the United States of America

10 9 8 7 6 5 4 3 2 1

To Tad Jankowski—To him I give the first dance, the last dance, and all the dances in between.

To my delightful mother, who read this manuscript and made excellent suggestions.

And to all of you who, when presenting, want to increase the likelihood of having your recommendations accepted and implemented.

TO THE READER

ABOUT YOU

You present your ideas and recommendations in many different settings. For instance, you present at work, at home, in civic organizations, and at committee meetings. Whatever the setting, you want to be heard; you want to feel confident. But most of all, you want people to accept your ideas and follow your recommendations. The American Management Association surveyed 2,800 executives with the question, What is the number one need for success in business today? The overwhelming response: *To persuade others of your value and the value of your ideas.*

I have written this book not only for the businessperson, but also for a more general audience that includes everyone from teenagers, who want to convince their parents they've earned an allowance increase, to presidents of companies, who must persuade a questioning and cautious board of directors to increase the operating budget. This book will help you to focus on your unique qualities and strengths and to use them in making effective and convincing presentations.

ABOUT YOUR LISTENERS

People listen with 25 percent efficiency. Information usually needs to be sent three times to people in order to be received and processed, because people distort 40 to 60 percent of what they hear. Few people have taken training in learning to listen effectively. Moreover, people react in different ways to the manner in which presentations are made; some people prefer to listen to facts while others need to see visual representations.

In view of this complex reality of how people listen, what can you do to "present" so your listeners are motivated to pay attention, to remember what you said, and to carry out your recommended actions? This book, with its focus on formats and modality preferences, will give you an effective framework in which to address and solve those issues.

Your Concerns Questionnaire

Following are some of the most common concerns people have when asked to speak. Rate your concerns.

> 1 = Not a Concern
> 2 = Slightly Concerned
> 3 = Concerned
> 4 = Very Concerned
> 5 = Extremely Concerned

_____ Step 1   I look and sound as if I am nervous; I want to feel more in charge.

_____ Step 2   My objective is unclear and vague; I do not have a format to fit my objective.

_____ Step 3   I am and/or act disorganized.

_____ Step 4   My visuals are mediocre; they do not enhance my talk.

_____ Step 5   My delivery and speaking ability are just passable; I want to look and sound more enthusiastic and confident.

_____ Step 6   I do not know how to keep the group's interest.

_____ Step 7   I do not conclude with conviction and excitement.

_____ Step 8   I do not know how to answer difficult questions.

_____ Step 9   My recommendations are not presented with enough organization and conviction.

_____ Step 10   Something vital is missing when I talk.

_____ Total

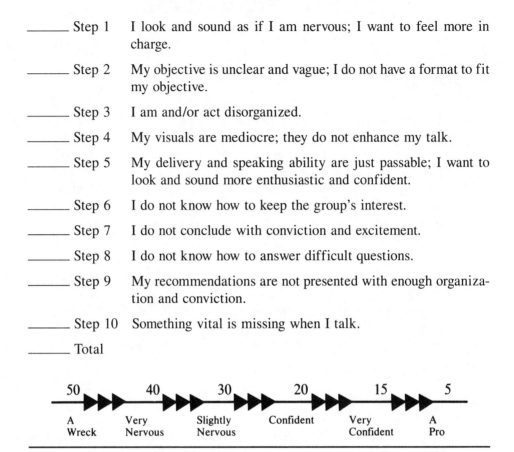

Look at the steps you rated as "Extremely Concerned." Read the corresponding steps in this book thoroughly. If you do not have time to read the whole text now, read only those steps of most immediate concern to you.

ACKNOWLEDGMENTS

I want to thank the following people for their information about presenting in other cultures: Paul Fahey, Yuri Kovalenko, Noriko Czaplicka, K. A. Maimani, and Rosa Barreiro. These companies have given me additional insight into the needs of the business presenters, and I thank them for their ongoing support: Gillette, Millipore, Banyan Systems, United Health Plans, Arbella Insurance, New England Deaconess Hospital, Interleaf, Polaroid, Aids Action Committee, United Way, Berlex Canada, Codex, Johnson & Johnson, and many others as well.

I thank my agent Michael Snell for his due diligence work and good humor.

These people added comments and suggestions for this revision, and I thank them for their time: Cindy Mills, Peter Lawson, Diane Chen, Elizabeth Brazell, Ron Foster, Ernie Pedersen, Phil Kay, Robert Levenson, and Ivelisse Rodriguez.

Tad Jankowski read and reread every page of this revision and offered excellent ideas. His ability to "keep at the task" helped me.

And thanks finally to my editor, John Mahaney.

CLAUDYNE WILDER

Jamaica Plain, Massachusetts
May 1994

The Presenter's Creed

Oh, mystery of life, keep me from the fatal habit of thinking my presentations are so important to the world that I make myself too nervous to captivate and convince my listeners.

Make me disciplined enough to define only one objective before I do anything else, and to use a format that encourages my listeners to want to follow what I am saying.

Give me the organizational ability to put everything together so that I do not run around like a person with no head a few hours before my talk.

Let me create relevant and entertaining visuals, then use those visuals with style and flair.

Energize my physical, emotional, and mental states so that I present with vitality and sparkle.

Teach me to pay attention to my listeners so, if they do not understand, I stop and explain, and if they need a break, I can accommodate them rather than make them sit for another hour.

Shut me up soon enough so I conclude with flair rather than out of desperation.

Let me answer the questions with zest and interest no matter how repetitive or hostile I perceive them to be.

Inspire me to do what I sometimes consider impossible: Make enthusiastic and motivating talks so people take action on my next steps.

And finally, after all this work and preparation, give *me* the courage to let myself shine through amidst all the data and recommendations.

CONTENTS

THE
PRESENTATIONS
KIT

STEP 1
CHANNELING YOUR NERVOUSNESS: INTROVERT AND EXTROVERT

KEY POINTS

1   Visualize giving a fantastic, motivating talk.

2   Sleep well so you feel refreshed and full of life for the presentation.

3   Make sure you are fully prepared.

4   Say positive comments to yourself before you start to present.

5   Breathe by pushing your stomach in and out.

6   Engage in enjoyable conversations before you start to present.

7   Greet your audience as they enter the room.

8   Pause as you talk so you can relax and take a breath.

9   Look at people and notice they are listening to you.

10   Know that no matter how nervous you feel, your listeners probably don't notice.

Robert Frost said, "The brain is a wonderful organ. It starts when you get up in the morning and does not stop until you get to work." Some people who present, however, would say, "No, mine only stops when I am asked to speak in meetings." If you are one of those presenters, Step 1 will help you. There are at least 10 myths that—if you believe them—will limit your ability to present with style and organization:

Myth 1. Good speakers are born, not made. I was not born a good speaker, so I am a hopeless case.
Reality. Good speakers take more time preparing and practicing than ineffective speakers.

Myth 2. I failed the first time I spoke in front of people, so I will fail from now on.
Reality. Many successes start with a failure. Thomas Watson, the president and founder of IBM says, "In order to succeed, double your failure rate."

Myth 3. If I just follow exactly what someone says and does, I will be as effective as that person.
Reality. Other people's styles are extremely useful as models but, in the end, you must present the way that feels and is most comfortable and effective for you.

Myth 4. People who speak and look confident are not nervous inside.
Reality. Most speakers experience some type of nervous energy that they accept and acknowledge and then use to energize themselves.

Myth 5. People who speak well in meetings have an innate talent for giving impromptu talks.
Reality. Impromptu speakers prepare as much as possible and use some type of structured format even when talking off-the-cuff.

Myth 6. Everyone has to love me and my talk or I am a failure.
Reality. It does not matter if everyone loves you or even likes you. Someone can dislike you or your talk but agree to do your next steps.

Myth 7. Every presentation I do must be perfect.
Reality. The talented speaker always knows something will go wrong and just continues anyway.

Myth 8. I am too old and set in my ways to learn.
Reality. You are never too old or too young to learn, as long as you have an open attitude and willingness to apply yourself.

Myth 9. I do not have enough chance to practice, so I will never feel confident.
Reality. If you really want to practice your presentation skills, you can find many situations.

Myth 10. Before I get up to talk, I feel physiological reactions—my heart beats faster and my breathing gets quicker. Those sensations mean fear.

Reality. The physiological reactions signal that you are energizing yourself (these are typical of Olympic athletes before they compete). They are normal, and you can draw on them to energize you, not to immobilize you.

The preceding myths hinder many people from taking the simple steps needed to reduce debilitating anxiety. How do you now take care of your presentation anxiety? What specific techniques can you use? You will be creating your own personal repertoire of anxiety-reducing techniques and behaviors.

Three essential points deserve to be mentioned first; (1) know your preferences toward introversion or extroversion, (2) have a positive attitude, and (3) pay attention to your breathing.

THE INTROVERT AND THE EXTROVERT: YOUR PREFERENCES

Most people are inclined toward being either more extroverted or more introverted. As you read this section and begin to understand your preferences, you will know how to care for yourself before, during, and after a presentation. The preferences detailed in the following lists are taken from the Myers-Briggs Inventory (MBTI). The MBTI is used in many Fortune 500 firms and government agencies. It is frequently used during team-building sessions as it provides a nonjudgmental framework for people to understand their differences and similarities. The inventory has four sets of preferences; usually a person fits into one of the 16 combinations. The MBTI is an excellent vehicle to help people understand why certain ways of being, doing, and thinking come easily for them while other ways take effort. This book discusses only one set of preferences: introversion and extroversion. For more information, see the References at the end of this book.

Identify Your Preferences

To begin identifying your preferences, complete the following questionnaires. There are no wrong or right answers. What matters is that you discover how you prefer to function in the world. Once you have a clearer sense of yourself, you will know better how to prepare yourself for those impromptu or planned talks.

Introversion

Check any of the following items that describe your way of being.

☐   1. Depending on the day, I may or may not say "hello" to a person I see on the street or in the hallway.

☐   2. When I am tired, being alone is rejuvenating to me.

☐　3. I enjoy doing written work more than giving oral presentations.

☐　4. I have a small number of carefully selected friends.

☐　5. I need my own space and privacy (that is, having a place of my own to work).

☐　6. People sometimes say that I am reserved and a bit difficult to get to know.

☐　7. I feel uneasy with spontaneous questioning.

☐　8. I enjoy the mental activity of formulating new plans and ideas.

☐　9. I like to reflect and consider all sides of an issue before acting.

☐　10. I like to work alone or with one person.

☐　11. I keep my emotions to myself.

☐　12. I prefer small group sit-down presentations over formal stand-up presentations.

☐　13. I like to pause and mentally consider an issue before talking.

☐　14. I like to work on one project for a long time.

☐　15. I dislike interruptions.

Extroversion

Check any of the following items that describe your way of being.

☐　1. I like varied and action-oriented work.

☐　2. When tired, I energize myself by interacting with people.

☐　3. I share my personal experiences.

☐　4. I am good at noticing people's responses.

☐　5. I do not mind interruptions.

☐　6. I usually greet people and say hello.

☐　7. I enjoy spending time, at least half the day, communicating with others and discussing issues.

☐　8. I express my emotions.

☐　9. I am easily distracted by the environment around me.

☐　10. I see myself as friendly, talkative, and easy to meet.

☐　11. Whenever possible, I choose to work with others.

☐　12. I like to see and talk about how other people do a task.

☐ 13. Most weekends I enjoy socializing.

☐ 14. I act quickly, sometimes without first reflecting.

☐ 15. I like to discuss ideas with people before I have thought them out in my mind.

Total Introversion Score _____   Total Extroversion Score _____

From your scores, is it obvious which way you prefer? Or do you belong somewhere between the two types?

Understand Your Preferences

An extrovert's essential stimulation is from the environment—the outer world of people and things. An introvert's essential stimulation is from within—the inner world of thoughts and reflections. Extroverts enjoy being salespeople, receptionists, politicians, and insurance agents. Introverts enjoy being electrical engineers, librarians, artists, attorneys, and computer programmers. Both forms of stimulation are used by everyone, yet most people gravitate toward one over the other. For example, an introverted manager would prefer to sit in her office and work in peace and quiet. She has learned to spend time with her staff, even though that is not her natural tendency. On the other hand, extroverted managers have to force themselves to stay in their offices to think and plan.

You may be one of those people who tends to be in between these two behavioral types. One day you say hello to someone, and the next day you walk across the street to avoid the person. One day you answer your phone all day, and the next day you refuse to do so. When you feel an almost desperate need for peace and quiet, you have temporarily "burned out" your extroverted tendencies.

Both extroverts and introverts do talk to others and can present ideas and suggestions with style and flair. Having extroverted tendencies does not necessarily mean that people are naturally good presenters. It does mean that they may be more at ease with 30 people watching and listening to them, whereas introverts may be more at ease with smaller presentations of three or four people. Persons with each preference do have habitual tendencies that help or hinder their presentation skills. How does each of these preferences manifest itself in a presenter?

Introvert Preferences.   If you lean more toward the introverted preferences, along with about 25 percent of the population, you must take good care of yourself before you speak. Here is what good care might mean for you. You need enough time alone to feel internally relaxed. You must believe you know your material and can answer any questions. You need to feel your talk is organized enough so that you can pay attention to your listeners. Finally, you must keep in mind that, after you are done, you can go home and have some space and privacy. If you do not find enough space for yourself at home, you can always feel comfort in knowing that you can stop your car for 15 minutes on the way home, just to be by yourself. This time alone is crucial for you as an introvert. If you conclude your presentation with feelings that you have been imprisoned, you have not taken good enough care of yourself. By having enough time alone, you will discover that you do a much more effective job creating an atmosphere for people to want to accept your next steps.

As an introvert, you like to dream things up, but actual implementation of those things is not of as much interest to you. Read Step 9 of this book for help with implementation. Step 2, on logical action formats, will give you structures in which to put your creative futuristic ideas. Since you want people to become motivated and help you carry out your ideas, do present a plan focused on action. Do not speak softly; speak loudly and project your voice to the back corners of the room. Be careful! You believe in the value of conciseness. You think words are precision instruments and sometimes struggle to find just the correct word. Avoid taxing people's patience as you stand there searching for the best word. That type of precision is not always necessary.

Extrovert Preferences.   If you are extroverted, along with about 75 percent of the population, you need to make certain you have spent enough time with people so you can feel energized and alive. When preparing, you have a tendency to do the research, gather all the details, and *then,* after all that work, create an outline. This way of putting together a presentation takes longer, since you may not have needed to collect all those materials. Organize your talk in a manner that lets you interact with the group. When presenting, be careful that you do not become distracted from your main objective. Discipline yourself to stay on the points. Do not succumb to an easy and seductive detour, which you enjoy. You also have a tendency to think out loud before your group. Remember that you probably were not asked to present because you are good at thinking out loud. You are there to communicate what you were supposed to have already thought about and organized *before* this time.

As an extrovert, you feel more at ease knowing that there will be support for your next steps. Be sure you have done your homework before you make your recommendations. Discussing the issues with participants prior to your talk will help you sort out the ramifications of your proposed next steps. Since your enthusiasm can sometimes overpower people, use it, but not with such intensity that people feel overwhelmed.

Balance Yourself

Now that you know your tendencies, you have just begun. Your presentation problems frequently do not stem from your preference, but more from not using the presentation strengths of the other preference. If you are an extrovert, you will forget to do what introverts do and vice versa. Here are four examples to give you an idea on how to use behaviors from your less-used preference.

INTROVERSION SITUATIONS

Jim dislikes and is uneasy with spontaneous questioning.

Idea. He writes out and practices responses to potential questions. He asks the listeners to write down their questions so he can answer them during the question-and-answer time.

Debbie feels uneasy not knowing her listeners.

Idea. She can greet people as they enter. If that is not possible, she can ask questions by a show of hands to assess people's interests and expectations.

EXTROVERSION SITUATIONS

Suzanne talks without reflection and sounds disorganized.

Idea. She needs more preparation. She can use a format in "Step 2, Defining Your Objective." Once she has the format, she should then take time to reflect on her talk.

Joe is easily distracted from his central points.

Idea. He can ask the listeners to hold their questions and objections to the end of his talk. Or, he can answer questions between each of his major points.

By having a clearer, more concise understanding of your personal preference, you can channel your energy into taking care of yourself. Use the characteristics of the other preference to enhance your repertoire of presentation behaviors. Understanding more about yourself and others helps you to get better and better as a communicator.

YOUR ATTITUDE

> Keep in mind always the present you are constructing.
> It should be the future you want.
>
> Ola
> Alice Walker, *The Temple of My Familiar*

The comments you make to yourself about a situation determine your attitude toward it. Consider those comments your beliefs. A positive attitude is fueled by beliefs that empower you. What are your beliefs about the people listening to you? The following statements need to be incorporated into your belief system:

- People want me to act and sound at ease so they will feel comfortable.

- People usually cannot tell if I am nervous.

- People want and/or need to learn what I am saying.

- As I begin, people will give me the benefit of the doubt.

Think back to the last time you had to sit and listen to a presenter who was obviously very nervous. How did you feel and what did you do? You probably did not know whether to look at the person as if he or she were doing an effective job or to look away. You felt awkward and found it difficult to concentrate. Even if you, as the presenter, feel nervous, do your participants a favor and act in a confident manner. Consider the lines from a song from *The King and I,* by Richard Rodgers and Oscar Hammerstein II: "Whenever I feel afraid, I hold my head erect and whistle a happy tune, so no one will suspect I'm afraid. . . . The result of this deception is very strange to tell, for when I fool the people I fear, I fool myself as well."

Attend a presentation program that includes making more than one videotape of you speaking. After seeing yourself on videotape, you will probably comment, "I did not sound or look as nervous as I felt." (This knowledge alone is worth the whole workshop.) Remember, you will almost never appear and sound as nervous to your listeners as you feel inside yourself.

Each time you present, you will become stronger and more confident. Helen Keller wrote, "Security is mostly a superstition. It does not exist in nature, nor do the children of men as a whole experience it. Avoiding danger is no safer in the long run than outright exposure. Life is either a daring adventure, or nothing." Be daring with yourself and enlarge your abilities and competencies. You cannot have a strong stomach by doing one sit-up a month, nor can you become a more confident presenter by practicing only once a month.

You will find that many people want to and/or need to know what you have to say. Particularly, as you begin, they will listen to you with respect because they hope that others will listen to them with similar respect. This is a fundamental form of communication courtesy. They will give you the opportunity to speak and share your points. Keep telling yourself, "These people need to hear what I am saying. I will make this talk as useful and interesting as possible."

BREATHE

Runners stretch before running. The batter swinging the bat in the on-deck circle is preparing for a turn at bat. Trapeze artists always stretch before a show, for once they are swinging on the bar it is too late to warm up. Athletes who forgo a warm-up period are more likely to suffer injuries when performing. You, as a presenter, must warm up by breathing.

There are many breathing exercises you can learn. The following is one of the easiest to practice:

Consciously push your stomach in and out. Feel your stomach going in and out, using your hand to be sure it is moving. This will make you breathe from the diaphragm, for as the stomach moves, the lungs fill. You can inhale through your nose and exhale through your mouth. Practice so you can breathe this way without being obvious. As you fill your lungs with air, your body will begin to calm down and your voice will reflect that inner calmness.

For those of you who want to refine your ability to breathe with greater ease, here are some guidelines from *Unlimited Power* by Anthony Robbins (New York: Ballantine, 1986):

> Let me share with you the most-effective way to breathe in order to cleanse your system. You should breathe in this ratio: inhale one count, hold four counts, exhale two counts. If you inhaled for four seconds, you would hold for 16 and exhale for eight. Why exhale for twice as long as you inhale? That's when you eliminate toxins via your lymphatic system. Why hold four times as long? That's how you can fully oxygenate the blood and activate your lymphatic system. . . . So here's the first key to healthy living. Stop and take 10 deep breaths, in the above ratio, at least three times a day. . . . See what numbers you can build up to by slowly developing greater lung capacity.

Try these breathing techniques, see which one feels best, and then use it on a regular basis. You will find that, if you use your technique before you speak, you will communicate in a forceful manner and be able to take charge of your presentations no matter what the circumstances.

Manage Your Nervousness

> There is perhaps nothing so bad and so dangerous in life as fear.
>
> Jawaharlal Nehru

When you practice the following hints, you will discover an inwardly focused energy giving you the ability to be in charge of yourself. Reading these hints is a beginning (about 10 percent of the task). To improve your confidence, you must do them (about 90 percent of the task).

In the Days before You Present

- Plan.
- Assess your participants.
- Make a logistics checklist.
- Practice! Practice! Practice!
- Prepare ahead.
- Visualize for success.
- Sleep well.
- Study successful presentations.
- Know the size of the group.
- Know where you are going.

- Practice desensitization.
- Find mentors.

On the Day of Your Presentation

- Check room and equipment.
- Anticipate negativity.
- Give yourself positive comments.
- Exercise.
- Have a small meal.

Just before You Present

- Practice relaxation exercises.
- Engage in enjoyable discussion.
- Greet people.
- Start on time.
- Eliminate physical barriers.
- Know people's names.
- Check your pockets and clothes.
- Go off by yourself.
- Verify time scheduled for your presentation.
- Find your adrenalin.

During Your Presentation

- Establish voice and eye contact with everyone.
- Pause to breathe.
- Trust your intuitive feelings.
- Speak through mental blanks.
- Take a sip of water.
- Have something familiar with you.
- Pay attention to your body.
- Look at people's body language.
- Keep your wits about you.

- End early.

- State the obvious.

- Smile, if appropriate.

IN THE DAYS BEFORE YOU PRESENT

> Nothing in life is to be feared. It is only to be understood.
>
> Marie Curie

Plan

How do you act before a trip? How well do you plan? Some people become very energetic before traveling. They hurry around organizing everything, making lists, and planning, planning, planning. Once they are on their way, they are relaxed and confident, since they have done everything possible to make the trip enjoyable for themselves and for anyone else traveling with them.

Other people prepare in a disorganized fashion and, after beginning the journey, feel a vague sense of anxiety, wondering if they may have forgotten something vital. Many times they discover that they *have* forgotten something vital.

For those of you who find yourselves very anxious for days before a talk, practice living this philosophy, as stated by Charlie Brown in the comic strip "Peanuts": "I have developed a new philosophy. . . . I only dread one day at a time." Try planning without dread. The dread comes from thinking that you should be planning while day after day you do nothing. Your anxiety mounts, and you worry since you have not yet written down the format for your talk. When you actually pick a format for your talk and start filling it in, your anxiety diminishes. In fact, at that point you may regret that you do not have more time, since you may begin to enjoy the planning. When you plan with enough time to digest your talk, you will do a better job, feel more relaxed, and experience less dread.

Systematic planning gives you time to make your revisions *before* your talk, not during it.

Assess Your Participants

Whenever possible, find out who will be attending your presentation. In Step 2, you will find a participant assessment list. If at the beginning of your presentation you do not know the participants or their reasons for attendance, ask for a show of hands. For example, ask, "How many are here to learn about the new computer system?" or "How many of you are technical computer specialists?" As you ask for a show of hands, raise your hand, which encourages others to do the same. Depending on the group size, you will now have a sense of each of your listeners. The better you "know" the person, the more opportunity you have of tailoring your talk to him or her.

Make a Logistics Checklist

Make a checklist and go over it thoroughly, or be sure the person in charge of logistics uses this checklist. If you are doing a presentation for the first time, ask an experienced presenter to double-check your list of equipment, supplies, and handouts. Checklists are included in Step 4.

Practice! Practice! Practice!

Imagine that you have decided to do a 15-mile race walk. You have never walked more than a couple of miles and that was a few months ago. The race walk is in three months. Many of your friends plan to participate and have asked you to join them. If you have any respect for your body, what will you do for the next three months? Yes, naturally, you will practice. You will start with a few miles, then gradually build up your stamina and leg strength. Now imagine that you have been asked to do a presentation in three weeks. How much practice will you do before the actual day of your presentation? You need to practice just as you would do for the race walk. Practice builds confidence. Without practice, you are bound to be nervous and less confident, and you might not achieve your objective.

Prepare Ahead

Remember this time-honored principle: Anything that could go wrong will go wrong, and no doubt, some things you would never have dreamed about will also occur.

This principle especially holds true when you need to get things done quickly. If you wait until the last minute to get those slides done, you may find the print shop machine has broken down and your slides will be unavailable. One manager waited until the day of her presentation to obtain final approval from her superior. Much to her dismay, the superior made some important major changes. Two hours before her presentation, she was in a total state of panic, redoing many of her overheads. A company lawyer attended a top-level management meeting where he was asked a question he should have been able to answer. Prior to the meeting, he had seen the agenda. Just ten minutes of preparation would have helped him sound as though he was on top of the issue.

Visualize for Success

One of John's first presentations was almost a disaster. His facts turned out to be outdated, he stuttered, he ran overtime, and the bulb on the overhead projector burned out. Now every time John has to present, he breaks out in a cold sweat. He reruns in his mind's eye that terrible day and scares himself into thinking he will experience all those feelings and that failure again. John is practicing the art of visualization, only he is visualizing a past failure rather than a future success. He needs to train himself to imagine the successful presentation he is about to give. As Sumner M. Redstone, Chairman of Viacom, said, "Real success is built on catastrophe." John has experienced the catastrophe, and now he needs to use that experience to get "unstuck" and go on with his life. Here is a process of visualization for success that John can practice:

> He answers these questions: "How do I want people to view me?" "What do I want people to say about my presentation?" "How do I want to look?" When John has ideas about how he wants to appear and what he wants to say, he is ready to visualize himself giving the talk. He sits down in a quiet room and runs through his presentation in his mind's eye. Essentially, he is creating a movie of the talk he will give. He can start the movie as he gets up to talk or start it days before, visualizing the preparation work as well.

If John still vividly reruns that "failure of a talk" during his visualization, he must change it. He can see a picture of that past day, then blur it or make it smaller. One person put a big furry dog in the picture, which causes him to smile when he sees himself back in that unpleasant situation. If John "feels" the unpleasant situation, he must find a way to interrupt those feelings. He looks anywhere but on the ground. He walks around and looks at the sky. If John hears his shaky voice inside his head, he changes it. He may hear a favorite song instead. He tells himself that the shaky voice was a radio station that has gone out of business. These are all ways to end those failure reruns in yourself and to start visualizing yourself as effectively communicating with others and convincing them of your next steps.

Who uses visualization? Actors and actresses, professional presenters, and athletes incorporate visualization into their training. World-famous skiers only have a few precious practice runs before they do a specific course. After those runs, they rehearse the track course about a hundred times in their mind. As they rehearse, they concentrate on the twists and turns and the difficult jumps. They visualize themselves going across the finish line and pouring on the energy toward the finish. Do the same. As you run through your talk in your mind, visualize those transitions from one point to another. Particularly focus on seeing yourself ending your talk full of energy.

Sleep Well

If you have trouble sleeping, here are some suggestions: (1) Take a nice warm bath before you go to bed; (2) find yourself a 10- to 15-minute meditation tape, and listen to it when you are in bed; (3) drink a warm glass of milk or take a natural remedy that will calm you down and allow you to sleep; (4) play some relaxing music; (5) exercise early in the evening so you are physically tired and want to lie down and sleep; (6) find someone to give you a nice, relaxing massage; (7) do yoga stretches before going to bed. I do not recommend drinking alcoholic beverages; many people find they do not wake refreshed, but groggy, lazy, and with a hazy mind.

Remember, you must sleep well for at least two nights. If you are awake until the early morning hours and have to present in two days, you may be in for a shock when you awake the day of your presentation and feel very tired. For some people, the full impact of a "late nighter" is not fully felt until two days later. Plan your schedule so that you know you will have energy. Be aware that the more presentations and talks you give in a row, the more you will need to be sure to sleep well between each one.

How to Have a Restful Sleep the Night before Your Presentation

The following relaxation exercise will take you about 10 minutes, depending how quickly or slowly you breathe:

1. Lie down in bed and put your hands behind your head. Place your thumbs on the indentation in the middle of the back of your neck (the occiput).

2. Start breathing in from your stomach. Feel your breath go from your stomach thru your diaphragm, then your lower rib cage and finally into your chest. Breathe out in reverse order: from your chest to lower rib cage to diaphragm to stomach. Do this five times.

3. Then put your left hand over the middle of your forehead and your right hand over your throat. Breathe five times.

4. Keep your left hand in the middle of your forehead and move your right hand to the middle of your chest. Breathe five times.

5. Keep your left hand in the middle of your forehead and move your right hand over your navel. Breathe five times.

6. Continue keeping your left hand in the middle of your forehead and move your right hand over your pubic bone. Breathe five times.

7. Now put your left hand on your pubic bone and your right hand on your coccyx, which is the spot at the bottom of your spine opposite your pubic bone. Breathe five times.

8. Put your arms by your sides and breathe five times.

Adapted from material by Loretta Levitz, Ayurvedic Practitioner, Boston.

Study Successful Presentations

A woman learned that her no-nonsense "time is money" sales presentation style just did not go over in her new department. They felt more comfortable with less structure, more feeling comments, and a relaxed "we have all the time in the world" approach. Even though she did not feel as productive, she modified her behavior to gain acceptance with the group.

Study the acceptable successful presentations in your setting. Watch those people who get good reviews. Watch people who are asked questions in your meetings. They are often the ones who have learned how to speak and share information in a way that is congruent with the organization's culture. Step 2 provides you with an example of an organizational assessment form.

Know the Size of the Group

Some people are nervous when speaking to a group of four or five of their colleagues. These people usually feel more relaxed talking to a hundred strangers. When speakers know the size of the group ahead of time, they can prepare themselves psychologically and determine the right visuals for that size group. If you have 10 people, you might use different visuals than if you have 100 people. You can also prepare more or less handouts depending on the size of the group. Making 10 copies on the morning of your talk might seem feasible for a group of 8 people. Making them for 200 people will be overwhelming.

Know Where You Are Going

Some of you have had the experience of being lost in a big building and not finding the conference room or of driving around and around and not finding the building. Getting lost is truly one of the most senseless ways to panic yourself. Have directions that you can follow and use. In fact, have a backup plan in case the directions prove to be inaccurate. For example, when going to a totally new place, carry a map and have a phone number to call.

Practice Desensitization

Desensitization is a technique used by people to overcome fears such as the fear of flying in airplanes or the fear of swimming. Following is a brief explanation of the desensitization process. If you feel your fears of speaking are especially strong, go to the bookstore and find a book on phobias that explains this process in detail.

Sit in your favorite chair and think about preparing for a presentation. If you feel your heart starting to pound, take a breath. If the breath is not enough to calm you, do not imagine yourself presenting. Stop for a moment. When you get over feeling nervous about imagining your preparation, go on to imagining yourself the day of your talk. If that feels too overwhelming, imagine yourself a week before the talk. By now you are probably getting the idea of how this works. When you start to feel nervous, back up a step, take a deep breath, and relax. Then go forward. Gradually, as you imagine getting closer to doing the presentation, you will find that your fear has shrunk and that the thought of giving a presentation does not immobilize your ability to prepare for it. Finally, you will be able to imagine yourself presenting with enthusiasm.

Find Mentors

A coach can make all the difference in the world to how a player plays. Steve Allen says about a coach he had in school, "I've had good luck. Good fortune is an accident. I had a high school teacher, Marguerite Byrne, who encouraged me to enter an essay contest that I won. She looked at my work, she smiled at me, and she said I was very good. She gave me friendly attention. A little kindness means a lot. . . . Kindness, you know, has a ripple effect."

With a mentor, you are asking for advice from someone you respect and trust. You may just need a word of encouragement about your talk or you may want someone to coach you on the two presentation elements you need: organization and style. When approaching someone, ask the person for specific help such as, "Will you look over my outline?" or "Will you listen to my talk and tell me what to continue, start, or stop doing?" Request that the listener fill out an evaluation sheet. When and if the person does critique you, accept the criticism. Do not be defensive or you will not receive another critique.

ON THE DAY OF YOUR PRESENTATION

Check Room and Equipment

Be sure you check all the equipment; try it. Avoid embarrassment. Test the equipment so you know *that* it works and *how* it works. A specific piece of equipment may look the same as the other types you have used, but it may be different. It is better to check it out before you are in front of people! Check the equipment each time. Within an organization, you never know what may have broken on a machine since you last used it. One man says he can never figure out how a videocassette recorder can break between the evening and the morning, but it seems to happen. He now checks the machine at 8:00 A.M., even if he had checked it at midnight the night before.

Ask about the heating system, and know who can adjust it should the room become too cold or too hot. Ask if any construction is going on in the area. One woman tried to give a talk to a group of senior managers while the room next door was being remodeled. Do not try competing with a power saw; you will lose. Then there is the doctor who, while he was explaining a new procedure to his staff, was constantly interrupted by the hospital's blaring page system. Consequently, he lost his train of thought, and the staff had trouble following his explanation. Even being able to turn down the intercom would have helped. No one knew if that was possible, let alone how to do it.

Nowadays, many presenters use very complicated high-technology equipment. If you are using new equipment, do two things: (1) Practice using it many times until you are comfortable and (2) have an equipment expert in the room with you to help fix any problems that may occur as you present. If the expert cannot stay in the room, know how to call for quick help. Almost nothing makes a presenter more nervous than to have equipment break and not be knowledgeable enough to fix it.

With technology, you prepare for the worst scenario of none of it working, make a backup plan, and know you could calmly and confidently carry out this plan with your audience watching.

Be sure to reconfirm your room reservation at least once. Make sure your participants know where the room is located and how to get there. Some buildings are so large that people can wander around for a half hour and never find the designated location. If that could happen to your participants, now is the time to mark a path to the room.

You or someone at your meeting should be able to answer the following questions (see detailed checklists in Step 4):

- Where are the light switches, and can the lights be dimmed?

- Is there a thermostat for the temperature and instructions on how to operate it?

- Where can people put their coats?

- Where are the restrooms?

- What phones can people use?

- Can the intercom be turned off or down?

- Where can people get coffee and tea?

- Will there be a meeting in the next room?

Anticipate Negativity

Do you feel your boss will disagree with everything you say? Are you afraid you will gauge your presentation over the heads of the nontechnical people? Before you present, sit down, face your fears, and make contingency plans in case the worst does occur. Better yet, take preventive actions before your presentation. For example, one manager, being afraid that no one would agree with her proposal, spent time with key managers. She discussed a number of the major decisions that she would ask them to make at the end of her talk. She knew, even before beginning her budget request, that five key managers out of seven were in favor of her request. Consequently, she was more able to enjoy the process of presenting her proposal, responding to questions, and asking for approval of her budget.

The more prepared you are, the easier time you will have in adapting to unforeseen circumstances. Remember that your listeners take their lead from you. If you act upset, then your listeners will feel upset. If you act confidently, then they will share in your confidence.

Give Yourself Positive Comments

How far and fast do you think a runner would go if she said the following comments to herself just before and during a race? "I can't finish the race. I am not as good an athlete as the person in front of me. I am tired. My legs are in lousy shape. I should have drunk more water." Some presenters say these same types of negative comments to themselves. They say things to themselves such as, "I do not know enough about this subject. I wish it were over now. I move my hands too much. I feel so nervous." Negative thinking is like a weed that grows and grows when unchecked. You must nip it in the bud. You do not need this dialogue in your head. Some people find it helpful to yell *stop* (in their mind). Those negative thoughts will actually stop. Other people drown out the negative thoughts by positive affirmations (which you will read about shortly).

Karl Wallenda, the famous high-wire aerialist, fell to his death in 1978. He had walked the tightrope for years. His wife said that, for three months prior to the fatal performance, Wallenda had thought of nothing but falling, an event that had never before been in his thoughts. Something changed in his attitude. It was as if he was just waiting for the moment when he was to make a mistake. In his case, it was a life-and-death mistake. Fortunately for most presenters, their life is not on the line when they present, although you would believe it was so by the way some of them look and sound. Remember, you are not on a high wire!

Consider your mind as a partner. Now I ask you, if you had the opportunity, would you hire your mind as a partner? Would you go into business with your mind? Guess what? You *are* in business with your mind, and you, for better or worse, cannot fire it. It is there to stay. You can teach it to stop attacking you and to become your best friend, or you can let yourself be food for your own school of mind sharks. It is your choice.

Think about the comments you say to yourself either before or during a talk. Practice saying these positive comments (also called affirmations). Select three or four that seem appropriate for you. Say them over and over to yourself. If you do not find any from the following list that you want to use, make up your own:

- I clearly communicate my recommendations.

- I am well organized. People are able to understand and absorb the information I present.

- I speak confidently and enthusiastically.

- I have excellent examples to share.

- I know there will be a difference when my listeners implement my idea or buy my product.

- Each time I present I know better how to convince others.

- I have an enthusiastic voice.

- I have skills and information others want and need to learn.

- When I make a suggestion in a meeting, I present in a systematic manner.

- I can be visible. People want to see me.

Exercise

Exercise can have such a calming effect. A playwright makes sure she swims on the days that she presents her plays to a new theater group. A salesperson on the road always walks five miles before seeing one particular customer. A social worker goes dancing the night before she must present her cases. An AIDS speaker always does his yoga before he gives talks to groups of 50 or more. All of these people have found ways to channel their nervous energy. They receive two benefits from regular aerobic exercise; their bodies become healthier, and they redirect nervous energy before a presentation.

Have a Small Meal

If you want to feel energetic when presenting, do not eat big meals that day. Perhaps the following scenario has happened to you. You are the first speaker after lunch. You eat a lunch consisting of chicken with cream sauce, a baked potato with sour cream, and a piece of apple pie. You not only have to keep yourself energetic, but you also have to fight off the intense desire to take a nap. Just imagine how the people sitting must feel if you feel that way and you are standing up.

Preparation

Woodrow Wilson was once asked how long he took to prepare a 10-minute speech. He said: "Two weeks." "How long for an hour speech?" "One week." "And how long for a two-hour speech?" "I am ready now."

Woodrow Wilson

It takes three weeks to deliver a good ad lib speech.

Mark Twain

I should never have made my success in life if I had not bestowed upon the least thing I have ever undertaken the same attention and care I have bestowed upon the greatest.

Charles Dickens

Get the facts, or the facts will get you.

Thomas Fuller

I am prepared for the worst but hope for the best.

Benjamin Disraeli

Practice is the best of all instructors.

Publius Ovidus (43 B.C.–A.D. 17)

Be careful. Carbonated beverages make you belch. This is not such a pleasant experience if you are standing in front of people. You can camouflage a yawn, but a belch has a nasty habit of escaping. Save the carbonated drinks for after your talk.

JUST BEFORE YOU PRESENT

Practice Relaxation Exercises

Some people work themselves into a frenzy before their presentation. For example, Mary, a nurse, is the fifth person to present on the program. She sits quietly all day and watches others. Her nervous energy increases. By the time she is ready to speak, she has ruined her blouse with perspiration. Her voice cracks and her hands shake. Through a series of countdown exercises and relaxation techniques, Mary can learn to sit in the conference room and practice relaxing while she listens to the other speakers. As a result she will be able to sound calm and collected as she begins her talk. Following are three different relaxation possibilities.

Scanning Your Body: Do Alone or with People

- Sit with your feet flat on the floor and legs straight. Relax your body. Put your hand over your diaphragm (if you can do this without being noticed), exhale, and empty your stomach and chest of air to the count of eight. Then breathe in for eight counts. Do this five or six times, and you will feel yourself relax.

- Now systematically scan through each of your body parts. Start at your feet and say slowly to yourself, "I relax my left foot, my right foot, my left ankle, my right ankle, my left calf, my right calf," and so on. By the time you finish scanning through your body, you will feel calm and centered.

Relaxation Countdown: Do Alone or with People

- Breathe out with a sign of relief when you shift to abdominal breathing. Take another deep breath and in your mind's eye, watch the breath fill your lungs completely, from bottom to top. As you breathe out, silently say "ten," letting go of tension as if it were a wave moving from your head, down your body, and out the soles of your feet. Imagine the feeling of letting go.

- On the next breath, repeat the images, saying "nine" on the out breath. Continue backward all the way down to one. If you lose count, do not worry. Pick up wherever you think you were.

- As you practice this technique, two or three breaths will leave you as relaxed as a full ten breaths (from *Minding the Body, Mending the Mind* by Joan Borysenko [New York: Bantam, 1988]).

Body Movement Exercises: Do Alone for Two to Five Minutes

It is difficult to sound enthusiastic if your body feels like dead weight. Doing the body movement exercises in a closed office or in the restroom (if you have no other place to go) will get your system going and your adrenalin moving so you feel energized. Never underestimate the importance of taking four minutes to get the energy moving throughout your body with the following exercises:

- *Head.* Gently roll your head from side to side and rub the back of your neck.

- *Shoulders.* Lift them up and down and roll them around.

- *Arms.* Swing them in a circular motion.

- *Torso.* Move your torso in a circular motion.

- *Legs.* Lift each leg off the ground and move it in a circular motion.

- *Whole body.* Move yourself in any way that will feel good.

Engage in Enjoyable Discussion

Here is a wonderful secret to relax. Before presenting, chat with someone who has traveled where you have been or has enjoyed activities you like. Calm yourself down by reminiscing about beautiful Hawaiian sandy beaches or quiet walks in the forest.

You will discover that your body naturally releases unnecessary tension when you discuss or think about some lovely experiences. If the situation does not permit a discussion with someone, sit and remember those places. Experience the happy, calming feelings that come with your good memories.

Greet People

Do not be aloof and act the way you think a great speaker (whatever that means to you) would behave. Be genuine when you greet people. If you have too large a group to be able to speak with individuals, you may want to begin by greeting the group as a whole or by saying hello to specific divisions within the group. For example, you could say, "I appreciate that you salespeople have taken the time to attend. I will be as brief and to the point as possible."

Start on Time

Organizations have different standards for being on time. I know two organizations whose meetings always begin 10 minutes after the announced time of the meeting. This is their way of being on time, and people who arrive after that are late. Consequently, when working in this organization, I always start at 10 past the hour, saying, "Well, now it is time to start. Anyone who comes after this is late." People laugh and nod their heads, realizing that I understand some things about the organization's culture. However, you had better be there and be ready to go at the scheduled time, even though you will not start for 5 or 10 minutes.

Eliminate Physical Barriers

To establish rapport and to feel connected to your group, try not to use lecterns or large tables that stand between you and the group. This makes you feel more "on the spot" and sets up a physical barrier between you and your group. If you do use a table, walk away from it occasionally. For example, Joe felt he needed his notes as he explained details. When he gave examples or analogies, however, he did not need his notes, so he could walk away from the table where they lay. Speakers who use podiums often walk around the stage when they tell stories. They only move back to the podium to see their next point.

Know People's Names

Do you forget a person's name as soon as you hear it? If so, how often, as soon as you meet the person, do you consciously repeat *out loud* that individual's name? You will have a better chance of remembering the name when you repeat it out loud. Here is the way to do it: "Sue, I want you to meet Charlene." Sue then says *out loud,* "I am glad to meet you, Charlene."

Another technique is to obtain a list of the participants a few days before your meeting. Say those names out loud. When you meet the people, you can more easily match the name with the face. When meeting people, some speakers make a mental note such as, "Charlene looks like my aunt," or "John reminds me of a writer I know." Finally, some people do well as long as they have really looked at the person. In their mind's eye they see Charlene as the one with black glasses or Sarah as the woman with red hair.

Whenever possible, have participants place name cards in front of themselves. I ask them to write their names on both sides of the card. If the cards get turned around, the participants and I can still see the person's name. You can also supply them with stick-on-tags. The stick-on tags are helpful because you can still see people's names during a break. Do not use pin-on tags since they leave holes in clothing. Supply magic markers so people can write their names large and dark enough for you and everyone else to read.

Find methods that work for you and use them.

Check Your Pockets and Clothes

A presenter had an interesting nervous gesture that would not have been noticed except for the change in his pocket. Every few seconds, he would slap his arm against his side and his change and keys would jingle. People became distracted by the noise. Another presenter had slips of paper falling out of his pocket. Checking your clothes means being sure that you are all dressed, buttons and zippers closed, collar down, and so on. Some mornings do not lend themselves to this careful scrutinization. Take some time anyway; better to correct something before than in the middle of your talk. You will feel more at ease knowing you look totally presentable.

Go Off by Yourself

Some people need time alone. If you are that kind of a person, do take the time. You will be amazed at what just 10 minutes alone can do for your mental and physical state. When you are driving, arrive 15 minutes early, sit in your car, and do some breathing by making your stomach go in and out. Compose yourself. There is always a way to find a few minutes for yourself, even if you have to hide out in the restroom.

Verify Time Scheduled for Your Presentation

Theoretically, people in a meeting situation have all agreed to attend and know the amount of time involved. That is the theory. In practice, you may need to confirm the ending time with all involved. You might say, "It is my understanding that I have 20 minutes to talk. Is that correct?" State this so you know how much time you really have.

Find Your Adrenalin

You need a certain amount of adrenalin so you can communicate with conviction. Be glad when you feel that adrenalin. It makes you sound motivated and eager to share your information. If you do not feel that way, do something about it. One presenter was tired, yet had to give a talk to two departments of about 40 people each. Before her talk, she walked briskly five times around the block and then felt ready. She certainly did not feel like walking around the block, but she did it anyway! Do whatever it takes to get yourself going. Here is what some people say about adrenalin before a presentation or performance:

> Advertising executive Roger Myers said, "If anxiety is there, I respond to it. If it isn't, I create it."

> Elizabeth Cady Stanton, at the first women's rights convention in Seneca Falls, New York, said, "I should feel exceedingly diffident to appear before you at this time, having never before spoken in public, were I not nerved by a sense of right and duty. . . ."

Stanton's adrenalin came from a sense of purpose and calling. We do not all get a chance to make historic talks, so we must summon up that energy in whatever way works for us. While the best way is to become excited about the material you will present, other ways may include taking a walk, talking to oneself or others, or eating energizing food.

DURING YOUR PRESENTATION

Rarely will you look and sound as nervous as you feel!

Establish Voice and Eye Contact with Everyone

When you really look around at people, you will feel calmer. Make friendly eye contact with everyone. People do like to be recognized and will react favorably. Remember, most of these people are glad that *you* are up there and that they are not (see Step 5 for information on eye contact).

Pause to Breathe

Pause at the end of your sentences. Do not say "ahh," or "umm," as a transition to the next sentence. Silence is much better. To remind yourself to pause and breathe, write a *P* in your notes or insert a symbol you will recognize. One person made herself a picture of someone with a hand up as if to say "halt." This reminded her to pause.

Someday you will have to present in an emotionally laden situation, be it in a work or a personal crisis. You will be glad you have practiced the skill of pausing to breathe. It will come in very handy. When my father died, I decided to speak at his memorial service, which was an emotionally charged experience. I managed to speak with humor and seriousness due to my ability to pause and take a breath whenever I felt that I was about to cry and to be unable to continue. I would stop, breathe, and then go on. I had learned this skill over time, and it was such a gift to be able to use it during those moments at the service.

Trust Your Intuitive Feelings

Do not be a victim of your own organization. "Good instincts usually tell you what to do long before your head has figured it out," says Michael Burke. You may have a very organized presentation, yet part way through you feel a need to change the order or to delete certain information. Do it. Trust your intuitive feelings. Do not get into the frame of mind, "I did all this preparation, and now the participants have to listen to me no matter what they do or do not already know." The better prepared you are, the easier time you will have of reorganizing all that preparation.

Speak through Mental Blanks

If you forget your next point, keep talking. As you speak, find your way back to your next point. No one has a script for your talk. No one will yell out that you

just lost your place and how dare you do that. Those thoughts are only in your mind. Out loud you can say, "Let me look at my notes and see where I want to go next." Or, you can take a sip of water and give yourself a moment to look down at your notes to see what is next or what makes sense to say next. If you are really brave you can ask your listeners, "Where was I?" (*Caution:* If you have written your notes too small or if they are disorganized, you will not be able to find your place. Your notes should be legible. You do not want to admit that you cannot read what you wrote.)

Take a Sip of Water

I am sure you have noticed that ever-present glass of water. It is there for many purposes. Water will keep your mouth moist. Stopping to drink will make you pause between sentences. Some people speak and act like nonstop express trains, others know enough to be the local line—stopping at appropriate points. If you are the "express train" type of speaker who talks faster and faster as you present, write on your notes, "Take a sip of water," or pencil in the abbreviation "H_2O." A sip of water will slow you down. It is not enough to tell yourself that you will remember to take a sip of water. You must write this on your notes. Sipping water is also useful if you feel like crying or yawning, and such behavior is inappropriate. Do not cry or yawn. Take a drink of water.

Have Something Familiar with You

To feel more at ease, you may want to have a familiar pen, your special clipboard, or some other favorite object with you. Think of how Johnny Carson always had his special coffee cup and pencil with him on his show. Carry your own herbal tea bags so that you can feel comfortable and nourished drinking a familiar beverage. One salesman carries his own magic markers to use during his presentations. Another woman takes a particular notepad when she goes into other people's offices.

Pay Attention to Your Body

Your Internal State.   Unless someone is monitoring you with an "emotional X-ray machine," you can look, act, and sound confident no matter how fast your heart beats or how cold your hands become. Be secretive, and keep your nervousness to yourself.

REMEMBER -- NO ONE IS X-RAYING YOUR STOMACH OR
MONITORING YOUR HEARTBEAT

Your Feet.   Notice your feet and what they are doing. Are you letting them support you? Can you feel them on the floor? Do you feel solid on them? When standing, some people cross their feet at their ankles. No wonder they feel nervous and unbalanced. They are no longer standing on two feet.

Red Face.   Some people break out with red spots on their face or neck. If you are one of these, a way to lessen or stop this is to practice the following suggestion: Pay attention to your feet. When your face turns red, all the energy is going up toward your face. At this point it is not helpful to say to yourself, "Oh, no, I am turning red again. This always happens." In doing this, you create a self-fulfilling prophecy. Instead, begin to move the energy in your body away from your face. Say such phrases to yourself as, "My feet are planted firmly on the ground. I send energy down my body and into the floor. I imagine two poles coming out of each of my feet and holding me firmly in the ground." All these phrases are ways to learn how to send your energy down instead of up. Rehearse these phrases so that, when you begin to speak, it will be natural for you to focus on your feet. One woman decided to focus on her hands instead of her feet. She said that she used to give piano recitals and never blushed, perhaps because all that nervous energy went into her hands. She reported success as she learned to see her excess energy no longer moving to her face, but going out her hands.

Your Shoulders.   If your shoulders tend to move up toward your ears, imagine wearing a big heavy arctic jacket on them. The jacket keeps your shoulders down.

Some people also practice pushing down on their lateral back muscles. (These are the muscles in your upper back.)

Cold or Shaky Hands.   When you find that your hands are cold, clammy, or shaky and you have to shake someone's hand very soon, be glad you are wearing a jacket with pockets. Use the pockets to warm, dry, or calm your hands. If you must hold a piece of paper in your hand and your hand shakes, put the paper on a clipboard. Then hold the clipboard. Your hand will shake less as you hold something heavy in it. You can also make a fist, then relax your hand. This will relax your hand and stop it from shaking.

Perspiration.   If you perspire noticeably, here are a few suggestions. Wear clothes that make it difficult to see any excess perspiration. Wear underarm pads if you have a real need. Find the coolest place, and stand there before your talk. Keep a tissue or handkerchief with you in case you need it for your face. If possible, exercise on the day of your talk; do some relaxation exercises to calm and balance yourself.

Dry Mouth.   If you find that your mouth has become quite dry, you can subtly chew on your tongue to produce some saliva. Just take a few bites and you will be lubricated. Better to always have a glass of water handy, but when desperate, chewing on your tongue does work.

Look at People's Body Language

Many books have been written about the importance of analyzing other people's body language. Take this information with a grain of salt. Someone sitting there with arms folded may just be cold, have a stomachache, or find that it is the only way to be comfortable in the chair. Do not let yourself be intimidated. Also, body language may mean something else in a different culture. The American nod for yes may mean no in another culture, for example, in India, people rock their heads just a little down to signify yes. Do not try to second-guess someone's body language, then allow yourself to feel uneasy as a result of your analysis. The final verdict of people's response to your presentation comes when each person agrees to your next steps.

This does not mean that body language is unimportant. We can all feel when an audience is bored or hostile. Use body language information as a guide in modifying your presentation, but use it with discrimination. You are at an advantage when you know some of the people in your group and how they typically act when agreeing or disagreeing with a recommendation. Use their body cues as information to change and modify your speech.

Some nervous presenters really do act as if their audience is pursuing them with daggers. This is definitely not true! Whether there are five listeners or a hundred listeners, they are only people. Most are interested in what you have to say, and most do hope that you are a lively and informative speaker. Remember, they came because they want or need to know what you have to say.

Keep Your Wits about You

The Interrupters.   Some speakers feel concerned about interrupters. "What can I do if someone keeps interrupting me? I just go to pieces," said one presenter. After the second interruption, say something like, "Excuse me, your comments are helpful but I have only a limited amount of time. Will you please wait until I am done?" If you still want to encourage questions add, "I will answer key questions as I talk, but that is about all the time we have." If the person starts to interrupt again, interrupt him or her and say, "Can you ask your question quickly please? We can spend time talking after this meeting," or "I am sure many people have opinions they would like to state now, but we do not have time. That is just the way it is today." Say these things graciously before you feel upset. Do not wait until your voice tone is edgy and you feel emotionally out of control.

The Goof.   When you do or say something that is not too dignified, such as misspell a word, say a word incorrectly, or actually trip over your feet, just go on with your presentation. Do not giggle or say, "Oops, I goofed!" One mistake is enough, so keep your dignity and go on. People forgive your mistakes more easily than your ineptness with long-winded apologies.

How do you keep your wits about you? Breathe deeply and, while breathing, consider your options; then speak. Look forward to being as poised as John Anderson, a presidential candidate who had an egg thrown at him. Anderson responded by saying, "Well, now that we've had breakfast . . ."

End Early

This technique has its foundations in grade school, when the teacher, to be appreciated, let the students out of class 5 minutes before the bell. It works brilliantly with adults as well. Finish your talk 5 minutes ahead of schedule. People appreciate this, and you will have a few more people positively disposed toward carrying out your recommended next steps. Know your ability to plan time. An architect who does 3-hour presentations never budgeted time correctly. She would consistently run 20 to 30 minutes late. Now she always tells herself that she will end a half hour before the stated ending time. As a result, she ends on time.

One way to really have everyone appreciate you *before* you even begin is to tell them you will end 5 to 30 minutes early. Try it. People smile, relax, and mumble comments to themselves such as, "Great, I have so much to do." (What some are really saying is that they want to go home early!)

State the Obvious

A well-respected man was speaking. Due to a physical handicap, he had trouble turning the pages of his speech. So he said just that—"I am having a bit of difficulty turning the pages." His comment relaxed the audience, and he appeared in charge of the situation.

Dare to say what is true, and do not ignore the obvious. For example, if you see a slide with incorrect numbers, say, "This slide is wrong." Take off the slide, then say, "Let me tell you the correct numbers." You will relax yourself and put the listeners at ease by communicating honestly. Following are some other comments you may need to say:

- "It seems as if you all need a 2-minute stretch before I continue with point 2."

- "I am a bit nervous about sharing my latest data with you due to the next steps it demands we take."

Smile, If Appropriate

Some books tell presenters to smile at everyone before starting a talk. This is great advice if you feel you can smile and look positive. If you feel too nervous at the beginning, then do not force yourself to smile. Also avoid smiling if it would

make you look insincere and phony. Women who try to force a smile may give a cute little-girl smile. Men, on the other hand, are less likely to attempt a weak smile. After a few moments into your talk, you will be able to relax and smile naturally.

Some presentation topics do not lend themselves to a smile. If you have to present a plan to lay off employees, or to convince others of your need for a larger budget when budget cuts are rampant, or to confront a difficult objection to your proposal, a smile is inappropriate. In *Speaking Up: A Book for Every Woman Who Wants to Speak Effectively* (New York: McGraw-Hill, 1977), the authors make these observations about women:

> If you make your argument while beaming at your opponent you neutralize it. When you know what you have to say isn't popular and put on a big apologetic smile you convey ambivalence, appeasement. Far worse than the apologetic smile is the mirthless sound that punctuates many women's talk. It isn't really giggling or laughing although it sounds vaguely like it. It is an apology; an apology for speaking and an apology for existing.

What they are saying—which applies to men as well—is that you must consciously choose when and how to smile.

Feel Good about Your Presentation

Here are some ways presenters have told me that they get themselves in a great mood in order to present:

I meditate.

I listen to humor tapes in the car. I find these especially useful when I feel worried or hassled. I forget my troubles.

I visualize a receptive, open audience. I imagine them nodding their heads as I talk and agreeing with what I am saying.

I picture myself wrapping up the presentation with everyone looking pleased. I imagine how good I will feel inside knowing that the preparation was worth the results.

I always have to exercise. That calms me down.

I do some voice exercises. These get my voice going.

I always arrive early enough to be sure the room is set up exactly as I want it. I always plan in my mind that I will have to rearrange it. That way I don't get upset when at least half the time I do have to rearrange it.

I tell myself not to take myself so seriously. I remind myself that I am a speck of dust in the universe—and that is an exaggeration even.

STEP 2 DEFINING YOUR OBJECTIVE: TEN FORMATS

KEY POINTS

1   Write down in one sentence your objective for the talk.

2   Consider the cultural backgrounds of your audience members.

3   Learn about your audience.

4   Find out about the cultures of the organizations from which participants come.

5   Call some of your audience members before you talk.

6   Tailor your talk to the specific audience needs.

7   Pick a format to use or customize your own.

8   Add unique examples and anecdotes.

9   Include the costs if they are relevant.

10   Be sure to have a visual that shows the agenda for your presentation.

THE TEN FORMATS

One secret to convincing people to act on your recommendations is to use the appropriate format; this takes you 50 percent of the way. The format has the power to lead you as well as your audience. It also has the internal structure to save you time. Remember when you learned to type instead of write? Remember when you learned to drive to the store instead of walk? In both cases, you learned a skill and saved some time. When you become proficient at using these formats, you will save yourself time and irritation. You will eliminate the unnecessary so as to concentrate on only the essential.

You will learn 10 specific formats to use when gathering, organizing, and presenting information. A format will "sculpt" your talk. Some of you will pick one of these formats and follow it just as it is. Others will tailor the formats to suit a particular need. Abraham Maslow said, "When the only tool you have is a hammer, you tend to treat everything like a nail." The 10 formats in Step 2 will give you other tools besides just a hammer.

Formats help you gather and organize your materials and present your materials to your participants. Formats help you gather your materials so that you will be able to save important time. By using a format, you will have a plan *before* you start researching and gathering information. They help you organize your materials so you can separate your "musts" from your "wants." Decide what absolutely must be included in your talk, then consider what else you want to include. Budget your preparation time accordingly. Finally, formats help you present materials to your participants in a particular logical order. This order keeps you on track and makes it easy for your listeners to follow your train of thought.

You choose a destination before beginning your vacation; do the same before giving your presentation. If you pride yourself on effective time and work management, always begin your presentation planning process by writing down a clearly defined objective! This advice seems elementary until you listen to many presentations and attempt to ascertain their objectives. Next time you present, ask your listeners to note what they consider your talk's major objective. You may be surprised at what they suggest.

A defined objective has the following benefits:

- Saves you time.

- Helps you to organize quickly.

- Makes you stop and plan before you start doing.

- Focuses and narrows your research so that you do not digress.

- Provides criteria for choosing your materials.

- Gives you a way to get going and to avoid procrastinating.

- Makes you sound credible and organized when presenting.

- Enables you to be more in charge of the information.

- Limits your audience since you can select the participants most appropriate for the subject matter.

- Gives you a way to measure the success of your presentation in analyzing how well you achieved your objective.

Defining an objective is one of the most important things you will do in connection with your presentation. To go about setting your objective, answer these questions: Who asked me to speak? Was I given the objective by someone else? What next steps do I want my listeners to take? Does one of these 10 objectives fit my talk?

1. *Identify the Problem.*   Discover the real problem amidst many issues.

2. *Present Strategy Recommendations.*   Decide on the best strategies.

3. *Sell a Product, Service, or Idea.*   Sell people on the benefits, to them or their group, of an idea, service, or product.

4. *Recommend Decision Alternatives.*   Present the best possible solution from among several alternatives.

5. *Identify Potential Problems.*   Identify some potential problems and suggest preventive actions.

6. *Teach Skills.*   Train people in new skills.

7. *Share Information.*   Share some information.

8. *Communicate Bad News.*   Tell someone unpleasant information.

9. *Report Progress.*   Report on the progress of a project or report.

10. *General Format.*   My objective does not fit any of the preceding categories and I need a way to organize my information.

Once you have set an objective, ask yourself, Is my objective attainable? How will I know that I have achieved my objective? With whom can I verify my objective's accuracy and applicability?

USING THE FORMATS

You are now ready to explore the 10 formats. The following sections explain each format and provide an example of its use. For variety, some of the format examples are shown as visuals that could be either slides or overheads. Of necessity, these presentations have been abbreviated for inclusion here, but you can see how to turn the format organization into a visual presentation.

The Ten Formats

Format	Objective	Order	Examples
1. Identify the Problem	Discover the real problem amidst many issues.	1. State what you want to have happening versus what is actually happening. 2. Specify what things are happening that are the same. 3. Specify what things changed about the time the problem started. 4. Suggest the underlying problem(s). 5. Present the potential solution(s). 6. Suggest the next steps.	• Identify problems due to rapid expansion. • Identify why research at a standstill.
2. Present Strategy Recommendations	Decide on the best strategy or strategies.	1. State the objective. 2. State the present situation. 3. State the desired outcome. 4. State the potential strategies. 5. List the advantages and disadvantages of each strategy. 6. Recommend one or more strategies and what to do next.	• Choose best strategy for handling rapid growth. • Choose best advertising strategy.
3. Sell a Product, Service, or Idea	Sell people on the benefits for them or their group of a product, service, or idea.	1. State the objective. 2. Determine and state the needs. 3. List the features. 4. List the appropriate benefits. 5. Specify the next steps.	• Sell multimedia training. • Sell boss on 4-day workweek in the summer.
4. Recommend Decision Alternatives	Present the best decision among several alternatives.	1. State the decision to be made. 2. List all the musts and wants. 3. Rate the importance of wants. 4. List the alternatives. 5. Eliminate alternatives not meeting the must criteria. 6. Compare the alternatives to see how much they satisfy the wants. 7. List any strong positive or negative consequences of each alternative. 8. Recommend one alternative and suggest steps for carrying it out.	• Choose a computer system from among three vendors. • Pick the best location for the company picnic.
5. Identify Potential Problems	Identify potential problems and suggest preventive and/or contingent actions.	1. State the goal. 2. List anticipated issues that may block achieving the goal.	• Identify what may go wrong with the computer installation.

The Ten Formats (continued)

Format	Objective	Order	Examples
		3. Rate the seriousness of the issues. 4. State preventive and/or contingent actions. 5. Identify a prime mover and deadlines.	• Identify problems with the trade show.
6. Teach Skills	Train people in new skills.	1. Give introduction. 2. State skill areas to learned. 3. Explain areas using key points, examples, anecdotes, handouts, questions, and exercises. 4. Summarize major lessons of the day. 5. Suggest the next steps in order for participants to apply the information.	• Train newly promoted managers. • Teach a new safety procedure.
7. Share Information	Share information.	1. List information to be shared. 2. Explain the task. 3. Define the buzzwords and jargon words. 4. Relate to your listeners' interests. 5. Explain its significance to the organization's goals.	• Explain purchasing department's needs to the financing department. • Share latest medical research with colleagues.
8. Communicate Bad News	Make the best out of the bad news.	1. Discuss the background. 2. State the bad news. 3. Present options to choose among. 4. Conclude reaffirming the options. 5. Guide audience into choosing most preferable option.	• Tell people the tasks they are doing are no longer needed. • Get boss's approval to change a deadline.
9. Report Progress	Report on the progress of something—a project or report.	1. Define the subject and the area. 2. List all the issues. 3. Categorize the issues. 4. Prioritize the issues. 5. Delineate the next action steps.	• Update the boss on the total quality project. • Share the results of the customer focus groups.
10. General Format	Present information in an organized, logical manner.	1. Open: State what talk is about. 2. Key Points: List the 3–4 major points of the talk. 3. Details: Go over the points in detail. 4. Example: Share anecdotes, examples for clarity. 5. Close: Restate major points. 6. Next steps: Suggest actions to take.	• Phone conversation. • 10-minute informal meeting presentation.

Objectives

Obstacles always show up when you take your eyes off the goal.

Publilius Syrus (circa 43 B.C.)

Whatsoever you attempt, consider your goal. Every path hath a puddle.

George Herbert

So I say, "every path has its puddle," and try to play gayly with the tadpoles in my puddle.

Louisa M. Alcott

The journey of a thousand miles begins with one step.

Lao Tsu

Speech that leads not to action, still more that hinders it, it is a nuisance on the earth.

Thomas Carlyle

The ancestor of every action is a thought.

Ralph Waldo Emerson

It is hard to fight an enemy who has outposts in your head.

Sally Kempton

The following format examples are used in this step:

- *Format 1:* Identify the Problem—The Rapid Increase in Outlets (page 39).

- *Format 2:* Present Strategy Recommendations—Develop a Nation of Job Creators! (page 42).

- *Format 3:* Sell a Product, Service, or Idea—The Polaroid LCD Panel (page 45).

- *Format 4:* Recommend Decision Alternatives—Choosing a Vendor (page 47).

- *Format 5:* Identify Potential Problems—The Case of No Presentation (page 48).

- *Format 6:* Teach Skills—The Franklin Quest Increasing Productivity Seminar (page 50).

- *Format 7:* Share Information—CD-ROM Training (page 52).

- *Format 8:* Communicate Bad News—Meat Eating and Deforestation (page 53).

- *Format 9:* Report Progress—Marketing to the Hispanic Market (page 55).

- *Format 10:* General Format—The Hallway Discussion; A 401(k) Plan (pages 57 and 58).

- A Format to Introduce Someone (page 61).

- Create Your Own Personalized Format—United Way (page 61).

Format 1: Identify the Problem

Format Objective.   Discover the real problem amidst many issues.

When to Use.   Use this format when, for no clear, apparent reason things are no longer going along as smoothly as they had been before. Examine what has been the cause of the turn of events. This format encourages you to spend time identifying the real problem rather than choosing the first problem that is suggested.

Order

1. State what you want to have happening versus what is actually happening.

2. Specify what things are happening that are the same.

3. Specify what things changed about the time the problem started.

4. Suggest the underlying problem(s).

5. Present potential solution(s).

6. Suggest the next steps.

Ideas for Presenting

- Show the list of brainstormed problems and ask the group to pick the real problem. Let them suggest ways to solve it.

- Present several potential solutions, or let the group, as a whole, come up with a list of potential solutions to your suggested problem.

- Present several solutions, including time deadlines, resources available, and the estimated cost for each solution. Let the group decide which one to implement.

Format 1: Identify the Problem—The Rapid Increase in Outlets

This company had 20 outlets last year; now there are 50, and the rapid increase has created many problems. You, as the president, are sorting out with your staff exactly what are the underlying problems.

1. *State what you want to have happening versus what is actually happening.*
   Sales projections should be close to what outlets actually sell. We should be able to accurately estimate our short-term borrowing and purchasing needs. With this fantastic growth, morale in the company should be high.

2. *Specify what things are happening that are the same.*
   • All managers asked to make projections and send to company headquarters.
   • Outlets being set up the same way.
   • Promoting from within.
   • Overnight mail being used to handle projections from managers.

3. *Specify what things changed about the time the problem started.*
   • Expanded by 10 outlets in 3 months.
   • Paying more interest than before (as an adjusted percentage of sales).
   • Complaints from the outlets about managers doubled.
   • Promoted 15 new managers (10 were never managers before).
   • Sales growth of 20 percent due to increased advertising.

4. *Suggest the underlying problem(s).*
   • Growth too rapid.
   • Inexperienced management.
   • Projections from outlets not timely enough.
   • Too much advertising.
   • No organized way to handle all the data.

5. *Present potential solution(s).*
   • Hire experienced managers and put them above the inexperienced ones.
   • Do less advertising; cut back on investment and expansion.
   • Computerize.

6. *Suggest next steps.*
   Address these potential solutions at the next board of directors meeting.

Extra Words about Problem Solving.   You may have been asked to solve a problem, yet no actions were taken on your recommendations. While the format on problem identification will be helpful in making presentations dealing with problems, fine-tune your presentation by incorporating into your talk the following four prerequisites for problem solving. These four prerequisites suggest that problems must be addressed in a specific order. When not addressed in this order, actions usually are not taken. The prerequisites are (1) the existence of a problem, (2) the significance of the problem, (3) the solvability of the problem, and (4) the self or others' competence and power to solve the problem. When these four prerequisites are not taken into account, the following negative consequences can occur:

1. *Existence of a Problem.* Everyone involved needs to agree that the problem exists. You may have been asked by one person to look into a problem, but when you present your solutions to a group, not all of them think the problem exists. For example, a large company was about to relocate one plant of 200 people to another building. During the process, people were going to move into smaller offices than they had before and would be assigned to new work groups. One person saw this future move as a potential loss of productivity for the people moving. He tried to present some solutions to the problems he could foresee, but no one listened. He first needed to convince people that a problem was about to exist.

2. *Significance of the Problem.* Everyone involved agrees that the problem is significant enough to examine and consents to spend some time brainstorming solutions. If this does not occur, the following scenario could happen. A long-time employee tells a new manager that a piece of machinery needs to be rebuilt this year because it is breaking down. The manager responds, "I am sure it is not that serious. We can wait until next year when our budget will permit it." A few weeks later, the machinery does break down. This puts everything behind schedule. The employee first needed to present the situation in such a way as to impress on the new manager the significance of the problem.

3. *Solvability of the Problem.* While ideally everyone involved should agree that the problem is solvable, it is crucial to convince at least the key people. When key people do not agree that a problem is solvable, comments such as the following are heard:

- We have always had that problem here, and I don't see it going away.

- Our customers don't mind that we're late. That's just how we do business.

- There just are not any other possibilities. We have tried everything.

If you hear the foregoing comments, focus on the key people and provide them with several ways to solve the problem. Communicate the benefits of solving the problem.

4. *Self or Others' Competence and Power to Solve the Problem.* The key people involved should believe that there is someone with authority, knowledge, expertise, or influence who can solve the problem. When people do not believe someone can do something, they make negative comments such as, "No one around here knows how to do that," or "We tried once and we just can't solve that issue," or "Our customers would never go along with that."

Since these comments are typical in problem-solving sessions, anticipate them and prepare a ready answer. By integrating these prerequisites into your problem-solving presentation, you will have a higher probability of convincing people to adopt your suggested solutions.

Format 2: Present Strategy Recommendations

Format Objective.   Decide on the best strategy or strategies.

When to Use.   Use this format when you are considering long-term issues, changes in policy, or a redirection of the present focus. It allows you to systematically present the potential strategies that the group needs to consider.

Order

1. State the objective.

2. State the present situation.

3. State the desired outcome.

4. State the potential strategies. These are ways to reach the desired outcome.

5. List the advantages and disadvantages of each strategy. Here you may include the cost, the amount of time required to implement each strategy (short-term and long-term time commitments), materials, and people needed.

6. Recommend one or more strategies and what to do next. You may propose one of the strategies, assign someone to look into another one of the strategies, or combine the strategies. Since the objective calls for a choice of strategies, guide your listeners into making the decision.

Ideas for Presenting.   You may use the following visual sequence with this format:

1. State the objective of your presentation.

2. Show the present state and desired outcome.

3. List the three strategies.

4. Delineate the advantages and disadvantages of each strategy (using one visual for all three or one visual for each).

5. Recommend a strategy.

6. State next steps to carry out the strategy.

Format 2: Present Strategy Recommendations—Develop a Nation of Job Creators!

This is a strategy presentation given by Gary Cogley who runs training programs for people who wish to become entrepreneurs. He believes entrepreneur training should start in first grade.

DEVELOP A NATION OF JOB CREATORS!

Present Situation

Creating a nation of wage earners in our educational system.

Desired Outcome

Create a nation of entrepreneurs who become job creators!

POSSIBLE STRATEGIES

1. Train entrepreneurs during college

2. Encourage entrepreneurship from first grade!

Strategy 1: Train entrepreneurs during college

Advantages
1. Colleges already have some programs in place
2. Students may have money to try some of their ideas

Disadvantages
1. Students' creativity already stifled
2. Students afraid to risk or make mistakes

Strategy 2: Encourage entrepreneurship from first grade!

Advantages
1. Learn responsibility
2. Appreciate parent's business
3. Become creative
4. Schools more connected to community

Disadvantages
1. None for students
2. Schools must change
3. Short-term start-up costs

RECOMMENDED STRATEGY

ENCOURAGE ENTREPRENEURSHIP FROM FIRST GRADE!

BENEFITS OF THIS STRATEGY

1. Train the next generation of small business owners
2. Keep small businesses a family business
3. Enlarge some small businesses
4. Encourage creativity, innovation, responsibility at a young age
5. Strengthen families

BLOCKS RUN INTO

Block 1. Outmoded system
How to manage it
  ‣ Fund system differently
  ‣ Set up school connections with community
Block 2. Teacher resistance
How to manage it
  ‣ Retrain teachers
  ‣ Modify profile of the ideal teacher
  ‣ Schedule time for teachers to get to know the community

NEXT STEPS

1. Retrain teachers
2. Connect small businesses to the school system
3. Encourage municipal support

Format 3: Sell a Product, Service, or Idea

Format Objective.   Sell people on the benefits for them or their group on a product, service, or idea.

When to Use.   You "sell" more than you realize. Unless you are *directly* involved in sales though, you probably have not taken a course or read a book on how to sell. Perhaps you consider yourself above learning sales techniques, but reflect on *all* the types of selling situations you are involved in during a week. You sell ideas to other people at work. You sell someone on volunteering his or her time. You sell a spouse on a vacation spot. You sell a colleague on helping you with a project. You sell a clerk on accepting a returned item. Each of these situations requires that you use your skill to convince others. Let the sales format help you. By just using this format you will have a higher success rate in selling your product, service, or idea.

Order

1. State the objective.

2. Determine and state the needs. Pick only the key needs of the people who will agree on the product, service, or idea.

3. List the features of your product, service, or idea. Relate those features as much as possible to the needs you have listed.

4. List the appropriate benefits. The benefits listed should address the specific problems, interests, and needs of the people or company. Include emotional as well as logical benefits. Emotional benefits include recognition, achievement, confidence, and security. For example, state your benefits as, "What this new insurance plan will mean for you is . . . ," then state the benefit.

5. Specify the next steps. Suggest steps such as buying the product on a trial basis or experimenting with the new process for two weeks, and then evaluating it.

Ideas for Presenting

• Use only the features and benefits appropriate to the needs of your listeners.

• Spend more time on benefits and less time of features. This is particularly true for those of you who are specialists. Speak only about those features that people can understand.

• Until you are accustomed to stating benefits, say before each benefit, "So what this means for you is . . . ." This phrasing forces you to speak to people about exactly what the product, service, or idea will do for them. One of the best ways to understand this skill is to see it in operation. Go to a used car lot or a stereo equipment shop and see the experts at work. If you plan to do this several times, leave your wallet at home!

- Use one visual for each step in this process.

Format 3: Sell a Product, Service, or Idea—The Polaroid LCD Panel

CHOOSING AN LCD PANEL

Why Polaroid is the best choice!

YOUR COMPANY'S LCD NEEDS

- Must work with Macintosh and IBM
- Must work with most overhead projectors
- Need sharp, ultrabright clear images
- Must be small and light for portability
- Must project video and television images in real time
- Must be easy to use

KEY FEATURES FOR YOUR TECHNOLOGY PEOPLE

1. Optional video to RGB adapter
2. Video adapter includes stereo loudspeakers
3. Weighs 4.8 pounds—smallest unit on the market
4. Whisper-quiet cooling system
5. Offers switch-selectable number of colors
6. Parallel viewing between the screen and the monitor

KEY BENFITS FOR NONTECHNOLOGY PEOPLE

1. Only one simple set-up
2. Set screen image once and it's done for the entire presentation
3. Adjustments easy to make on the front of control panel

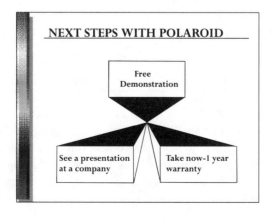

NEXT STEPS WITH POLAROID

Free Demonstration

See a presentation at a company

Take now-1 year warranty

Format 4: Recommend Decision Alternatives

Format Objective.   Present the best decision among several alternatives.

When to Use.   Use this format when you have several concrete choices and want to do a systematic analysis. Some of you will use this analysis to confirm your "gut feeling." Possible situations include purchasing materials, hiring someone, and choosing a location for an office.

Order

1. State the decision to be made.

2. List all the musts and wants. The musts concerning the decision are measurable, specific, and mandatory. The musts are those things that you absolutely *must* have whereas the wants are those things that are desirable but not essential.

3. Rate the importance of wants. Use a scale of 1 to 10.

   1 = Not an important want

   10 = A very important want

4. List the alternatives. You may already have your alternatives in mind, or you may have to do research to find them.

5. Eliminate alternatives not meeting the must criteria.

6. Compare the alternatives to see how much they satisfy the wants. You may have to do some research if you do not know the answers.

   a. Rate each alternative against each want on a scale of 0 to 10:

      0 = Will not meet my want at all

      5 = May somewhat meet my want

      10 = Really meets my want

   b. Multiply the value you gave your want by the rating of your alternative. Total the points. For each alternative, you will now have a total number that you can compare with the other alternative's total number.

7. List any strong positive or negative consequences of each alternative.

8. Recommend one alternative and suggest steps for carrying it out.

Ideas for Presenting.   The decision-making process you go through here is not the process you necessarily will share with your group. You must do this analysis so you can adequately support your recommendation. Most people do not want to be taken through the laborious process of sharing all your analyses and calculations. Share the most relevant of the must and want criteria, and discuss the positive and negative consequences.

Following are three different strategies to use as you present:

1. If alternatives are close, present the best couple of alternatives. Let the group discuss them and decide on the best one.

2. Present all the alternatives and recommend one of them.

3. Only present the chosen alternative, and have backup material on the other alternatives should you be questioned.

Format 4: Recommend Decision Alternatives—Choosing a Vendor

Decision Buy a computer system for the company		Alternative A Quick Systems	Alternative B Reliable Systems	Alternative C Easy Access Systems
Key Musts				
Handle expansion from 20 to 40 offices		✓	✓	✓
All outlets see information		✓	✓	✓
All offices able to input information		✓	✓	✓
Good training on computer		✓	✓	✓
Well-known name		✓	✓	–
Key Wants and Values*				
Easy to operate	9	$(9) \times 4 = 36$	$(9) \times 6 = 54$	$(9) \times 8 = 72$
Compact	4	$(4) \times 3 = 12$	$(4) \times 8 = 32$	$(4) \times 9 = 36$
Makes graphics and charts	3	$(3) \times 10 = 30$	$(3) \times 6 = 18$	$(3) \times 1 = 3$
Reliable support and service	10	$(10) \times 8 = 80$	$(10) \times 9 = 90$	$(10) \times 7 = 70$
Total		158	194	181
Strong Positive or Negative Consequences		*Negative:* Poor service reputation	*Positive:* In business six years *Negative:* Have to send our people to their training; will not come to our outlets	*Negative:* In business for one year; no graphics; not sure about training
Recommended Alternative with Next Steps Buy from Reliable Systems as long as references check out well and we like the training				

* Values rated on a scale of 1 to 10.

Format 5: Identify Potential Problems

Format Objective.   Identify potential problems and suggest preventive and/or contingent actions.

When to Use.   Use this format when you have made a decision to implement something new or when you are redirecting your efforts to a new orientation. You want to ferret out what could go wrong and suggest remedial action.

Order

1. State the goal.

2. List anticipated issues that may block achieving the goal.

3. Rate the seriousness of the issues. Use a scale of high, medium, or low to help you decide on which issues to concentrate most of your time.

4. State preventive and/or contingent actions. Deal with the most serious issues. For example, smoke detectors are preventive measures that warn you of smoke before a fire begins. Fire escapes are contingent measures that provide you with a way to escape from a fire.

5. Identify a prime mover and deadlines. The prime mover will carry out and/or delegate the actions needed. Before your presentation, if you know who must be the prime movers for some actions, talk to these people so they are prepared and committed to take actions.

Ideas for Presenting

- List the issues, then do the rest of the format with the group.

- Brainstorm preventive and/or contingent plans with your group.

- Let the group rate the seriousness of the issues.

- Let the group decide who will be the prime mover on the different actions that need to be executed.

Format 5: Identify Potential Problems—The Case of No Presentation

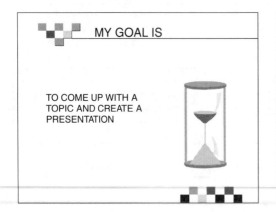

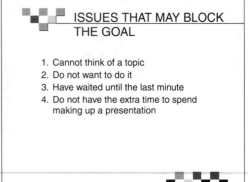

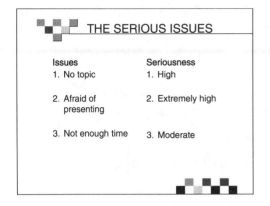

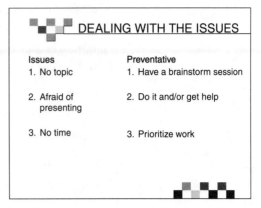

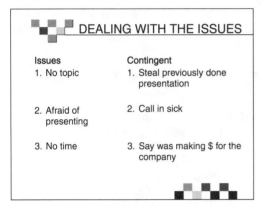

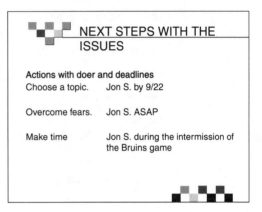

Format 6: Teach Skills

Format Objective.   Train people in new skills.

When to Use.   Use this format whenever you are teaching people new skills. Modify it based on your training situation.

Order

1. Give a specific introduction. Plan your introduction and how you will establish rapport with the group. Tell the participants the advantages they will have in learning the skills you are teaching.

2. State skill areas to be learned.

   a. What are the *key points* you plan to cover?

   b. Give *examples* and *anecdotes*. Relate the training to experiences and ideas participants can understand. Do not just talk theory. Use examples people can relate to.

    c. Will you have any *handouts?* Will you hand them out before, during, or after the skills training?

    d. What nonthreatening *questions* can you ask to determine if the group understands what you have said?

    e. Do you have any hands-on *exercises* so participants can learn the skill? An exercise can last 5 minutes to 3 hours.

3. Conclude with summary of major lessons of the day.

4. Suggest the next steps in order for participants to apply the information.

Ideas for Presenting

- The most important part of training is not how much you talk, but how little you talk. Encourage the participants to share their knowledge and experience. Create situations so that, as participants are learning, they can practice the skills.

- People remember stories and examples much longer than an hour lecture on theory.

- Be sure to say, "As a result of this 2-hour training, you will be able to . . . ." Then tell the people what they will be able to do that they cannot do now.

- Have a good time. If you do, your group will also.

- Use acronyms that help people recall the central points. For example, Roko Paskov, who teaches public speaking programs, used OASIS:

O = Organize your attitudes toward fear.

A = Analyze yourself and the audience.

S = Set goals and the purpose of the talk.

I = Integrate your materials.

S = Start, your future is here now.

Format 6: Teach Skills—The Franklin Quest Increasing Productivity Seminar

Here is a short lesson plan for teaching a segment of the seminar on how to use a product, in this case, the Franklin Day Planner:

1. *Introduction* Creative negotiations are filled with asking questions and brainstorming options.		
2. *Skill Areas*	Asking Questions	Brainstorming Options
Points to cover	• Open questions give the other party an opportunity to talk. • Find out the other party's interests by asking questions.	• Brainstorming helps you get out of taking a rigid position. • Make sure the other party agrees you are brainstorming, not deciding.
Anecdotes and examples	Joe at Gillette Japanese delegation	Father and son Fish tank
Handouts	List of open ended questions to ask.	The brainstorming process.
Questions to ask	• Are you a question asker? Why or why not? • What messages do you hear in your head about asking questions?	• When was the last time you thought of other options rather than stick with your first negotiating position? • What meetings at work hold brainstorming sessions?
Exercises to do	• Think of a future negotiation and list six questions you can ask during that negotiation.	• At your table brainstorm all the ways to get from this building to the Prudential Tower.
3. *Conclusion* When you ask questions and brainstorm options during a negotiation, you discover the interests of the other party and sometimes come up with options no one had yet considered. 4. *Next Steps* Think about your next negotiation and the questions you can ask. Before negotiating consider the other options to the first recommendation you are about to make.		

Format 7: Share Information

Format Objective.   Share information.

When to Use.   Use this format when you are asked to share information. This could be with another department or committee, another person, or another organization.

Order

1. List the information to be shared. List the tasks, products, and/or projects you are working on. Item 2 shows how this format can be used to share information about a task.

2. Explain the task:

   a. Describe the task.

   b. Give a clear example of how to do the task.

   c. Specify how doing the task benefits the organization and the group of people you are addressing.

3. Define the buzzwords and jargon words. Put a list of the buzzwords and jargon words on the board or on a flip chart so people can look at them as you speak. Write the definitions next to the words.

4. Relate to your listeners' interests. Explain how your task connects to the tasks they are doing.

5. Explain its significance to the organization's goals.

Ideas for Presenting

- Use any props you can create or bring. These visuals can make the information more understandable.

- Encourage people to ask questions; then modify the information you share based on people's interest.

Format 7: Share Information—CD-ROM Training

---

1. *List the information to be shared.*
   CD—ROM training in the company.

2. *Explain the task.*
   - Decide what training programs to start putting on CD—ROM.
   - Survey our training centers to find out which ones have CD—ROM drives now.
   - Choose the operating platform for the courseware.
   - Make a budget.

3. *Define the buzzwords and jargon words.*
   CD—ROM = Compact Disc—Read Only Memory.
   Platform   = What the CD—ROM needs in order to work. There are now different platforms. We need a standard platform for all training centers.

4. *Relate to your listeners' interests.*
   - Some of you are members of the Interactive Multimedia Association, and I know you have been following the growth of the CD—ROM industry.
   - Holiday Inn Worldwide is putting multimedia training stations in the chain's 1,600 hotels.
   - Each of you as managers must have your employees in training 40 hours a year. CD—ROM will make this goal easier to reach.

5. *Explain its significance to the organization's goals.*
   - Education will be available to more people in their own time frame.
   - Cost of training will go down so we save money over the long term. With large numbers of trainees, interactive videodisc instruction costs 64 percent less than conventional training.
   - We will be able to compete as our people are trained quicker in real time.
   - There will be consistent instructional materials and delivery.

Format 8: Communicate Bad News

Format Objective.   Make the best out of the bad news.

When to Use.   Use this format when you must tell people unexpected and unpleasant news.

Order

1. Discuss the background. Give facts, history, and other strategies that were considered.

2. State the bad news. Speak in clear and simple terms. Do not beat around the bush.

3. Present options to choose among. List the potential negative and positive consequences of each.

4. Conclude reaffirming the options.

5. Guide audience into choosing most preferable option. This may happen during the presentation, or the audience may want to think about the choices before deciding.

Ideas for Presenting

- At any point during your presentation, your listeners may want to vent their feelings. Allow them to vent, but retain control of the situation.

- If you are not affected, do not say you know how people must feel. They will not believe you.

- If it makes sense, you can ask people if they can think of any other options.

Format 8: Communicate the Bad News—Meat Eating and Deforestation

1. *Discuss the background.*
   Today we are here to discuss the impact of our meat-eating habits on the environment. One third of all the raw materials (including energy) consumed in the United States is used in the production and distribution of meat, eggs, and dairy products. In contrast, growing grains, fruits, and vegetables for human consumption uses less than 2 percent of all raw materials.

2. *State the bad news.*
   It takes 20 times as much land to feed one person on the standard American diet as it would to feed someone whose diet included no meat, eggs or dairy products. The United States has lost 75 percent of its original topsoil, and we are still losing it at an incredible rate of 60,000 lbs per person per year. Of this loss, 85 percent is directly associated with the raising of livestock.

3. *Present options.*
There are at least three things we can do to reduce this impact:

- Stop eating meat now.
    Positive: You would be casting a clear vote against waste.
    Negative: You wouldn't give yourself time to learn how to balance your diet properly.
- Eat 7 lbs less beef per year.
    Positive: Be similar to reducing your household water consumption by 33 percent.
    Negative: You would still be contributing to the environmental problem.
- Make a plan to become a total vegetarian by a year's time.
    Positive: You can adjust slowly to a vegetarian diet.
    Negative: It is sometimes harder to do things gradually than all at once.

4. *Conclude.*
Did you know cattle raising is responsible for at least 12 percent of the clearing of tropical forests and that deforestation is probably the most critical environmental problem that we face in this century? I know that we are all probably concerned about the deforestation. Each one of us can have an impact on changing this by making a simple choice. You can stop eating meat, you can eat less meat, or you can make a plan to become a vegetarian by a year's time.

5. *Give person the choice.*
What other information do you need before choosing an option?

Format 9: Report Progress

Format Objective.   Report on the progress of something—a project or report.

When to Use.   Progress report presentations are for the purpose of updating your audience. Your major goal is to have everyone leave feeling confident that you are doing and will continue to do a competent job. You want participants to say to themselves, "Yes, she is effective. Today I heard that those areas are being managed productively. I agree with the direction they are headed."

Order

1.   Define the subject and the area.

2.   List all the issues.

3.   Categorize the issues.

4.   Prioritize the issues. Use a scale of high, medium, or low. You may choose not to list your reasons for these priority ratings, but know them in case you are asked.

5. Delineate the next action steps. List the prime mover (person who will direct or perform the action). State the projected completion date.

Ideas for Presenting

- Have one page listing the issues in categories and in order of priority. Use a separate piece of paper to list each issue, the next steps to be taken on that issue, the deadline, and the designated prime mover.

- Before you begin, decide if you will stop for discussion after each next step, to gain approval, or if you will wait until the end of your talk. If you wait until the end, you can say, "I will begin implementing all these next steps unless someone has a question or concern."

Format 9: Report Progress—Marketing to the Hispanic Market

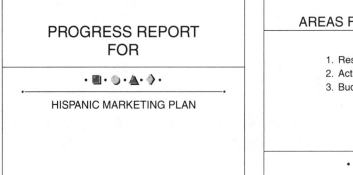

PROGRESS REPORT
FOR

· ■ · ◐ · ▲ · ◆ ·

HISPANIC MARKETING PLAN

AREAS FOR DISCUSSION

1. Research
2. Action plan
3. Budget

· ■ · ◐ · ▲ · ◆ ·

1. RESEARCH

► Issues & priority   ► Next steps

■ Market selection–High   ■ Identify top 10 regions for marketing

■ Timing–High   ■ Finish by end of October

· ■ · ◐ · ▲ · ◆ ·

2. ACTION PLAN

► Issues & priority   ► Next steps

■ Markets–High   ■ Create promotions

■ Events–Medium   ■ Identify festivals

■ Community–Medium   ■ Select key programs and organizations

· ■ · ◐ · ▲ · ◆ ·

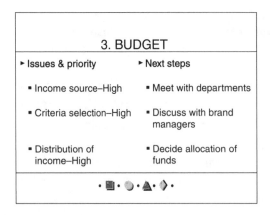

Format 10: General Format

Format Objective.   Present information in an organized, logical manner.

When to Use.   Use this format when none of the other formats seems appropriate.

Order

1. *Open.* Give the objective of your talk. If you cannot give this in one sentence, you are not ready for your talk. Yes, you can have two sentences, but no more!
2. *Key Points.* State the three or four major points. When you have only a few major points, people remember them. If you have numerous points, people will feel too saturated with information and will not be able to grasp your whole talk. Most facts and details can be categorized into three or four major groupings.
3. *Details.* Explain each of the key points.
4. *Example or Anecdote.* Share information and stories to add interest and clarity.
5. *Close.* Restate your major points. If you do not state your points at the opening of your talk and then again in closing, your listener's retention will be a great deal less than it could have been. Rather than boring your audience, you will make them feel delighted with your organization and with their ability to understand the key elements you are presenting.
6. *Next Steps.* Tell the group what must be done next.

Ideas for Presenting

- Be sure to list and mention your three or four major points before you explain them.

- Use this outline when asked to give a 3- to 10-minute talk in a meeting. It keeps you on track. You must practice this format to master it. Out of 10 people first using this format, 6 or 7 do not follow the format's order the first time.

They forget to enumerate the key points *before* explaining them. They leave out an anecdote or example. Consequently, their talk is usually less clear-cut and certainly less interesting to their listeners. They close with a shrug of the shoulders, saying things such as, "Well, that's it," or "I have nothing else to say about this." The format is deceptively simple, yet it requires a high level of focus, organization, and discipline.

- This format is an extremely powerful tool. Generally people, and in particular visually oriented people, will retain information better if they are given a general structure first and then exposed to the details later. Also, sharing an example or anecdote is not only for your listeners' enjoyment or education, it is for your benefit as well. If you worry about not sounding enthusiastic, sharing an example or anecdote will help overcome that impression.

- Think about the general format as a train. The engine is the objective chugging toward its goal. It is followed by the key points, details, a story, a recap, a closing, and finally, by your recommended next steps.

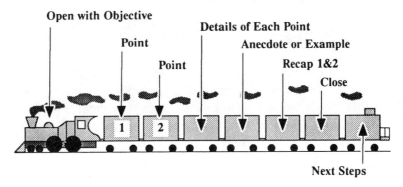

The General Format

Following are two examples of how to use the general format.

Format 10: General Format—The Hallway Discussion

Sue stops you in the hallway and asks you about your project. You answer her question using the general format:

- *Open.* Let me tell you about the project's deadlines.

- *Key Points.* There are two deadlines that I feel we can meet—the research paper deadline and the sample deadline.

- *Details.* The research paper is almost complete, and I know that after John takes the trip to California to gather the rest of the information, we will complete the paper. The samples are nearly complete. To wrap up the samples, we will have a focus group of about 10 employees and let them taste the products.

- *Anecdote or Example.* Last week, Mary had 4 employees tasting products all day. We found that, after about four tastes, they lost all objectivity and said things such as, "This is better than the last batch," when, in reality, it was the same batch as previously prepared. With 10 employees, we will receive a more accurate sample on how people will react to the product.

- *Close.* As you can hear, we can meet the deadlines shortly.

- *Next Steps.* I will have the research paper on your desk before the deadline. As for the samples, please give your approval for me to select 10 employees to participate in a focus group. I will have the approval paper on your desk this afternoon.

Note how the key points were repeated in the conclusion and how the speaker recommended certain next steps to keep the project moving.

Format 10: General Format—A 401(k) Plan

Frequently, the benefits of a company must be explained to employees. Some of these benefits are excellent, but because of a poor presentation, employees don't understand how to take advantage of them. The following example of a general format was used to discuss 401(k) plans with company employees. The presenter tried to make it simple so that employees would not be scared away by the numbers.

In some of the sessions, the presenter added a section on filling out the forms, and the audience filled out parts of them in the seminar. That way, no one felt intimidated about the forms. The presenter wanted to make it as easy as possible for people to understand the advantages of a 401(k) and know how to go about investing.

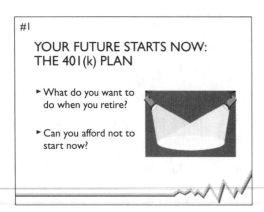

#1:   This encourages people to start thinking about retiring. Rather than beginning with an unfamiliar concept, the presenter starts by having the members of the audience think about themselves. When the session was after lunch and people looked tired, the presenter had them turn to the person sitting next to them and share ideas about their retirement.

#2:   The presenter talks about how people look at savings, from putting their money in the piggy bank to keeping it in a bank to investing it.

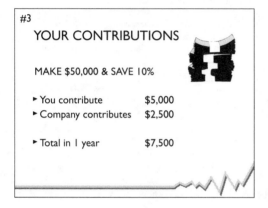

#3:   This shows what the company contributes. The presenter picks an employee in the group and says, "Jim, let's look at how much money you'd have as you save. Now suppose you make . . . ." If time permits, the presenter will have each person calculate what they could receive in a year if they put away 10 percent of their pay.

#4:   Changing to numbers instead of bullets enables the presenter to walk to the back of the room and still talk. Without having to point to the screen, she can say, "Now let's discuss point 3."

#5:   The presenter hands out some information about the various funds employees can invest in.

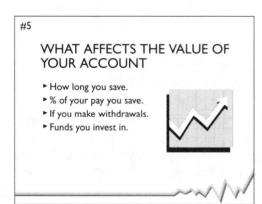

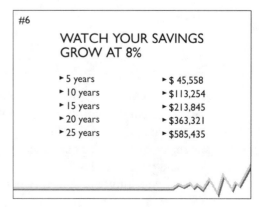

#6: After showing these numbers, the presenter turns off the projector and gives some examples of what people retired with after 25 years, without the names, of course! This adds human interest. The examples run the spectrum from people in manufacturing to senior executives.

#7

YOUR TRANSFERS AMONG FUNDS

- One transfer a calendar year
- 25% increments
- Exception = eligible for retirement

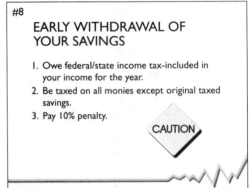

#8

EARLY WITHDRAWAL OF YOUR SAVINGS

1. Owe federal/state income tax-included in your income for the year.
2. Be taxed on all monies except original taxed savings.
3. Pay 10% penalty.

CAUTION

#7: The telephone and pad are supposed to convey how easy it is to transfer among funds.

#8: This visual is necessary so people really understand that they can't just take out the money when the mood strikes them.

#9: The word *beneficiary* is explained.

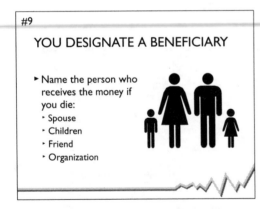

#9

YOU DESIGNATE A BENEFICIARY

- Name the person who receives the money if you die:
  - Spouse
  - Children
  - Friend
  - Organization

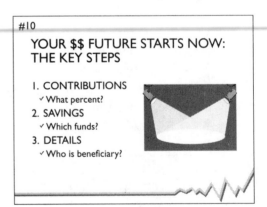

#10

YOUR $$ FUTURE STARTS NOW: THE KEY STEPS

1. CONTRIBUTIONS
   - What percent?
2. SAVINGS
   - Which funds?
3. DETAILS
   - Who is beneficiary?

#10: The summary visual reviews the agenda and also suggests the key steps for people who choose to open a 401(k). Notice the same picture that was used for the opening visual. This ties the talk together. The presenter ends with a statement such as, "You are center stage in your world. Only you can decide how you want your future to be. You have an excellent opportunity at this company to save for your future. I sincerely hope you take it."

A FORMAT TO INTRODUCE SOMEONE

The following format works well for most introductions:

- *The Topic.* State the name of the subject or title of the talk the presenter will be giving.

- *The Importance to the Audience.* Say why this topic is important to the audience.

- *Speaker.* So people will remember something about the speaker, divide your comments about the speaker into three or four major areas. For example, you can say, "Our speaker today has accomplished much in the areas of writing books, giving speeches around the world, and researching the AIDS virus. The books she has written include . . . ." Mention those accomplishments that will give the speaker credibility with that specific audience.

- *What the Speaker Will Do for Them.* Tell the audience what the speaker will do to make them more motivated, educated, informed, and so on. Here you are giving your audience reasons to want to listen to the speaker.

- *Final Words.* Say to the audience, "Now let me present to you [name of the speaker]." Say the person's name last. Make your introduction short, lively, and energetic. There is nothing worse than having someone introduce you who puts the group to sleep during a 5-minute introduction.

CREATE YOUR OWN PERSONALIZED FORMAT—UNITED WAY

Every year, United Way conducts a campaign to raise funds. Employees from the different United Way agencies are asked to speak at company meetings. These speakers have no training in presenting and feel intimidated when they see anywhere from 30 to 200 people looking at them. In addition, they are frequently not told how much (or little) time they have to talk until right before they start to speak. We developed the following format to enable these speakers to give fantastic, motivating talks:

- *Open.* I want to tell you about my agency's (name of agency) services.

- *The Services.* The three services I want to tell you about are:

  1.

  2.

  3.

- *About the Services.* Let me give you some specific examples of how these services help people:

1. Service 1 with an example.

2. Service 2 with an example.

3. Service 3 with an example.

(Each speaker is prepared to say a couple words about the service and then give a specific example. If they have 15 minutes, they will go through all the services with one or two examples of how people are helped. If they only have 5 minutes, they will share only one of the services along with an example.)

- *Close and Next Steps.* These three services are just a few of the many we provide. Your contributions make them possible. I thank you for supporting people in need. Just a little bit from you makes a major difference in our clients' lives. (Most presenters make up their own close, but this one is here just in case. They repeat the services and then do their close.)

One speaker commented, "I couldn't believe the difference in my level of confidence when I gave my last talk for United Way. I had 15 minutes planned and they only gave me 10. I cut out talking about one of the services. I kept my examples and could see a couple people deeply moved by the stories I told. I want to give more of these talks."

PRESENTATION CONTENT QUESTIONS

As you put together your information in the formats, consider the following questions:

- Do you need to give any background about the situation? Are people up-to-date on the topic?

- Do you need to say what you will not cover? Some people may be concerned about what you will say. If you do have to talk about an uncomfortable issue, let people know so they have a chance to psychologically prepare themselves. If you know you are not going to discuss something that would put some people in an uncomfortable position, say so in the beginning. They will be relieved.

- Do you need to give detail on your topic? Do you have to discuss its history, what makes it an issue, what has been tried so far, the consequences so far, how you are qualified to help, and how they, the listeners, can participate in examining the situation?

- Do you have a cost? This is especially important if the option that you are recommending costs much more than another option. You may have to justify the higher cost.

- Do you need proof that what you are suggesting will work? Do you have any proof?

- Have you clearly stated the benefits in terms of what they mean for each of the listeners?

- Have you included a reminder to breathe deeply when you say that most difficult statement?

- Is there an order to the events? If so, have you presented them in chronological order, which is usually easier for people to grasp?

OVERALL FORMAT CONSIDERATIONS

Think of the general format as the general organizing tool as well as a specific format. No matter which of the specific formats you use or how you combine the different formats, always have these ingredients in your presentation:

- *An Opening.* You state the objective of your talk.

- *An Agenda.* These are the key areas you plan to cover.

- *Examples and Anecdotes.* When you share anecdotes, this is for human interest. Also you keep your voice from becoming monotone.

- *A Conclusion.* You are repeating the key areas you covered.

- *Next Steps* (if appropriate).

You have now seen all the formats in use. You can see how they can be used to focus, to save time, and, particularly, to provide the foundation for a well-organized and convincing presentation. Use them and you will be surprised at how comfortable you feel preparing and communicating your information and recommendations to others.

PARTICIPANT ASSESSMENT

You have invited people to a picnic lunch with you as the host. You provide varied and delicious foods for everyone. As the host, you have done your homework so that everyone's food needs are considered and taken into account.

You are the host when you present. You must know your group so you can meet their needs. A participant assessment enables you to learn about your participants. With this information, you can choose the most appropriate ways to communicate your objective to your participants.

Chris Roden, one of the most successful salespersons for State Farm Insurance and now a certified financial planner and consultant, says this about gathering information:

> The early part of the interview is best spent by the salesperson asking probing questions designed to reveal not only the facts of the prospective buyer's or client's situation, but also his or her attitudes, beliefs, and objectives in

the area of the presentation. Upon completion of this important and time-consuming segment of the presentation, the salesperson has a solid basis for identifying accurately the prospect's problems and view of the world. Thus the basis for presenting a professional proposed solution or alternate solutions that are truly client-centered has been laid. The salesperson has established a feeling of trust on the part of the client. The close of the presentation, during which the desired action is requested and implemented, is usually brief and almost automatic if the suggested preliminary steps have been thoroughly conducted.

How do you gather information about your participants? Whenever possible and appropriate, meet with them and discuss their interests and levels of knowledge regarding your subject. Ask them what they want to know about your topic. Do not rely on someone else to tell you what he or she believes are the interests and concerns of the participants. By doing this, not only will you have accurate information, but you will also establish a positive rapport with the participants before your presentation. Knowing your participants' needs will help you assemble the correct level and number of materials necessary for a successful talk, which is one in which people accept your next steps. Remember, if you are in a situation where your words are translated into another language, you must be precise. Some phrases, such as "There are many ways to skin a cat," just do not translate well. Know your audience, and leave out expressions and examples that have no relevance to them. The following list gives you some questions to use when you do your participant assessment:

Participant Assessment

1. *Presentation Objective.*

    a. Has anyone else tried to achieve this objective with the group you will be talking to?

2. *The People.*

    a. Number of people?

    b. Same or different levels of skill, technical knowledge, education?

    c. Responsibilities and job titles?

    d. What do they currently know about your subject? Do they have any prejudices one way or the other about your subject?

    e. What is the number of men and women?

    f. What are the people's ages?

    g. What are their cultural backgrounds?

3. *Potential Issues.*

    a. Who will help support your objective?

    b. Who needs to be convinced to support your objective?

     c. Who should you talk to before your presentation?

     d. Will people be agreeable? Disagreeable? Neutral?

     e. What time of day is your talk? How will people feel then?

     f. Will people be asked to do any of these things: give up control, space, money, or resources, receive more work without extra pay, or accept more responsibility with no authority?

4. *Decision Makers.*

     a. Who are the decision makers?

     b. Can you be sure the decision makers will be at meeting?

     c. What can you say or do to establish rapport with them?

     d. Who can you talk to ahead of time and receive support?

     e. What, if any, preconceived ideas will they have about you or your subject?

5. *Other Issues.*

     a. Any particular way you should dress to establish rapport?

     b. Any words, hot buttons, or examples you should be aware of?

     c. Any regional differences for you to consider if you are presenting in a part of the country other than the one you are familiar with?

6. *Next Steps.*

     a. What next steps will you propose at the end of your talk?

     b. Can you obtain approval for those next steps before the meeting?

7. *Revised Objective or Compromise Plan.*

     a. What next steps will you compromise on? (For example, change deadline)

ORGANIZATIONAL ASSESSMENT

> My greatest strength as a consultant is to be ignorant and
> to ask a few questions.
>
>   Peter Drucker

An organizational assessment helps you examine the organization and determine exactly what type of presentation is the most appropriate. Perhaps you have recently changed jobs. In your previous job, you always made stand-up presentations with intricate overheads. Before you proceed in the same way in your new company, look around. Ask questions to discover the types of presentations used in this company. Learn about the idiosyncrasies of the organization. Focus on learning the most successful way to present proposals to senior managers. Set yourself up for success. Eliminate the uneasiness that accompanies walking into unknown territory without a map. You can use a cultural assessment form if you are going to speak to a culture other than your own. Following is an example of a completed assessment form:

1. *Objective Set.* Obtain agreement on design of theater.

2. *Visuals to Use.* Audience is not technically oriented. Use a detailed model. Bring blueprints for company engineers to examine.

3. *People Generally Invited.* Attending are vice presidents, who will be making decision, engineers, and booking staff.

4. *Meeting Tone.* Company is entertainment oriented. Use informal tone. Meet around the table; do not do stand-up formal talk. Encourage people to share their opinions.

5. *Things to Always Do.* Put model in easily accessible location so everyone can see it throughout the talk.

6. *Clothes to Wear.* Though informal, company is known for no-nonsense approach. Wear suit. Can take jacket off during meeting.

7. *Things to Never Do.* Do not challenge operational criticism of design.

8. *Language Acceptable.* Use informal tone; avoid technical.

9. *Communication between People.* Encourage roundtable discussions.

10. *People to Talk to Ahead of Time.* Talk to construction vice president. He will be hardest to convince due to preconceptions. His opinion carries a lot of weight.

11. *Informal Network (Who to Talk to off the Record).* Talk to bookers who easily get positively excited about new designs.

12. *Decision-Making Process.* Expect no decision this meeting. Bring calendar to schedule another meeting so can decide to take action at the second meeting.

13. *Other Considerations.* Keep meeting less than two hours. Leave model with construction vice president to handle and return. (He likes hands-on examples.) Schedule follow-up meeting as soon as possible. Structure presentation so another meeting is necessary.

14. *Scheduled Meetings.* Everyone brings calendars so next meetings are scheduled.

15. *Meeting Focus.* People are expected to share their opinions. Decisions are made by whole group, but if undecided, senior person decides.

COSTS

Some people leave out the issue of costs when they are thinking about how to reach an objective. Sam, who wants a new color printer, defines his objective as, "Getting a new color printer." Perhaps a more realistic and attainable objective is, "Present three alternative color printers for purchasing department to choose from."

You must do your homework about costs if you want people to agree on your recommendation. Some people feel they must first obtain approval to go ahead before researching the costs. This is a mistake. If you do not know the costs, people may not take you seriously. The more preparation you can do, the better chance you have of people agreeing to go ahead with the costs you are proposing.

STEP 3 ORGANIZING EVERYTHING

KEY POINTS

1   Look over your information and take out all the jargon.

2   Prepare the presentation for the amount of time you've been told you have, then prepare it in case you have 5 to 15 minutes less time.

3   Don't make a lot of extra notes for yourself to go with your visuals. You won't have time to look at them once you start talking.

4   Be sure you have transition phrases you can say as you move from one topic to another.

5   Create a presentation checklist and check off every item!

6   Copyright your handouts, if appropriate.

7   Decide when to give out the handouts so they best complement your talk.

8   Find ways to establish your credibility.

9   Tailor your presentation to influence key people in the room.

10   If you must read a speech, learn how to write it up so it will be easy to read.

You have just taken the first two steps on your journey by (1) transforming your anxiety into focused energy and (2) selecting the format that would best meet your objective and focus your organizing efforts. Both steps are equally important. Step 3 covers all the other details you need to consider to communicate convincingly.

YOUR BEST NOTES

Before we discuss the best notes to use when presenting, remember this: When you are in the process of preparing for a presentation, ideas will come to you in the strangest places. Carry some notepaper so you capture those ideas. Paper works better than the back of deposit slips from a checking account. Jim Bucci, Vice President of Human Relations, says about notes:

> Getting organized is a process, not something you make an appointment to do. It is evolutionary over time and begins as soon as you agree to speak. Capture ideas as they come into your mind by jotting them down on note cards. Your best ideas will come at the most unusual times. Always carry blank paper. You will be amazed at how much material you will have accumulated when you start this process early.

One woman told the story of her attempt to use index cards for a management presentation. She had read somewhere that the best way to present was to put her speech on 3-by-5-inch index cards, and she had 20 of them. Part way through, she jumped ahead, so her cards were out of order. She had written too much detail on them, and as a result, she had to squint at the cards and look at them frequently. To top it off, she had to ad lib her conclusion. She had forgotten to put headings on the cards and could not find the conclusion card. Her mediocre talk distressed her, since she had done her homework and knew the information.

She later discovered that if she used one piece of paper and listed all the major headings and the key points below each major heading, she could do an excellent job. While index cards may work for some people, in her case the constant shuffling and lack of an overall outline were confusing. Visually, for comfort's sake, she needed to see her entire outline throughout her talk.

Look through and use the different ways of organizing your notes. Enjoy finding several that make you comfortable when speaking.

Use Index Cards

People use index cards for speeches, presentations with overheads, flip charts, or slides. Some people enjoy them, and others find them too confusing to organize and follow. If you do decide to use index cards, be sure to write your major points large enough so that you can read them without squinting. Number your cards so you can easily put them back in order if you drop them. Of course, you think you will never drop them, but number them anyway. Following are two examples of how index cards might look.

#5		#10	
	BENEFITS		**NEXT STEPS**
	1. Quicker customer service		1. Set due date
	2. Save $$$		2. Meet with marketing
	3. Happier employees		3. Call 4 clients
			**Story about Sam

Write Out Your Talk

If you want to have a profound impact on your listeners, you are setting an almost impossible task by making yourself read your talk verbatim. Some people write out every word they intend to say and are able to follow the written words with ease. If your mind races off in 10 directions at once or if you retain many visual images in your mind simultaneously, reading from a written-out speech may not work for you. You will lose track of where you are on the page.

People who *read* speeches usually have several *ineffective* presentation habits. Half the time, they look down at their notes, they use few gestures (and those gestures are usually smaller and less interesting than the ones people make when speaking from notes); they speak in a monotonous voice tone; and they act flustered and apologetic when they lose their place. Reading a speech is an art. The art consists of coming across to your listeners as not reading the speech. This takes more practice than using notes! If you do decide to use a written speech (or have to for some special reason), apply the key points that are discussed here.

This true story is worth mentioning. A law student was listening to a speech by a famous judge who was talking about the students' commitment as lawyers to give something to the community and to use their talents not only for themselves. Halfway through his talk, he began telling them what excellent doctors they would make. The remainder of his talk was directed toward them as doctors. No one in the audience said a word. Evidently the judge had more than one speech to give and some of his notes got switched!

Don't read your opening comments. I saw a speaker get up and open his talk by reading these words, "It gives me a great deal of pleasure . . ." He certainly should have been able to do such an introduction without notes. This simple mistake lost him his rapport and cost him dearly in his efforts to convince his audience. Here are guidelines for writing out a speech, if you really must:

- Begin every sentence on the left-hand side of the page.
- Triple-space the sentences; you may want to space them even more apart.
- Use large type, but not upper case; upper case is harder to read.

This is the size of the font you need to use. It is 20 point. You may even want it bigger.

- Use a font that is easy to read.

- A word of warning: Don't make up a fancy system that signals you to emphasize words, to look around, or to pause because you won't remember the meaning of the cues when you get up to talk.

- For emphasis, use **bold.**

- For pauses, use a row of periods (ellipses). For example, say: "Now let me relate an example from a client's business. . . ."

- Put down your notes to share an example. The anecdote should not be written out since it is more personal and is intended to bring you into direct rapport with your audience. Feel free to walk around while telling the story or anecdote. This gets you away from behind the podium and gives the audience the feeling that you are one of them.

- Don't use the bottom third of the page. You will lower your voice too much as you look down. Make notes to yourself at the bottom of the page such as *Smile; Look at People; Pause.*

- And finally, be sure to number your pages!

Ad Lib or Memorize?

Some people scare themselves into believing that they have to memorize their talk. They believe that this will then show their true effectiveness as speakers. In reality, nobody even cares. Moreover, memorizing a speech is a surefire way to increase nervousness and anxiety. If you decide to memorize it, first consider some of the disadvantages. You cannot adjust it to the audience, or you will forget where you are. You may get lost. How will you find your place? Fortunately, memorizing is unnecessary as long as you can scan your outlined notes and follow them with ease while maintaining eye contact with individuals in the group.

Many people do impromptu presentations without notes. They get an idea and make some notes about it. They leave their desk without taking their notes, walk into someone else's office, and then discuss their idea. Under those circumstances, the presentation has more of an impromptu feel to it and can be effective without notes. For a planned presentation, make notes for yourself to follow. You will feel more relaxed, even if you never look at them!

Use Flip Charts

The flip chart serves as your guide. You can write very small notes in the upper corners of the flip chart. These serve as memory jogs for you. The advantage with a flip chart is that people can visually follow along with you. Plus, you see your presentation structure with every page you turn.

Use Overhead Transparencies

You can put the major points on the transparencies, and write reminder notes to yourself on the frames. Keep your reminder notes brief and in large print so you can read them easily.

You can write on the borders of your overheads. The following illustration shows an overhead. Your overhead will be either a 3M flip frame or in a cardboard frame. You can write notes on the frames. To send away for a free sample of the 3M flip frame, see "Visuals" in the References.

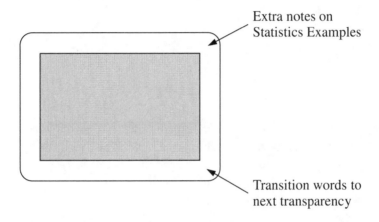

Extra notes on
Statistics Examples

Transition words to
next transparency

Some presenters make notes on plain paper between their transparencies. Other presenters make notes on a hard copy of their overheads and use those notes as they speak. Sometimes, though, these notes are too small and hard to read. The fewer notes you have the better.

Use Slides

If you have a mind that goes in many directions and you show slides and talk from notes at the same time, you may end up feeling confused and disorganized. If you have enough information on your slides, you will need very few notes.

Your notes can be organized in many ways. Three common methods involve using index cards or hard copy. Use an index card for each slide.

1. *Index Cards.* Put the heading of each slide on each index card, and number the cards in sequence with your slides. One presenter had 20 slides and 20 index cards. Half the index cards were blank. He found it easier to keep his place if he turned a card every time he showed a slide.

2. *Hard Copy.* Make an 8½-by-1-inch hard copy of each of your slides with notes on the hard copy. This is useful if you aren't that familiar with your

slides. You can see the hard copy of the slide ahead of time. A word of warning: Many companies make up standard company presentations. They send them out with the picture of the slides on one side of the page and the words to say opposite each slide. Usually, these supplied notes are too small to be legible, so the presenter should not rely on them during a presentation. Don't be fooled into thinking these notes will be usable—they are too small to read. You need to make up your own bullets to speak from if you need extra notes besides the slides.

3. *Speaker Notes Created on a Computer Graphics Program.* On most computer graphics programs, you can make speaker notes to go with each visual. The program prints the visual at the top of the page with the speaker notes below.

Buy a Small Group Presentation Book

When you go into a stationery store, the sales clerk can show you something that looks like a binder but can stand up on a table. This is excellent to use when you do the same presentation over and over to one or two people. For small groups of people, a presentation book set up on a table is much more intimate and informal than slides or flip charts.

Make Outlines

In the next several pages, information is organized in vertical, horizontal, and "mind-mapped" outlines. Experiment with each outline form. Certain presentations may lend themselves more to one form than the other. Or, you may prefer to use only one type of outline for every talk. When you find an outline form that feels right for you and your particular presentation, you will communicate with confidence.

Horizontal Outline.   The horizontal outline provides the key for many people to begin making exquisite presentations. People who are whizzes at impromptu talks, but dull when reading a speech or following a vertical outline, generally do well with horizontal outlines. This outline is preferred by lateral, left-brained people who think "across" rather than "down." They prefer to see their complete talk on one page with the outline of major headings and key points made horizontally, not vertically. This comforts them, as they can quickly see where to return to should they get sidetracked. Following is an example of a horizontal outline. As you can see, this book itself is the subject of the outline. Five main headings are listed horizontally. Set forth under each of the main headings are the 10 steps, also listed horizontally. Below each step are some key points related to that step.

10 Steps to Successful Presentations

Opening		Organizing		Pacing	
1 Channel Nervousness	2 Define Objective	3 Materials	4 Visuals	5 Yourself	6 Group
Introvert and extrovert Days before talk Day of talk Just before talk During talk	Ten formats One sentence Assess participants	Best notes State transitions All relevant information included Specialist hints	Readable Enhance presentation Pictures	Easy to listen to voice Movements appropriate Breathe Sip water	Control room Visual, auditory, and kinesthetic modalities

Concluding		The Future	
7 Conclude	8 Questions and Objections	9 Next Steps	10 Taking the Leap
Conclusion ideas Addressing ego states	Do's and don'ts Phrases for answering	Restate next steps Negotiating Mediating conflict	Use humor Be yourself Persevere Personalize Find your passion

Vertical Outline.   You probably learned this outline form in school. Some people are comfortable using it. If you are one of those people, then keep using it.

I.   *Opening*
    A. Channeling your nervousness
        1. Introvert and extrovert
        2. Days before talk
        3. Day of talk
        4. Just before talk
        5. During talk
    B. Define objective
        1. Ten formats
        2. One sentence
        3. Assess participants

II. *Organizing*
    A. Materials
        1. Best notes
        2. State transitions
        3. All relevant information included
        4. Specialist hints
    B. Visuals
        1. Readable
        2. Enhance presentation
        3. Pictures

III. *Pacing*
    A. Yourself
        1. Easy to listen to voice
        2. Movements appropriate
        3. Breathe
        4. Sip water

Mind Mapped Outline.   Users of mind mapping say it has several benefits. It improves learning and recall and stimulates creativity. Some people use mind mapping as a way of organizing their thoughts, since they do not have to redo the outline with every new thought. They just add another line. You can mind map any of the ten formats and, if you choose, use the maps as notes to talk from when giving a presentation.

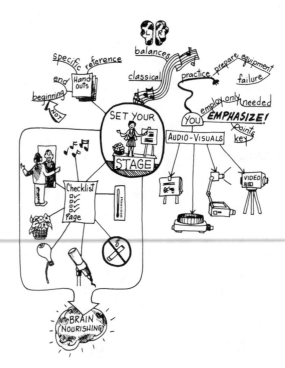

Reprinted with permission from *Present Yourself* by Michael Gelb, © 1988 B. L. Winch and Associates/ Jalmar Press.

Never say or do these things:

- "I wish I had more time."

- "I know we've been on the phone for an hour. I'm trying to hurry through this because I have so much information."

- "I may not finish on time, so we may have to take a bit longer."

- "I am halfway through my talk, and I have not even covered one-third of the materials."

All those types of comment only make your listeners nervous. Be brief. Know how long each part of your talk will be. Decide how much you need to say in order to reach that objective.

You don't endear yourself to people when your presentation runs over its allotted time. When you are asked to speak, usually you are told how much time you will have. Don't believe what you are told. For example, if you are told you have 20 minutes, plan a 20-minute talk, a 15-minute talk, and a 10-minute talk. Then, if you are told that the schedule is behind, you will know what points you must eliminate to go from a 20- to a 15-minute talk. Unless a miracle occurs, you will never get your full time if you are the last speaker in a day—maybe half of it with luck. Be prepared, so you are not caught off guard.

Plan on concluding 5 minutes early. People will appreciate you for that. Ideally, a talk should last 20 to 30 minutes. An hour is the limit any group can sit and comfortably pay attention. Most people are not used to sitting for long periods; be good to your audience and give them a stretch break. When you are talking on the phone, you do not have the advantage of seeing a person's nonverbal behavior. Conclude almost before you think you should. You can then ask, "Have I given you enough information to make a decision?" or "That covers the essentials regarding those two mutual funds you asked about. What else can I tell you?"

If you plan to discuss specific issues and questions with participants after you speak, save some energy for that purpose. Too many salespeople speak too long, then neither they nor their audience have enough energy left to discuss the actual purchase. Most people have experienced a salesperson talking them into and out of a purchase.

The following examples may motivate you to make your talk as brief as possible:

- The shortest inaugural address was George Washington's—just 135 words. The longest was William Henry Harrison's speech in 1841. He delivered a 2-hour, 9,000-word speech in the freezing northeast wind. He came down with a cold the following day, and a month later he died of pneumonia.

- Paul LeRoux, author of *Selling to a Group* (New York: Harper & Row, 1984), wrote, "Most presentations are 10 to 30 percent too long. 'Too long' can be only a few minutes. A good 20-minute presentation might have been made excellent by pruning five minutes."

- Mark Twain was at a meeting where a speaker was asking for money. Twain decided to donate $100 to the cause. As the speaker droned on, however, the author decided to cut it to $50. As the speaker continued, Twain again cut his intended offer to $10. Finally, the speaker finished, and the collection basket was passed around. When it reached Twain, he *took* a dollar out of the basket.

- A certain African tribe considers long talks injurious to both the presenter and the audience. To protect both, there is an unwritten law that every speaker must stand on one leg while addressing the listeners.

Length

The more you say, the less people remember.

François Fénelon

If you tell every step, you will make a long journey of it.

Thomas Fuller

Charm + wit + levity may help you at the start;
But at the end, it's brevity that wins the public's heart.

R. Cheney

I'm sorry it's such a long letter. I didn't have time to write a short one.

George Bernard Shaw

HINTS TO TECHNICAL PEOPLE AND SPECIALISTS

Remember the last time you had the experience of buying an object you knew nothing about? If you do not remember, then go into a stereo or computer shop and have that experience. The salesperson may have given you all the jargon about the product you wanted to buy. You smiled to show interest but did not understand half of the terminology. You walked away feeling frustrated and probably intimidated. When you finally found a salesperson who could explain the product in terms you understood, you felt motivated to buy it.

If you specialize in an area that many people in your audience are not familiar with, then you are a technical, or specialty, person at least to those people. The following is a list of some specialists:

- The computer specialist who presents a system revision to the managers of a department.

- The art design specialist who has designed an advertising piece for the marketing group.

- The volunteer who knows all about the latest research done by her organization and is asked to talk at a community meeting.

You must be careful when you know a lot of data about one subject. This is hard because the longer you have been in a field, the more you assume everyone uses and understands your words. Have you ever noticed that sometimes the person who is new to a subject has the best rapport with those unfamiliar with the topic? The speaker does not yet know enough of the jargon to bore or confuse others.

Not speaking to the level of your group can have serious consequences. A technical manager lost his promotion because he always presented information in such a cryptic fashion. His speech was filled with acronyms and professional jargon. No one but his closest associates could follow him. Management would not promote him, knowing his conversations filled with jargon would make it impossible for him to establish rapport with people outside his specialty.

Time is precious; audiences judge the presenter more and more on the ability to synthesize material into only what is necessary for them to hear in order to choose the next steps with confidence. If you are a specialist, your tendency may be to tell all or perhaps even to show off. Some specialists when they speak are like gamblers: they do not have enough sense to quit while they are ahead. A general rule is to say less rather than more. Then ask questions such as, "Would you like to know more about this?" or "Which points shall I explain in more technical terms?" or "Technically, would you like to know why I reached this conclusion?" You will feel people's approval when you effectively impart the right amount of information. The focus, as any successful salesperson knows, needs to be on the listener's desire to have more information, not on covering everything there is to say on the subject.

Be sure to select the materials that will motivate the participants to easily and enthusiastically want to reach the objective. For example, a pickax is necessary for climbing the ice-capped Matterhorn, but it is useless for walking the rolling, manicured slopes of the Vermont hills. A 10-page statistical analysis of the business at hand may be necessary for the board of directors meeting, but not for the Friday afternoon company update meeting.

The next time you speak to a person or a group unfamiliar with your topic, keep the cartoon on page 80 in mind, along with the points that follow it.

Use Your Own Experience, Analogies, and Examples

The dryer and more foreign the material, the more examples and analogies you will need so that participants can comprehend and enjoy paying attention. Take the time to plan your examples. Speak to people in terms of their own experience. Use analogies your listeners will understand. Analogies compare the known with the unknown, the concrete with the abstract. They increase and illustrate understanding. The following analogies make you listen:

- Dr. Jesse Steinfeld, a former U.S. surgeon general, said, "Imagine four commercial airplanes with 250 people aboard each, crashing every day in our country and killing everybody aboard. That's how many people die prematurely from smoking cigarettes every single day in our country— more than 1,000 people!" His analogy, although gruesome, is excellent. It really drives the point home.

- Mike Simmons former vice president of Fidelity Systems Company explained, "Maintaining and upgrading the computer systems in this company is like a person driving to Florida while attempting to change the

"For Better or For Worse," copyright © 1989, Universal Press Syndicate. Reprinted with permission. All rights reserved.

battery, overhaul the engine, and clean the car—all of this without stopping the car. This is the challenge systems people will encounter as they work on upgrading our computers during the next year."

These analogies are ways to make the unfamiliar familiar to people. Each analogy serves as a bridge so that a person can walk from the known to the unknown feeling safe and secure. The appropriate analogy can save you hours of explanation, convince people more quickly, and sometimes entertain as well. Relating analogies helps you—the presenter—speak with more emotion.

Limit Details

Reasonable facts and details are what nontechnical people need to know, not all the nitty-gritty details that intrigue you. As you consider which details to include, ask yourself if each particular detail is a must to know or just a nice thing to know. "The secret of being a bore is to tell everything," said Voltaire. Leave some mystery in your talk. Stop before you have people wishing you would! People who are bored or intimidated by all your information will not be supportive of your objective. They will not care about anything but getting out of the room as soon as possible. You want the audience to absorb and understand your presentation. Keep asking yourself, "Does the audience really need to know this detail?"

Write Out Acronyms

If you must use acronyms, abbreviations, and other jargon, write their full name on the flip chart or the board for all to see. If you do not write them out, the audience will find some way to pay you back.

Reprinted by permission: Tribune Media Services.

Use Familiar and Simple Language

Galen said, "The chief virtue that language can have is its clearness, and nothing detracts from it so much as the use of unfamiliar words." Ask yourself, "Can people understand what I am about to say?" Rather than say, "Cable 10A will link to cable SKC for user interchange," say, "The 100 people in Arizona will be able to send information to the 50 people in New York." You may use familiar words but in a context foreign to your listeners. For those of you who use computers, do you remember the first time someone told you to look for the pop-up menus? All you may have seen in your mind was a menu of your favorite restaurant. Keep your words short. In the *Tao of Pooh* by Benjamin Hoff (New York: Dutton, 1982), the reader learns the following about scholarly speech:

> Now the one rather annoying thing about scholars is that they are always using Big
> Words that some of us can't understand. . . .
> "Well," said Owl, "the customary procedure in such cases is as follows."
> "What does Crustimoney Proceedcake mean?" said Pooh.
> "For I am a Bear of Very Little
> Brain, and long words bother me."
> "It means the Thing to do."
> "As long as it means that, I do not mind," said Pooh.

Save your big words for the appropriate occasions—for Scrabble.

Prepare Participants

If you have to use unfamiliar language, prepare your audience by telling them the degree of detail you will present. Tell them that you will be using technical words but will also give a nontechnical overview. This explanation informs the nontechnical people that later you will explain what you are saying in words they can understand.

Use Visuals

Whenever possible, use visuals such as charts and graphs or even props. Use anything to make the unfamiliar familiar. Notice how the show-and-tell programs on television always show the implements they are discussing. The carpenters show their tools, and the chefs show their utensils. The following is an excellent example from *The Laughter Prescription* by Dr. Lawrence Peter and Bill Dana (New York: Ballantine, 1982):

> The statistician was worried because the pilots never paid much attention to his statistical displays. Further, he suspected that they did not understand what the curves on the charts meant and seemed confused as to whether an ascending curve was good or bad. His illustrator hit upon the novel idea of placing small thunder clouds on the poor performance side and shining sunbursts on the good performance side. The pilots were amused, paid much better attention, and seemed to derive more meaning from the statistics thereafter.

Use Clear, Short Sentences

The shorter you make your sentences, the less likely you are to lead your listeners into a technical jungle. Your technical jungle may be so full of "stuff" that you, due to your skill, can hack your way through it; but no one else may want to join you in that arduous process. Sometimes, talks feel that way to participants: a dense jungle of impenetrable, undefined "stuff." Give your participants the feeling of walking on a nice wide path with plenty of space. Keep it clear.

Ask for Questions

When you are sharing information and do not know how much detail to include, speak about the essential points, then ask, "Who wants more detail about this area?" Do not say, "Does anyone have any questions?" Most people will not ask. They do not want to appear uninformed in front of their colleagues or friends.

The following examples are of two talks—one in technical language and the other in language most people, although unfamiliar with the specialty, could comprehend. Marty Barrett of Interleaf actually used these two talks in a presentation program:

- *The Technical Talk.* "Compensation philosophy is influenced by several variables that exist external and internal to a business enterprise. Primary external influences surround the competitive, economic, and regulatory environments. Primary internal influences surround corporate strategies and goals, culture, and available resources. A compensation philosophy is effective if it is synergistic with the above and achieves the balance between corporate desired results and individual employee needs."

- *The Nontechnical Talk.* "Organizations have to decide how to pay employees so that they feel they are being paid fairly. The issues a company considers when setting up a pay scale include federal and state laws, the economic and geographical area where the work is done, the type of business a company is in, and the company's management goals and philosophy."

As can be seen from the preceding examples, there is nothing inherently wrong in using specialized language. For presentations before nonspecialists, however, it can be your kiss of death. You may be tempted to give a full explanation, but if the audience even begins to look perplexed, do not do it. When someone asks for a piece of paper, do not tell them how the paper is made. When someone asks what movies you have seen lately, do not give them a synopsis of your last year of moviegoing. Be judicious. That is the major job for all of you who are specialists. Weed out the necessary from the unnecessary.

When you have two different levels of expertise in your group, consider giving a background session before the planned presentation. Those who need the background can attend that session. As a consequence, when you are forced to use some technical language during your presentation, they will have a basic understanding. Alan Day, president of Systems Engineering Inc., Waltham, Massachusetts, a computer consulting firm, tells how his consultants are trained: "At

Systems Engineering Inc., we use a solutions-oriented approach to working on our customers' problems. We teach our consultants to ask open-ended questions and then *listen* to the customer, noting the language they use in defining the problem. Then when we present the solution to the customer, we take care to use the same language they use."

INFLUENCE OTHERS CHECKLIST AND MODEL

Put yourself in the shoes of one of your participants. Now, as that participant, experience yourself listening to yourself as the speaker. As a participant, how do you react to your presentation? Do you know what you are being asked to do? Do you understand the advantages for you in going along with the recommendations? This exercise will help you as you prepare to speak. In the following two scenarios, neither presenter was adequately prepared:

- *Joe's Raise.* Joe went in to ask his boss for a raise. After some discussion, he said, "I want a 10 percent raise." His boss said, "I can't now. The company just froze all salaries." Joe didn't know what to say next. If Joe had anticipated the objection and planned his response, it is likely that he would have received something more than just the naked no.

- *Tim's Project Date Change.* Tim went to the manager of another department to suggest they change the due dates for a project. The manager stubbornly refused. Tim left feeling frustrated.

These examples have the same thread running through them. The presenter did not plan a strategy for influencing the person. Better to plan ahead than to hear a no and then have to plan on how to overcome that no. That may take twice as much effort. With the "Influence Others Model," you can consider how to influence people the first time around.

Influence Others Model

1. State the product, service, or idea.

   _____

   _____

   _____

2. What do you want the person or persons to do about the idea?

   _____

   _____

   _____

3. What are the advantages for them in accepting the idea?

_____

_____

_____

_____

_____

4. What possible objections may they have? Write a response for each objection.

   Objection: _____

   _____

   Response: _____

   _____

   Objection: _____

   _____

   Response: _____

   _____

Using this model, let us look at how Joe and Tim could have improved their chances for a positive response.

Joe's Raise

1. *State the product, service, or idea.*
   Joe wants a raise.

2. *What does Joe want his boss to do about the idea?*
   Joe wants his boss to get him the raise.

3. *What are the advantages for the boss in accepting the idea?*
   The boss will have a motivated worker. The boss will feel pleased he got a raise for an employee. Joe will work harder.

4. *What possible objections may Joe's boss have?*
   Objection: The company has frozen salaries.
   Response: When will they be unfrozen? Can a raise be given now that is paid retroactively?
   Objection: We cannot do it now.
   Response: Can you do any of these things for me now—a new office, a special training program, or a few extra personal days?

Tim's Project Date Change

1. *State the product, service, or idea.*
   Change the due date for the project.

2. *What does Tim want the person to do about the idea?*
   Tim wants the manager to agree to the change in dates.

3. *What are the advantages for the manager in accepting Tim's idea?*
   Project manager's group will have a longer time to finish the project.
   Better chance of the work being done accurately with little revision
   necessary.

4. *What possible objections may Tim's manager have?*
   Objection: Can't tell group they do not have to do it on time. They have
   been working so hard.
   Response: I would be glad to come and explain why the dates need to be
   changed.
   Objection: This will cause some people to have to change their vacation
   times.
   Response: Well, can those people be compensated for their willingness to
   be flexible?

   While Tim may seem to be overly insistent, in actuality he is supplying the
manager with practical alternatives that he hopes will influence the manager into
agreeing with him.
   A word about influence and networks in organizations. In *Corporate Cultures* by Terrence Deal and Allan Kennedy (Reading, MA: Addison-Wesley,
1982), the authors say the following about accomplishing objectives:

> We have found that many "modern" managers only deal with the tip of the
> iceberg as far as communications are concerned. They send a flurry of
> memos, letters, reports, and policy statements, hold premeetings and man-
> agement sessions where they use flip charts, decision trees, and statistical
> analysis to accomplish . . . well, sometimes they do not accomplish much.
> We think that 90 percent of what goes on in an organization has nothing to
> do with formal events. The real business goes on in the cultural net-
> work. . . . Even in the context of a highly controlled meeting, there is a
> lot of informal communication going on—bonding rituals, glances, innuen-
> does, and so forth. . . . Top managers need to recognize and tap into this
> cultural network to accomplish their goals. Especially in a large corpora-
> tion, working the network can be the only way to get a job done.

LINKING POINTS TOGETHER

Remember the last time you were listening to someone present and, all of a sudden, you felt lost? The speaker probably moved on to another point without warning you. You did not realize that he or she had finished with the first point. To

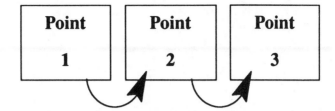

cause even more confusion, the speaker did not explain to you how the next point followed from the previous one.

Some people have more problems making clear transitions than others do. You will know if you are one of these people by how often people look at you as if to ask, "Where did that idea come from?" or "How did you get to that point?" You may also be the type of person who frequently puts parentheses in the middle of your sentences. You will be talking about one subject and when a different thought occurs to you, you add it in the middle of the sentence before returning to your original subject. Practice logic and order when speaking to people. Watch your "side trips." If you make them, at least explain them. When preparing for a presentation, write down your transition sentences.

The following ideas will help you link your points together and make clear transitions:

- Write out the sentences that link your points together. I rarely write sentences about each of my points, but I frequently write out the transition sentences.

- If each point is long and somewhat detailed, give a minisummary with each transition.

- Pause or move around with each transition. Your movement becomes a visual clue that you have changed the subject. You might stand in the center of the room as you talk about point 1. Then, as you begin point 2, you might move to the right, then back to the center. For point 3, you might move to the right again and then back to the center. This type of moving is a pleasure to do. Another effective moving technique is to stand on the right whenever you say all the positive points and stand on the left whenever you say the negative points. This is called *anchoring* your group. In effect, your group is learning that, whenever you step to the right, your point will be positive.

- Use a new visual with each transition.

- If each of your points is lengthy (that is, over 30 minutes), change your media when you change points. For example, use an overhead, then a flip chart, then go back to an overhead.

- Use phrases such as,
  "To move on to the next point . . . ."
  "Point 3 is . . . ."

"My last three points covered . . . My next three will cover . . . ."
"Next . . . ."
"In addition to . . . ."
"In the next section, we will cover . . . ."

Although these phrases may sound somewhat stilted to you, they indicate to people the transition points in your talk. *Caution:* There is a time and place for sounding so organized. A colleague of mine had a boss who constantly talked in numbers at work. She also began to talk this way in every situation. One day, she said to her husband, "I suggest we go to the Vegetarian Delight for lunch and there are three reasons—*A* . . . , *B* . . . , and *C.*" Her husband countered every reason with an objection and then in a humorous tone told her that, judging from the way she sounded, perhaps it would be more appropriate for them to have a business lunch!

GROUP PRESENTATIONS

A group presentation is a special type of presentation demanding a particular set of organizing skills. Group presentations take place for many different reasons. There are sales presentations to a potential customer where a number of people present from the diverse functions of the same company. There is the "Tell us about your project, or idea," presentation, in which people together attempt to "sell" a project in order to receive funding. There is the organizational information training type of presentation, where people spend several days hearing from the different departments in the organization. The following is a scenario of one group presentation:

The day was a success. Pauline's group presented the condition of each director's department to the board. Beforehand, all the directors met and decided on the key areas that each person had to include. They also agreed to relate one or two anecdotes describing how the parent company had helped each department. To add variety, one director gave a 15-minute slide show about a research project in his section. Another director distributed a 10-point questionnaire asking the board to guess the answers. Some questions were "true or false" questions, and other required percentage answers. This director told the board members that they would hear the correct answers to the questionnaire during his talk. At the afternoon break, still another director brought a large bowl of fresh fruit for the participants to enjoy. Every director felt his or her presentation had contributed to the total success of the day.

Accomplish two things with group presentations: (1) Keep the presentations interesting by varying them and (2) help each presenter to shine. Either you or another person designated as the group organizer must do the following things:

- Set up structured planning meetings. The organizer holds a brief first meeting (about 20 minutes long), assigning each presenter the key points to cover, then sets up a second meeting to rehearse. (This first meeting may take longer if people need to discuss what should be covered.)

- Make sure everyone has a role and that the role is perceived by the audience as necessary and important.

- Check to be certain that the speaker's materials do not overlap. It is almost impossible to follow someone who has said half of what you planned to say. At that moment, it is not too wise to say, "Well, so and so just presented half of my talk." This makes one of you look disorganized. In any case, it is a no-win situation.

- Help people pace their talks so there is variety and interest within and between the individual presentations.

- Motivate the presentation team to deliver with enthusiasm.

- Set up a *real* trial practice run, with time for evaluating each talk and the overall flow of the total presentation. The organizer makes sure people *really rehearse* and does not just allow people to say, "I'll be talking about . . . ." Each person must get up and *do* his or her talk as if it were the real thing, and in the right amount of time.

- Effectively and briefly introduce each speaker.

- Spotlight people who will have the most future contact with the listeners. This will enhance their credibility.

- Assure that the specialist in the group speaks in a language everyone comprehends.

A well-rehearsed and organized group presentation is a strong credible force. The sheer power of the whole presentation is sometimes enough to convince people!

LOGISTICS

> One piece of trouble is worth a thousand pieces of advice.
>
> Turkish Saying

Why discuss logistics in a chapter on organizing? It is never too early to be aware of all the logistical issues that may block your being able to communicate effectively. Anyone organizing a meeting needs a checklist. The following paragraphs illustrate the problems that occur when you do not have a list.

Prepare Yourself

The Handout Dilemma.   Sue thought that there were to be 8 people at the meeting, so she made 10 handouts. When she arrived, there were 20 people. She did not arrive early enough to make more copies. She had created the handouts to be utilized by the participants as she spoke. Ten people had to take copious notes while she spoke, and they were irritated by her lack of organization. She should have confirmed the number of people attending.

The Extension Cord.   Sam had a superb slide show. He arrived 5 minutes early. The room was excellent, but the only plug for his slide projector was in back of the room. He needed a long extension cord. One could not be found, and the nearest hardware store was 10 minutes away. Someone had to go buy the cord while Sam ad libbed the first 15 minutes of his talk.

Locate Yourself

To have the seating arrangements help, not hinder, your communication with people, keep in mind the following hints:

- *Be Able to See Everyone.* When possible, have the participants seated so that they can see each other.

- *Avoid Window Glare.* Arrange seating so people do not face the windows. The glare is hard on the eyes.

- *Keep the Door at the Rear.* Arrange seating so the door is to the rear or to the side of the group. This way, latecomers can arrive without distracting the group, and people who need to leave early can do so unobtrusively.

- *Take Away Extra Chairs.* Be sure you have taken away any extra chairs. You want a cozy feeling, not a feeling that the empty chairs represent people who did not come.

- *Have Comfortable Chairs.* Try to make sure the chairs are comfortable; and if they are not, take frequent 2-minute breaks so people can stand up.

Arrange Seating

If you send your seating requirements to someone, incorporate the preceding suggestions into your request. The following are some possible seating arrangement configurations:

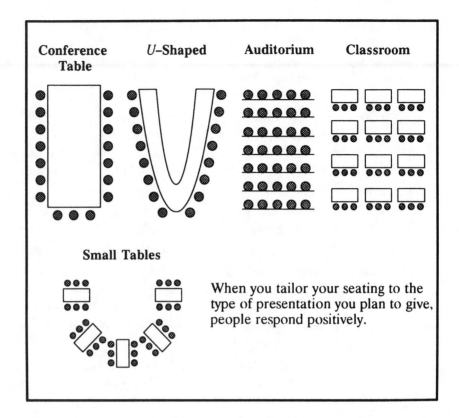

When you tailor your seating to the type of presentation you plan to give, people respond positively.

- *Use a Conference Table.* This setup suggests to participants, "We are all in this together." Be sure everyone has a seat at the table. This also facilitates easy interaction between participants. Sometimes the conference table is just too long, and you do not have that many participants. Ask them to sit on each side of the table as close to the front as possible.

- *Use* U-*Shaped Seating.* This works well even if you do not have a table. The participants will have the feeling of sitting at a conference table.

- *Avoid Auditorium or Classroom Table Styles.* This suggests to everyone, "I'll talk and you listen." Most of the time, this is inappropriate for a business setting. If you end up in a hotel with this type of arrangement, change it.

- *Use Small Tables.* This lets everyone see the front and lets them work in small groups at their table.

YOUR INTRODUCTION AND CREDIBILITY

You cannot convince people if they wonder about your competence! You may need to establish your credibility as the expert in the field. Many people believe it is enough to state their credentials at the opening of their presentation. This is not true. People forget all those details very quickly. A better way to have people remember your expertise is by referencing your skills during your talk. The following list will give you some ideas:

- *Mention People's Names.* If you have worked with someone in your field who is well respected, you may say, about halfway through your speech, "When I was working with _____ on this project, she seemed to feel that we needed to take a little more time to explore some other possibilities."

- *Mention Places You Have Worked or Visited.* If certain areas are well known to your group, say, "While visiting the Center, I learned . . . ," or "When I was working with *X* Company I led the project on . . . ."

- *Mention Academic Knowledge.* Your degrees or professional studies may help your listeners believe in what you say. You may want to state, "My three weeks of study at the Institute gave me a basis for the work I have been doing." You can also quote journals or newspaper articles that demonstrate you are keeping abreast with the current information.

- *Include Third-Party Endorsements.* As you consider your objective and the audience, you may want to include some third-party endorsements. You can refer to another organization that uses the product you want your audience to buy, you can tell people to call a certain person for more information, or you can say that someone who is not at the meeting endorses your recommendation.

There is a time and a place for these comments. There are also ways to establish your credentials without appearing to be a name-dropper or a self-centered individual. Remember, people may not know about you. For you to be taken seriously, they need to understand that you do have expertise and experience in the subject. Some people, once they are in an organization, forget to sell themselves as competent professionals. Many people do not know them. They should surreptitiously let people know about their expertise. Make notes, in one or two places, such as, "Refer to study at institute," or "Mention my degrees," or whatever you consider appropriate. This kind of referencing is particularly important when you are quite a bit younger than your audience. They want to know that you have had some experience. When you stop and think a moment, you will know how much you should state your credentials to the group.

Some speakers may feel that their credentials are threatening to the group, or they at least want to minimize them in some way. Jack Valenti, who represents the Motion Picture Association of America, after being introduced, said, "If I had known you were going to eulogize me, I'd have at least died first." This was his way of having people realize he takes his accomplishments lightly. He put himself on an equal basis with the audience rather than above them.

If someone asks for some information about you in order to introduce you, do that person a favor and give him or her an outline to speak from. Do not just give that person your résumé. He or she does not know what to emphasize. When you go to speak that day, take a copy of the outline you sent. If the person has lost the copy you sent and asks at the last minute what should be said, you will be prepared.

When someone is introducing you, look at that person. This will usually be the most comfortable thing to do. If you look at the audience, the audience members will not know whether to focus their attention on the person introducing you or on you. Do not give them that option. Look at the person speaking at the moment.

HANDOUTS

Handouts can include an outline of your presentation, detailed notes of your talk, definitions and acronyms spelled out, charts, quizzes, a bibliography, articles for further reading, brochures, and so on. Do not hand out so many pieces of paper that nothing gets read. A couple of pages may be read; 10 pages may not.

Ask yourself the following questions about your handouts:

Do I send them out ahead of time?

- If you send people handouts to read ahead of time, tell them what you want them to do (for example, "Please read and star any items you have questions about, since I will not be discussing this information unless there are questions.").

Do I hand them out at the beginning?

- Rarely distribute detailed materials that you are going to use in your talk just before you start talking. "Why?" you may ask. As soon as most people have something in their hands, they begin to look at it, which means they stop paying attention to what you are saying. Also, they may scrutinize the material and ask you more pointed questions than you anticipated.

- If the participants must have the materials at the beginning of your presentation, ask them, "Will you please follow along with me so you can make notes on the appropriate pages? This will save time for all of us."

- Some presenters give their audience a black-and-white copy of their slides or overheads. They say, "Should you choose, you can now make notes as I elaborate on each of these points."

What do I do about questions relating to the handouts?

- If the president looks through the materials and starts to ask questions about information on page 10 when you are only on page 6, you will do better to answer his questions than to request that he follow along with you. Pace the key people at your presentation. Do not expect them to pace you.

How can the handouts enhance my talk?

- If you are competing for business with another firm, your handouts will serve as a memory jog and subtly continue to persuade as people peruse them at a later date. This is especially true when you have some effective pictures and graphs, and reinforce their message with appropriate anecdotes.

- If your audience does not know your name, put your address and phone number on every handout page. You put it on every page in case they lose the title page with your name and phone number. This is particularly useful if you are the lunch or dinner speaker at a conference. Someone listening may want to ask you to speak, and he or she needs your address or phone number. A handout can serve as a nonobvious selling technique for the professional speaker. It also helps those in big organizations who forgot your last name and want to contact you.

- Put only the key words on your handouts, and tell participants they can follow along, writing in their own comments as you speak.

- Do not let the handout remain a mystery. Explain it. As Paul LeRoux says in *Selling to a Group* (New York: Harper & Row, 1984), "Take the 'news value' out of a handout before you pass it out. . . . Destroying the news value includes showing each page you plan to review. Summarize each page just as you would a visual." Naturally this advice depends on the situation and on how many pages of handouts you have.

- Handouts can also be used to inform people who are not at your talk. This is especially useful for the decision maker who cannot make your meeting.

Should I distribute them afterward?

- If the handouts are used just for the record, distribute them after the presentation.

- Be sure you do not act as if you are secretly keeping the handouts. I hear people complain that the presenter acted as if the handouts were a secret by saying, "I do have these handouts to give you later." When people hear that there are handouts, they will want them right away. If they do not get them right then, they later complain.

- Be careful when you tell people that, at the end of your talk, they will receive handouts of all you are about to say. This is an effective way to lose your audience's attention even before you begin.

What do all these seemingly contradictory comments mean for you as the speaker? Each situation is unique and demands that you decide how to manage the handouts. There is no right way. While you are choosing how to manage them, keep asking yourself, "What is the best way to use the handouts so that my communication is most effective?" Finally, consider whether you need to put a copyright notice on your handouts.

STEP 4

CREATING AND USING VISUALS

KEY POINTS

1   Make your visuals so they clearly guide you through your talk.

2   Make your visuals simple without a lot of words.

3   Never use complete sentences on a visual.

4   Edit your visuals at least 4 times.

5   Ask someone else to edit your visuals for word choice and for graphic layout.

6   Vary your visuals and don't use the same template over and over again (e.g., don't show six pie charts in a row).

7   Use fancy technology only when you know how to use it or you have a qualified assistant.

8   Your visuals may be gorgeous, but you need an enthusiastic voice tone and presentation manner to go with them.

9   If you use a computer graphics package, attend training and really learn how to use it.

10   Do not conclude while picking up your visuals. Conclude looking at your audience.

Step 4 is about creating and using visual aids. The visuals we will discuss in this step are designed to help you reach your objective. They cannot do *your* work of establishing audience rapport and convincing your listeners. Visuals only add to a well-organized talk.

Recent developments in computer graphics and multimedia presentations have made available some remarkable tools to assist us in making presentations. While it may be tempting to abdicate your role as the center of your presentation in favor of those technological marvels, keep in mind that many people in your audience see and experience a virtual onslaught of incredible images on a daily basis. The best policy is a judicious use of the new technologies to support your points and to bring out your unique nature as a presenter.

The most beautiful visuals in the world hardly matter if you speak in a monotone voice and do not establish rapport with your listeners. Visuals still demand that you be the center of the talk. They will help participants remember more for a longer period of time, but you are the center attraction whether you want to be or not. Visuals are the icing; *you* are still the cake.

YOU ARE YOUR OWN GRAPHICS DEPARTMENT

Many companies are moving away from having a graphics department. Employees are expected to make their own visuals. This is good and bad news. The good news is that you have control over your visuals. The bad news is that you have to learn how to make graphics. How do you start?

1. *Find Out What's Expected.* Look around your company. How are people expected to present? What do people at your level use when they present? What does the president of your organization use when he or she presents? Now you have a sense of what is expected of you.

2. *Do It Yourself.* If you are expected to put together your own presentation, get yourself an easy-to-use graphics program. Then attend a training class or have someone show you how to use it. You don't want to waste hours learning how to do something that someone can show you in 10 minutes. This is the first mistake most people make. They don't spend the time learning the program well enough so they can use it quickly and effectively. Unless you are the graphics person in the company, learn *one* program well. Your job is to make effective presentations, not learn every graphics package on the market. Here are the options for making and showing your visuals:

   • *Thermoprinters.* This is a machine that makes one-color overheads.

   • *Copier.* You can buy one-color transparencies and run them through the copier. Then you'll have a color transparency with black letters.

   • *Color Printer.* Find out if there is one in your company.

- *Slide Maker.* Find out if someone has one you can use or ask where your company get their slides made. Here is what a Polaroid slide maker (film recorder) looks like:

Used by permission of Polaroid.

- *LCD Projection Panel.* Does your company have one and will it work for your presentation? (LCD panels are explained later in Step 4.)

3. *Go to a Creative Service Bureau.* Companies that specialize in creating presentations are called service bureaus. You can find them listed in the yellow pages under graphics. You need to shop around for prices. Some can be very expensive, especially if you need a rush job. Also, you should really know what you want to put on each visual. For those of you who like to edit and reedit your work, remember you'll pay each time the service bureau makes the changes.

EFFECTIVE VISUALS

Keep your visuals *simple.* Visuals are for understanding, not for attempting to win prizes in abstract modern art. Use this simple touchstone for distinguishing whether a particular visual should be used: Will this visual make it easier for my audience to understand and enjoy my talk? The following checklist, along with the analysis of these requirements on the next few pages, will help you create motivating visuals for your audience.

Requirements for Effective Visuals

1. Use readable, consistent typeface.

2. Limit text to a few phrases on a page.

3. Use some color.

4. Write phrases, not sentences.

5. Vary between numbering and using bullets with phrases.

6. Put one heading on each visual.

7. Use pictures or charts whenever possible.

8. Be prepared to supplement the visual with comments about it.

9. Use parallel structure on each visual.

10. Vary the look of the visuals. Don't make every visual look the same!

Use Readable, Consistent Typeface

There are many exciting typefaces, but beware of mixing more than two to four different types. When you mix too many styles, you are asking your group to hopscotch all the way to your destination. Although variety is interesting, too much of it can distract your audience from the main path. This may seem to be a rather trite rule, but stop and consider how many overheads you have had difficulty reading because of this very problem.

Limit Text to a Few Phrases on a Page

Do not put too many points on a page; it causes the visual to become difficult to read and overwhelming to look at. People may see it and think, "Oh no, he is going to discuss all those points!" Don Keough, the president of Coca-Cola Company, when interviewed by Sandy Linver of Speakeasy, Inc., said, "Some pictures may be worth a thousand words, but a picture of a thousand words isn't worth much." Here's a rule from *PC* magazine: "We came up with the 'Coppertone Rule'—don't pack any more into a visual than you could read off a billboard as you're driving by at 40 miles per hour."

Use Some Color

According to Genigraphics Corporation, the supporters of PowerPoint, "A color ad is read by 80 percent more people than a black-and-white ad. Using color in a visual presentation increases recognition by 78 percent and comprehension by 73 percent. In short, color adds clout."

There are some considerations though as you use color. Don't use green and red together. They look the same to people who are color-blind.

Use color for emphasis, and change colors only if you have a logical reason for doing so. Otherwise, you may confuse your audience. A presenter having discovered colored transparencies, varied his presentation with red and blue transparencies. The change in colors had no apparent logic except that the presenter believed the colors added spice. Meanwhile, the participants spent much of their time trying to figure out what the different colors were supposed to signify rather than listening to the substance of the presentation.

Write Phrases, Not Sentences

Have you ever attempted to read an overhead that was copied from a typewritten page? Some people think that it is all right to use sentences, as long as you apologize by saying something like, "I know this is difficult to read, but I will read it to you." That is ineffective communication. Shorten everything to phrases. The following two examples illustrate this point.

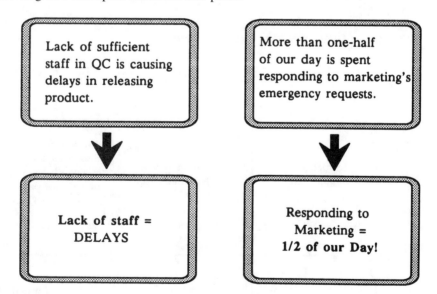

Vary between Numbering and Using Bullets with Phrases

You have a real advantage when you number your phrases. You can easily say things like this, "Let's look at point 5." or "Here are all the issues we decided are blocking our reaching the goal; I will talk about number 7." You don't have to go through each point. You can also direct your audience to the phrase you want to discuss in detail. This saves you from the tedious task of reading off each one until you get to the one that you really want to discuss.

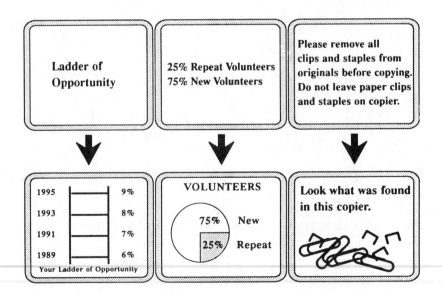

Put One Heading on Each Visual

When you have headings on each visual, people have an easier time following your overall framework. They see the major heading, then the points underneath. As you can see in the preceding examples, the one with a heading is easier to grasp. Whenever possible have a different heading on each visual. The heading should be directly related to the information on that visual.

Use Pictures or Charts Whenever Possible

Pictures are much more interesting than text. The following examples illustrate this.

If you put people in your pictures, the pictures will look more like a cartoon. This may be fine depending on your situation. You must be the judge of that.

Be Prepared to Supplement the Visual with Comments about It

Have you ever suffered through a presentation where the presenter just went through visual after visual and only read the words on each one, never adding any extra comments? Although many speakers think this approach is sufficient, it can be boring for both the presenter and the audience. Add comments to your visuals. It increases rapport and also shows that you have something to say. Sometimes, you may just want your audience to be aware of key points, but keep in mind that the audience wants to hear you, not read the detailed notes that you have made into visuals. If they didn't need to hear you, you could hand out the presentation visuals, sit down, and save time.

Use Parallel Structure on Each Visual

On each separate visual, use the same structure. Have every bullet begin with a verb. Or have every phrase begin with a noun. Or have every phrase begin with a gerund (verbs ending in "ing" such as encouraging, providing, building). Why? It's easier for you to talk as you go through the points. Also, the audience's comprehension is better. But don't make all your presentation visuals with phrases that start with a verb. You need variety in the structure of your phrases from visual to visual.

Vary the Look of the Visuals

Most graphic packages have a slide sorter in which you can see a thumbnail view of each of your visuals. As you work on your presentation, keep looking back at all the visuals together. You don't want five pie charts in a row. You don't want six consecutive visuals with just bulleted phrases on them. You want variety. Another way to see how your whole presentation flows is to print out hard copy and lay them all out on a table or the floor. Look at the total presentation at once and ask yourself these questions:

- Would this be interesting to look at?
- Is there enough variety among the visuals?
- Do I include some visuals with bulleted phrases, some with numbers, some with pictures, some with charts?
- Finally, will this presentation be motivating for me to give?

I find that until a presenter lays out the talk and sees it all, he or she isn't really aware of its total flow.

CRITERIA FOR VISUALS

As you create visuals using the guidelines in the previous section, the following criteria will help you decide whether or not to include a visual:

- Can the point really be visualized?

- Is the visual (or, are at least a few of the individual visuals) funny or entertaining in some way?

- Does the visual make my objective easier to understand?

- Will the visual enhance my verbal presentation?

- Will the visual be offensive or distracting to anyone?

- Does the visual fit with my other visuals?

EFFECTIVE VISUAL EXAMPLES

Examples 1 and 2 on pages 105 and 106 show alternative ways of presenting visuals. Choose the visual example that illustrates the point most effectively.

CHOOSING THE TYPE OF VISUAL

Many presenters agonize over the best method for presenting a visual: overheads, props, slides, flip charts, video, LCD panel, multimedia with sounds and animation, laser show, and so on. The list of possibilities is becoming endless. The answer usually becomes apparent as you consider the following criteria:

- *Size of Group.* Do not use a flip chart for a group of more than 25 to 30 people. Not everyone will be able to see the chart.

- *Presentation Mode.* If you are selling in competition with other firms, find out how those firms present. You want to give at least the same quality presentation or, when feasible, a more professional one.

- *Time Constraints.* Be realistic about the kind of visuals you really can put together within your alloted time span. Consider the principle that anything that can go wrong, will. Visuals completed a day after your talk are useless.

- *Organizational Culture.* What type of visuals are expected by your organization or by the group of people to whom you will be presenting?

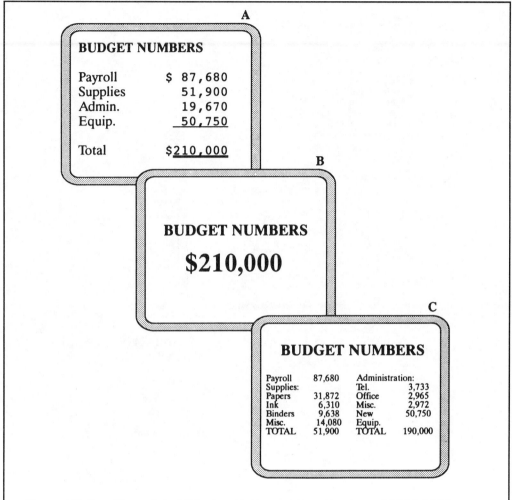

Example 1.   The point of this visual is the proposed budget of $210,000 for next year. Which visual best serves the point—*A, B,* or *C?*

Overhead *A* provides just enough information. To emphasize the information when you talk, highlight the total amount with a colored marker. This will help people remember the number even more. Overhead *B* does not have enough information to warrant an overhead, and overhead *C* has too much detail. You may want to have this for backup in case someone requests more detail. Also, the total is incorrect.

- *Presentation Objective.* Will the visuals you use enhance your objective or only get in the way?

- *Available Resources.* Know what resources (for example, people) you can truly count on.

- *Budget.* All visuals cost something; budget your time and money accordingly.

- *Your Comfort.* Will you be thoroughly comfortable with creating and using the particular visuals you have chosen? Don't tackle a complex

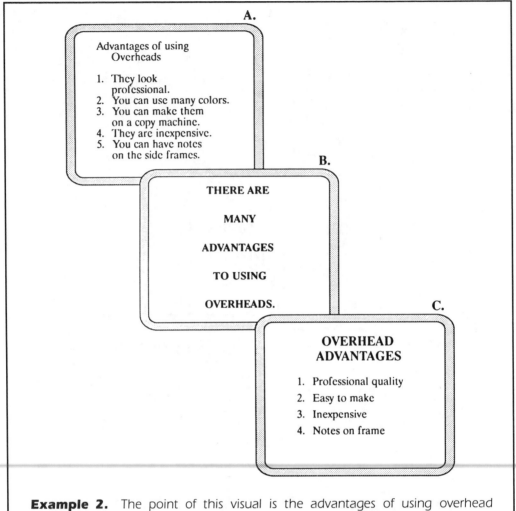

Example 2. The point of this visual is the advantages of using overhead transparencies. Which visual best serves the point—*A, B,* or *C?*

The sentences in overhead *A* clutter the visual; overhead *B* is difficult to read and visually boring; but overhead *C* provides just enough information.

multimedia presentation if you are new to that technology. Or at least, have an expert do it with you the first time.

- *The Lights.* Can you control the lights in the room? Overheads and, even more, slides and LCD panels need a fairly dark setting. If you can't close out the window light, your audience won't be able to see what is on the screen. But you don't want a room that only has an on-and-off light setting. Presenting to a totally dark room puts people to sleep and doesn't let you see the reactions of your audience.

- *The Room.* What is the room setup? Will everyone be able to see? If you are presenting in a hotel meeting room and are not familiar with the room, ask the catering manager or AV director to sketch out the room for you so you can explain how you want it arranged.

- *The Equipment.* Is there a decent overhead projector? For LCD panels, you need a projector with 4,000 lumens or greater. Don't assume the hotel will have this type. You need to ask and get confirmation in writing that they will supply the equipment you need. Also, be sure that the projector comes with an extra bulb. Most people who spend a lot of time presenting, invest in their own equipment. Why? They know it works, and they know it makes their visuals look great. There is nothing like a decrepit, yellowed-out overhead projector to wreck your gorgeous colored overheads. And finally, make sure there is a screen or a good wall on which to project your image.

FLIP CHARTS

Use when you have a small group (no more than 25 people). Be sure you have the time to make readable flip charts.

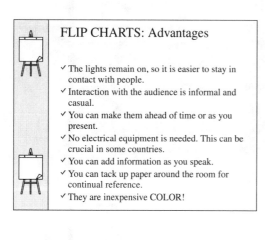

FLIP CHARTS: Advantages

✓ The lights remain on, so it is easier to stay in contact with people.
✓ Interaction with the audience is informal and casual.
✓ You can make them ahead of time or as you present.
✓ No electrical equipment is needed. This can be crucial in some countries.
✓ You can add information as you speak.
✓ You can tack up paper around the room for continual reference.
✓ They are inexpensive COLOR!

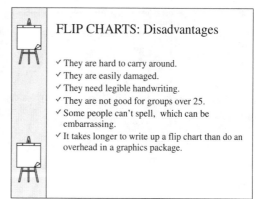

FLIP CHARTS: Disadvantages

✓ They are hard to carry around.
✓ They are easily damaged.
✓ They need legible handwriting.
✓ They are not good for groups over 25.
✓ Some people can't spell, which can be embarrassing.
✓ It takes longer to write up a flip chart than do an overhead in a graphics package.

Comments about Flip Charts

- When you walk into a person's office and see a flip chart stand, chances are that person processes information visually. Instead of sitting down and talking about your idea, put some notes, pictures, or phrases on the chart. Flip charts are great for this type of impromptu talk. The visually oriented person will think that you are a great communicator.

- Realize that, if you make a permanent set of fancy flip charts, you might end up forever changing what is so nicely written on the chart. They might not serve your purpose. Also, carrying the charts on airplanes might be a nuisance. So buy some good quality magic markers and try making your own charts as you go along. If, on the other hand, you are sure the information will remain unchanged for a while and you do not have to lug them about, go ahead and have some charts made. You can have them laminated so they last longer.

Creating Flip Charts

Choose a chart size appropriate for the amount of material you have.

While preparing the charts, leave every other page blank so that the next visual does not show through.

For turning, tape two pages (the prepared page and a blank page) together in the bottom corner.

For easy reading, alternate colors between points.

Make lettering dark enough and large enough to be read by everyone in the audience.

Distribute the graphs or words evenly over the whole chart page.

Do not use a red marker (it reminds some people of school).

Use headings to reinforce points.

When lettering, put an extra sheet under the page so that color does not bleed onto the next page (especially if you are writing on a wall).

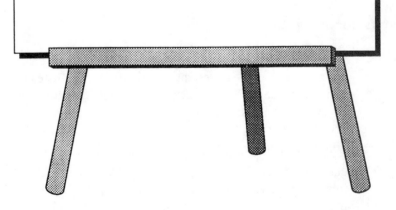

Using Flip Charts

Securely attach the flip chart to the easel.

Have the topic on the first page for all to see when entering room.

Make sure everyone in the group can easily read the chart.

Turn to a blank page when the visual on the flip chart is not relevant to what you are currently talking about.

Have extra paper in case you want to add points.

Leave blank pages in the middle and at the end of the flip chart.

Grasp the visual by the tape to flip it.

Stand to the left side of the easel to explain information on chart. People are used to looking from left to right.

Talk to people, not to the flip chart.

Use progressive disclosure (see "Comments about Flip Charts").

Use two charts: one for questions and one for facts.

- You can use the technique of progressive disclosure when you have already written your information on the flip chart. Tape a piece of paper over the material you do not want people to see and then move the tape and piece of paper down as you uncover the points in your talk. Or, you can fold the flip chart paper part way and reveal each point as you discuss it. Use paper clips to keep it partially folded up. Do not crease it; just fold it up easily.

OVERHEADS

Overheads are fun to use, especially now with all the fancy computer graphics packages available. However, do not be tempted to go overboard with them. Keep them simple. The purpose is to share information and have people follow your talk, not to bombard your audience with sights, colors, and graphs that more closely resemble an experience in a discotheque! Usually, you do not want people's heads reeling after your talk.

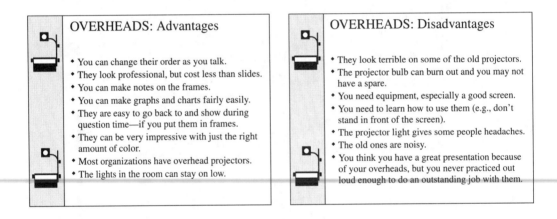

OVERHEADS: Advantages

- You can change their order as you talk.
- They look professional, but cost less than slides.
- You can make notes on the frames.
- You can make graphs and charts fairly easily.
- They are easy to go back to and show during question time—if you put them in frames.
- They can be very impressive with just the right amount of color.
- Most organizations have overhead projectors.
- The lights in the room can stay on low.

OVERHEADS: Disadvantages

- They look terrible on some of the old projectors.
- The projector bulb can burn out and you may not have a spare.
- You need equipment, especially a good screen.
- You need to learn how to use them (e.g., don't stand in front of the screen).
- The projector light gives some people headaches.
- The old ones are noisy.
- You think you have a great presentation because of your overheads, but you never practiced out loud enough to do an outstanding job with them.

Comments about Overheads

- Use frames around transparencies. A frame keeps a transparency straight on the projector. Frames also border the transparency so there is a finished look on the screen. They are much easier to pick up and use than the transparency alone. When you want to go back and find a transparency to show again on the screen, they are easy to sort through. There is room to write a few words or phrases on the frames, which serve to remind you exactly what you want to say when you show the transparency. You can buy cardboard frames or 3M flip frames. See References under "visuals."

- Dorothy Sarnoff in *Never Be Nervous Again* (New York: Ivy Books, 1987) suggests this excellent idea for keeping transparencies straight: "To get your acetate slides straight on the projector on your first try, make a slide guide for the projector. Cut a strip of cardboard about an inch wide. Attach it with masking tape on the upper edge of the projector to act as a straight edge for the acetate. Place your acetate right up against this guide and it will always be straight."

- When you use progressive disclosure with overheads, be sure you do not cover the material with only one piece of paper. As you move down the transparency, the paper will blow off. Use a pad of paper or put a pen on the one piece of paper. It is hard to dramatically uncover points when, halfway through, your paper flies off the projector. Only use progressive disclosure once or twice during your talk.

- If you like to write notes on the frames of the overheads, make a copy of those notes. In one case, a presenter had put all her notes on the frames. When she arrived to give her talk, she was told that the overhead projector was in the back of the room and that someone else would be putting her overheads on for her. Fortunately, she was early enough to make copies of her notes from the frames. Modern technology can sometimes ruin the best of your preparations.

- Colored pens can be used for emphasis. Underline points with them. Another word of caution: underline the transparency on the projector, not the words on the screen. One presenter started to underline the words appearing on the screen. Fortunately, someone yelled out, "Do not do that. It will not come off."

- For a presentation to a large group in a big room, use 2 overhead projectors. It becomes more like a show!

- Turn off the overhead when you linger on certain points. If you leave it on during your whole talk, there is no change of pace. In addition, the people sitting nearest the overhead will be lulled by the sound of the fan in the projector.

- If you are considering what type of equipment to buy, the following drawings show two types of overhead projectors. The transmission overhead is heavier to carry and stands higher, so it is more likely to block a person's view of the screen.

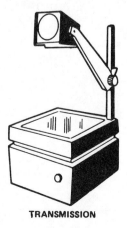
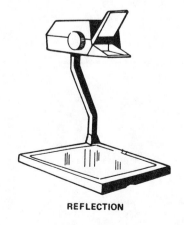

TRANSMISSION   **REFLECTION**

Creating Overheads

Learn how to use one computer graphics program.

Use phrases; never use whole sentences.

Make sure your overheads flow one to another.

Make hard copies, practice with them out loud, and then make the transparencies.

Put the overheads in frames.

If you don't have a color printer, use a colored transparency pen to add color to the overhead. Emphasize charts, key words with the color marker.

Proof your overheads and have someone else proof them as well.

Typefaces smaller than 18 point are too small!

Avoid using red type.

Be consistent—same size headings, same font throughout the visuals.

Only use clip art that helps make your points.

Using Overheads

Have the first transparency on the machine before you turn it on.

Have an extra bulb with you.

Make sure everyone can see the overheads. Ask: Who can't see?

Be sure the transparency is straight.

Use a pencil, not your finger, when pointing on the transparency.

Turn the projector off whenever you are not discussing the points shown on the transparency.

Don't read all the transparencies verbatim.

Talk to the audience, not to the screen.

Read from the screen, not the projector.

For variety, introduce the next visual before you show it.

The reflector projector comes in a portable carrying case. It does not stand as high, so it is not as likely to block a person's view of the screen. It sits flat on the table so you can slide your overheads on without having to move them up and down as with the transmission projector. The only disadvantage is that the plate scratches easier than the transmission plate.

- When you are showing an overhead, be sure the people in the back of the room can see. If they can't, you have two choices. Move the overhead up as you talk. Since this creates a big white space at the bottom of the projector, cover it with a piece of paper or cardboard. The bright light can bother some people to the extent that they will end up with a migraine after a few hours of presentations. Or, if you are using a screen, put the screen on a table so that it is up high the whole time. This works well when you are presenting in a big room, such as a conference or banquet room in a hotel.

- If your time is limited, mark the most important transparencies with Post-it notes. You will then easily find them as you talk.

SLIDES

Slide presenters sometimes ignore the necessity of telling interesting anecdotes. They think that their pretty colored slides exempt them from being animated speakers.

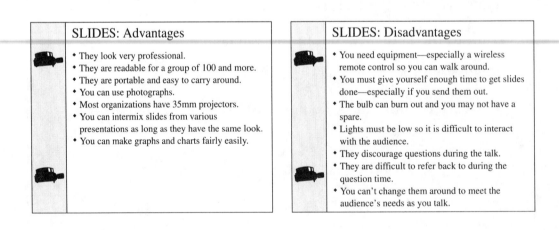

SLIDES: Advantages	SLIDES: Disadvantages
• They look very professional. • They are readable for a group of 100 and more. • They are portable and easy to carry around. • You can use photographs. • Most organizations have 35mm projectors. • You can intermix slides from various presentations as long as they have the same look. • You can make graphs and charts fairly easily.	• You need equipment—especially a wireless remote control so you can walk around. • You must give yourself enough time to get slides done—especially if you send them out. • The bulb can burn out and you may not have a spare. • Lights must be low so it is difficult to interact with the audience. • They discourage questions during the talk. • They are difficult to refer back to during the question time. • You can't change them around to meet the audience's needs as you talk.

Comments about Slides

- Many companies spend fortunes putting together slide presentations for their field and branch offices. These presentations are usually for the purpose of communicating information in order to convince people to "buy." Most people who design these slides have never taken courses on presentation skills, the design of graphics for an audience, or script writing geared to sales presentations. They do not have to give the presentation they created and watch people's bored expressions!

To make those presentations dynamic, the company should send the manager two outlines (one horizontal and one vertical) of the talk along with the entire script. Why? Some people like to see the information vertically and others like it horizontally. Then the presenter must use at least three of the following ideas:

- ☐ Tell a story about a customer.

- ☐ Give a personal view of how you like the product or service.

- ☐ Turn off the projector and take questions after this section.

- ☐ Ask for a show of hands when you read these questions.

- ☐ Give people a quiz here.

- ☐ Discuss how you, personally, or the office, will provide special service with this product.

Salespeople must relate to their audience even with a canned script. Or else they will be like a salesperson who went to Gillette and talked about how happy he was to be at General Electric. What he should have done when he started is to hold up a Gillette Sensor razor and said, "I love this razor. You've got a great product." Just do anything to tell the audience you know about them.

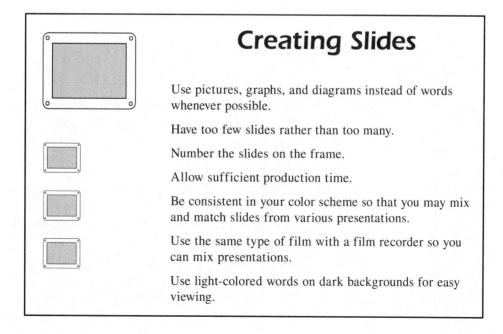

Creating Slides

Use pictures, graphs, and diagrams instead of words whenever possible.

Have too few slides rather than too many.

Number the slides on the frame.

Allow sufficient production time.

Be consistent in your color scheme so that you may mix and match slides from various presentations.

Use the same type of film with a film recorder so you can mix presentations.

Use light-colored words on dark backgrounds for easy viewing.

- Receive your slides soon enough to have time to check them for accuracy. Proofread your work by reading the words backward (that is, right to left). Someone lost his job because his statistics were incorrect too many times. He never budgeted his time to proof the slides. You may get away with presenting wrong data to management once, making the excuse that the slides just came back from the print shop. But three times may be pushing the goodwill of the president.

- Avoid having anyone else operate your slide machine. The person will get out of synch with you unless you have practiced together. If you have to let someone else run the slide projector, don't say, "Next slide, please." This destroys your presentation's flow. Use a head or a hand signal instead.

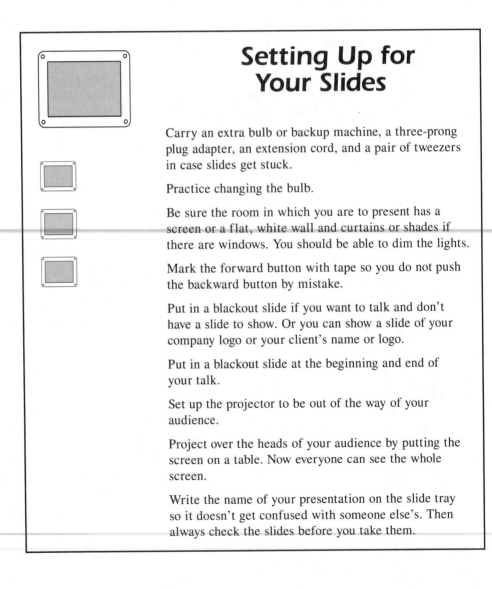

Setting Up for Your Slides

Carry an extra bulb or backup machine, a three-prong plug adapter, an extension cord, and a pair of tweezers in case slides get stuck.

Practice changing the bulb.

Be sure the room in which you are to present has a screen or a flat, white wall and curtains or shades if there are windows. You should be able to dim the lights.

Mark the forward button with tape so you do not push the backward button by mistake.

Put in a blackout slide if you want to talk and don't have a slide to show. Or you can show a slide of your company logo or your client's name or logo.

Put in a blackout slide at the beginning and end of your talk.

Set up the projector to be out of the way of your audience.

Project over the heads of your audience by putting the screen on a table. Now everyone can see the whole screen.

Write the name of your presentation on the slide tray so it doesn't get confused with someone else's. Then always check the slides before you take them.

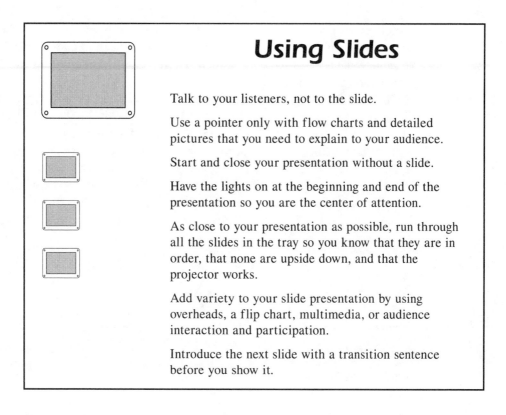

Using Slides

Talk to your listeners, not to the slide.

Use a pointer only with flow charts and detailed pictures that you need to explain to your audience.

Start and close your presentation without a slide.

Have the lights on at the beginning and end of the presentation so you are the center of attention.

As close to your presentation as possible, run through all the slides in the tray so you know that they are in order, that none are upside down, and that the projector works.

Add variety to your slide presentation by using overheads, a flip chart, multimedia, or audience interaction and participation.

Introduce the next slide with a transition sentence before you show it.

- You can make your own slides with a film recorder. The advantages are that you can make them at the last minute, you needn't wait to get them back, and it is more cost effective. Moreover, you are in control of the process.

LCD PANELS

What is an LCD panel? It looks like a square plate and you set it on top of an overhead projector. The panel connects to your computer. The graphics presentation you have created in your computer goes directly through the panel and is projected onto the screen. You don't need to have overheads or slides. This means you must have a computer available in the room where you will do your presentation. Many presenters carry their own notebook computer with them. Where are LCD panels used the most? They are very useful when training people on computer programs. The trainer can instantly change something on the computer and everyone can see it right then. They are becoming more popular with presenters.

Another thing you can do with an LCD panel is to hook your video into it. Why would you want to? Let's say you want to show a video to an audience of 60 people, and you have a small TV screen. By hooking the video into the LCD panel, you can show it on a large screen.

LCD panels fall into two categories: (1) active-matrix and (2) passive-matrix. Active-matrix panels are the best and most expensive. LCD panels simply display what is on your computer screen. The more features your computer has (e.g., 24-bit color card and fast processing), the more impressive will be your presentation. You also need to have a good overhead projector (4,000 lumens or greater) to get really good color. Passive-matrix panels are less expensive and suffer from poor performance and lack of processing speed. This can be frustrating for both the presenter and audience. You also can't show a video through a passive-matrix panel.

LCD PANEL: Advantages	LCD PANEL: Disadvantages
• It is lightweight and portable. • It can be used with all sizes of audiences. • Your presentation is live and interactive as it comes from the computer right to the screen. • Your presentation visuals can be quickly updated. • You can easily customize using client names and so on. • You can incorporate audience feedback as you present. • You don't need to spend time or money making slides or overheads. • The LCD panel can display anything that is on your computer.	• LCD panels have a high acquisition cost. • It is fragile as it is glass. • You must have a computer with enough memory and disk space to handle the graphics programs. • You need to bring your equipment just to be sure it all works right. • The room has to be somewhat dark so the images show up well. • You must have all this equipment: computer, excellent overhead projector, LCD panel.

Comments about LCD Panels

- You want to buy a panel that is reliable and easy to set up and operate. It is very hard to give an effective presentation if you must worry about the equipment 10 minutes before starting your program. Don't let anyone tell you it is easy to use and operate until you try it!

- This is a wonderful new technology, but as with any new equipment, to really know what you are doing, you must practice, practice, practice, *before* you use it in front of a real audience. Become very comfortable with your computer, the "air mouse," and/or the handheld control device (cursor). Depending on your cursor, you may have to stay close to the computer. If you are a presenter who enjoys walking around, you need to get a feel for how this presentation may be different for you.

- You really need to know the room setup ahead of time. LCD panels can look great and dazzle your audience, or they can detract from a presentation in a room full of windows with no blinds on them. You have more variables to consider when you use an LCD panel. If the room is too light, you won't be able to see the images on the screen.

- Just as it is important to chose a graphics program and stay with it, the same is true for presentations using the LCD panel. This approach will allow you to mix and match your presentations, and they will all have the same look and feel.

- Finally, to the extent feasible, set up your equipment beforehand and try it out. Then, if possible, try it again 30 minutes before you are on. Equipment has a way of breaking down between the setup, breakfast, and the presentation. No one has ever figured out how this happens!

PROPS

The major issue with props is to be sure that they have not been popularized— they need to be unique. If you have read about the prop, chances are that some of your audience have seen it or heard about it. Let your creative self think of something as you consider the audience and the type of next steps you wish to propose and have accepted.

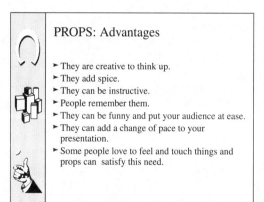

PROPS: Advantages

- ► They are creative to think up.
- ► They add spice.
- ► They can be instructive.
- ► People remember them.
- ► They can be funny and put your audience at ease.
- ► They can add a change of pace to your presentation.
- ► Some people love to feel and touch things and props can satisfy this need.

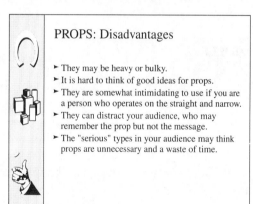

PROPS: Disadvantages

- ► They may be heavy or bulky.
- ► It is hard to think of good ideas for props.
- ► They are somewhat intimidating to use if you are a person who operates on the straight and narrow.
- ► They can distract your audience, who may remember the prop but not the message.
- ► The "serious" types in your audience may think props are unnecessary and a waste of time.

Comments about Props

- If possible, think about props you can bring and use. One supervisor came with a 5-inch stack of customer request forms and a telephone off the hook. She said that she had a way to reduce this stack and to get the phone back on the hook. Due to the processing delays, the customers had been calling to find out why they had not received quicker replies. Her props caught people's attention. Match your prop to the situation. The following are some examples:

  The Travel Agent. A travel agent dressed in a Hawaiian vacation outfit while telling a group of executives how his company markets affordable vacation packages. His clothes were a funny prop and appropriate to the situation.

The 100 Pennies. One speaker threw 100 pennies on the floor. He explained that executives throw away money every day by not paying attention to their employees' suggestions.

Earth Day. At a rally gearing up for Earth Day 1990, one activist painted a picture of conservationist Aldo Leopold on the pavement. Another activist drove up to the stage in a SOLECTRIA 5B solar racing car.

Dr. Land. Dr. Land, in 1977, introduced the Polaroid movie camera by having a woman dance while he filmed her. Ninety seconds later, the audience was able to see the color movie of the woman who had just danced.

The Computer Cables. One person brought a cluster of computer cables to her presentation. She wanted everyone to see what they looked like.

• When you are in a meeting with one or two people you can use an 8½-by-11-inch piece of paper as a prop. Make diagrams, draw a picture, or list a few key phrases that capture the flow of the conversation.

• Skits are fun to create and are especially interesting when you utilize people from your audience.

VIDEO

Videos can be an excellent way to break up your presentation and add some spice to it. Think about the most appropriate time to show it. I was recently in a very hot room and someone put on a video that was to last 60 minutes. This was just after lunch. It was almost impossible to stay awake with a full stomach in that stuffy room, especially since some of us were still suffering from jet lag. Thankfully, after 30 minutes, the presenter looked around at us and turned it off.

VIDEO: Advantages
* When you create it yourself, you can add personal touches.
* When you show people in the company, they like to see themselves.
* You can send the same message to many locations.
* Video equipment is easy to get and use.
* A video is easy to carry around.
* Videos can be shown via an LCD panel or very large monitor for a big audience.
* Videos can be incorporated into your presentation for a change of pace.

VIDEO: Disadvantages
* It is not great for retention.
* People can go to sleep when watching one.
* You need an expert to make it look professional.
* Experts are expensive to hire.
* It can be dated very quickly.
* The lights must be dim so you miss people's reactions.
* It gets boring easily if not done well.

Comments about Video

- If you want to make a video, get professional help. It is great to use your own employees for actors, but get a video production company to help you create your video.

- With companies all getting leaner and tightening travel budgets, videos have become a way to train staff. But it shouldn't take the place of interaction within the group that is watching the video. You can't just show a video and assume people are trained, just as you can't stand up and do a one-hour presentation on new products and assume people are now adequately trained on the new product.

- Videos have become a way to market products in the place of a company representative. You want to be sure that the video is excellent so at least have a professional video producer work with you on the project.

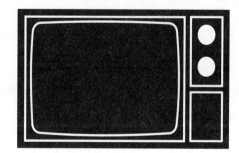

Using a Video

Queue the video beforehand.

Make sure everyone can see and hear.

Know how to use the pause buttons or remote control.

Have an LCD panel in position. The overhead projector should be 4,000 lumens or brighter.

Make the color adjustments for the LCD panel before starting your presentation.

When introducing the video, let the audience know its purpose and why you are showing it.

Be prepared to conclude the video showing with questions, an exercise, or some other group activity.

TELECONFERENCING AND USING A TELEPROMPTER

Because you are an excellent presenter, your company has asked you to take part in a teleconference. You are going to be speaking to people all around the world. What is the proper way to talk to a camera? Your company has told you a Tele-PrompTer will be available if you want to use it. The TelePrompTer is a box that is plugged into a computer. The speech you have written on the computer gets shown through the TelePrompTer either on a video monitor underneath the camera lens or on a flat screen that goes over the camera lens. As you look directly at the camera, you can read the words in the TelePrompTer.

What type of notes will you use? Will you look down at your notes or will you use a TelePrompTer? If you have written out notes, go back and read the information on writing out a speech. I strongly suggest you not write out your talk, but just write up some key points using the general format outline in Step 2. You want to appear relaxed, and reading a speech won't help you do that. If you plan to use the TelePrompTer, keep the following in mind:

1. Go at your own pace; the person moving the script will adjust to you. If you have to speed up as the copy races by or slow down because the copy is moving too slowly, stop and discuss how the operator can move the copy at your pace.

2. Put in the cues just as you would for any other speech: Use **bold** or underlinings for emphasis and several periods in a row (. . .) to suggest a pause. The more you pause and emphasize words, the less you will sound and look as if you are reading.

3. How do you avoid looking as if you are talking to a camera? There are many techniques: Some speakers imagine a whole audience behind the words they are reading; others imagine they are speaking to just one very special person who wants to hear every word. Some people have an excellent producer who helps them smile and look natural, or they may bring pictures of their family or friends so they can see someone by the camera lens. You can also look back on one of your most enthusiastic and motivating presentations. Recreate your feelings from that experience as you present now with the TelePrompTer.

4. Make sure you don't squint when reading the TelePrompTer. Some fonts are easier to read than others. Be sure you have a font you can easily read so you won't have to wonder if a word is *end* or *and*.

5. You must act the same way you do in front of a live audience. Gesture and smile. You won't be able to walk around a lot because you will be reading from the TelePrompTer. But if you have an example that you can relate without reading it from the TelePrompTer, then at that point, you can walk around. Just warn the camera crew ahead of time. This activity makes you look more natural and lets you get rid of some excess energy.

6. Take a break once in a while. At first, you will feel a little tense reading from the TelePrompTer, so practice for 10 minutes, stop and look at yourself, and then start over and do it for real. You'll be surprised at how natural you look. If you have props you can show, they will add a little variety.

7. Practice out loud at least two times before you use the TelePrompTer. You'll have a sense of where you want to pause and what phrases or words you want to emphasize. You will also begin to consider the gestures you can use.

8. Vary the talk. Try not to be a talking head for a whole hour. That is just too long. Vary the presentation just as you would vary a presentation in front of a live group.

MULTIMEDIA

Many books have been written about multimedia and all its different possibilities. *PC World,* August 1993, says, "Multimedia represents a convergence of different disciplines such as videography, computer programming, visual and audio arts." From simple to complex, here are some possible multimedia applications:

1. You are using an LCD panel to do your presentation and you have fade-ins and fade-outs between each of your visuals. This might mean the image on the screen fades out slowly with a blue pattern of lines, and the next image comes on as the blue pattern of lines dissolves.

2. Now you get fancy and add a little sound as well. At certain points in the talk, you have some music come on.

3. You include photographs made by someone in your company.

MULTIMEDIA: Advantages

* The material stimulates the audience.
* It is fun to put together—once you learn the programs.
* You can add much variety to a presentation.
* It is impressive to use during a sales presentation.
* You can engage the audience.

MULTIMEDIA: Disadvantages

* It is costly to buy the software and hardware.
* It takes time to learn the programs.
* Equipment can break down.
* You may not be able to customize it on the spot for an audience.
* You can get carried away and spend too much time creating a multimedia presentation.
* You can't depend on someone else for equipment, should carry your own, just in case.
* The audience gets lost in the "technology", and they miss the "message" of your presentation.

4. With certain programs, you are able to bring into your computer moving images from a video.

5. You can animate certain portions of your presentation with specialized programs.

Besides presentations, multimedia is being used to create self-paced interactive multimedia training. Many multimedia companies will take your training videotapes and make them into PC-based, interactive multimedia.

Comments about Multimedia

- *The Graphics.* Do not add graphics just because you like some images. Only use graphics to illustrate a point. Unless you have a clear reason, don't add a photo, clip art, or some image to every visual. That's overkill.

- *The Video.* Using a video as part of your multimedia presentation can be exciting, but creating one can be time consuming and frustrating if you don't understand the equipment well. You may need an expert to help you. If you cannot work on the multimedia presentation without feeling pressured, wait until you have more time.

- *The Sound.* Sound can be exciting to add into a presentation. Decide what you want to use the sound for. Do you want to excite the audience? What kind of mood do you want to set? Do you want to use it as an introduction to the major point of your presentation? What are the music or sound tastes of your audience?

- *The Overhead Projector.* Make certain that the right type of overhead projector is available. Many people will not hear you when you say that you need a certain type of projector. Write them a letter, simple and with big print, then follow up with a phone call. Protect yourself, if you can, by having an expert presenter readily available.

- *The Perfectionist.* If you are a perfectionist, you may have a tendency to keep refining a multimedia presentation over and over. You get an idea to add a little more music. Then you choose to put in another video image. Set limits, decide when you are done, and stop.

HINTS FOR USING VISUALS

- *The Screen.* Whenever possible, keep the screen angled off to the side. You want to remain center stage. This is great advice, and about half the time you might have that luxury in a conference room. When the screen is right behind you, always stand off to the side, changing sides once in a while so you're close to both sides of your audience.

- *Hand Gestures.* If you do not use a pointer, gesture to the screen with the arm nearest the screen. Do not reach across in front of your body to gesture with your arm. A person could miss seeing some vital information!

- *Orderly Visuals.* Have you ever seen a presenter conclude speaking with overheads scattered all over the table? The presentation may have been effective, but the sloppy looking table detracted from it. Create two stacks: one stack of overheads that you *will* use and one stack of overheads that you *have* used.

- *Lights.* If the room is too light and the lights only switch off and on (with no dimmer), remove some ceiling bulbs to lessen the light.

- *Bad Seats.* Before you talk, sit in some of the chairs you think are the worst in the room. You want to know that people sitting in those chairs will still be able to see the visuals. Also be sure that the screen is high enough to be seen by everyone.

- *Surprises.* Your first task is to take the surprise and mystery away from your visual, especially if its meaning is not obvious. People will not pay attention to you until they figure out that meaning. Tell them what it is as soon as you show it.

- *Variety.* Vary your talk. Use visuals, then none, then use them again.

- *Pointers.* Hold the pointer in the hand nearest to the screen. Pointers are great as long as you do not fiddle with them or wave them about.

    If you use your hands a lot, do not hold the pointer all the time or you will feel restrained. You can use it, then *leaving it open,* put it down.

A Presenter, Not a Conductor

Pick it up again when you want to point to something else on the screen. Be sure not to bang the pointer against the screen or white board. If you have numbers by your key issues, you will not need to use the pointer as much, since you can refer to each issue by saying, "Now, as you can see, the fourth issue I have listed is . . . ."

- *Talking.* Should you talk or not talk when changing your overheads, slides, or flip chart pages? Three presentation books will give you three different answers. Remember that when you talk and change your visuals at the same time, your attention is not fully focused on the group. Also remember that an unchanging pace gets boring, so you may want to talk sometimes and to remain silent sometimes. If you really want to emphasize something, then do not talk as you put up your visual. Show it, pause for two or three seconds, then discuss it.

- *Pacing.* When you are explaining your visual, you should try to stand by the screen or flip chart. Given the layout of some rooms, you may have to stand by the projector. If you have to stand by the projector, be sure everyone can see the screen. Remember the cardinal rule of visuals: Do not block the view! If you need to move around the room so everyone can have an opportunity to see the screen, do so. Try not to distract your audience with unnecessary movement.

- *Concluding.* End *without* a visual. Do not have a visual up for your concluding sentence. You started center stage, and you should end the same way.

- *No Visuals.* Be prepared to do your whole talk without any visuals. Then, if the equipment breaks or the power goes out, you will have a backup plan.

THE COMPANY STANDARD PRESENTATION

More and more divisions or certain groups of people in a company are doing 1- to 5-day presentations to either another group in the company or to customers. While they may be advertised as some type of training, they are generally a means of providing information. Unfortunately, these seminars are defective in that the flow of information only goes in one direction. Theoretically, this passive audience is supposed to remain attentive and interested hour after hour. To add insult to injury, the company has probably standardized its templates for the presentations, so each overhead looks basically the same hour after hour. This is known as the modern company presentation. It costs a lot to make, and yet it only produces nothing but boredom and, for some people, torture.

Here are some simple basics that the person in charge of these events needs to consider:

1. *Presentation Objective.* The marketing managers in a company were asked to present the latest product information to the sales force. Each manager put together 20 to 40 overheads for an hour-long presentation. One by one, the marketing managers presented in monologue fashion. The audience of salespeople sat for hours with glazed looks on their faces. The managers talked the whole time, and the salespeople had very little opportunity to interact with them. When asked to state their objective, the managers who presented said they were training the salespeople how best to sell the latest products. If that was their presentation objective, they failed to meet it. What they really "achieved" was to give the salespeople every bit of detail possible on these products without giving them a moment to interact. Although 10 presentations were involved not one of the managers did any real homework such as calling up the salespeople and asking them what they really needed to know about the products. No one let them practice discussing a new product with someone else so they could get a sense of the problems they might have as they attempted to sell to a customer. This is basically true for many company presentations. Everyone is just being busy putting together information without considering whether it's needed and how it might best be presented.

Make sure the presenters have specific objectives. They should discuss their objectives and then develop the means for best communicating them to their audience. Homework is essential. Find out what your audience needs to hear, not what you want to tell them. A sales staff is not going to be interested in the detailed manufacturing process or the detailed financing of the company. Always keep your eyes on your objective. Make each word and visual count. Time is valuable, and people have a short attention span. Make them glad they attended the presentation!

2. *How Much Detail.* You have two basic choices when putting together a presentation. Do you put every detail on your visuals so that someone who wasn't at the presentation can see all the details? Or do you put just enough information on the visual that you can speak to what is shown? People who put together companywide presentations for customers say that they want to hand out books with all the details of the presentations in them. However, how often do those potential customers actually go back and look things up? Do you know if your customers even looked at the materials? And finally, does the book have an index so people can actually find the information they are looking for? How many of us would feel enticed to open a binder of 200 pages with page after page of hard copy overheads, all looking the same? That sort of book is custom-made to sit unopened on the back of a shelf gathering dust and be thrown out when it is discovered years later.

3. *Standard Templates.* Don't make everyone use the same template design. If you want some order, give people a choice of three to five different template designs. And then tell people that they must have at least two visuals that don't fit the chosen design. Why? It is extremely boring to look at the same design hour after hour. Have two people look over the presentations and eliminate redundant sentences, phrases, and unnecessary detail. This means that people have to prepare early enough to make changes in the presentations.

4. *Interaction.* Presenters ask people to do what all studies show doesn't work: sit and process data hour after hour. Very few people can stay tuned in even after a single hour in a darkened room, let alone 2 days! The people who put these conferences together say that every minute counts. This truism gets translated into the fallacy that someone should be talking to the group every minute. The idea of interaction as a valuable and useful way to process information and learn seems to be a concept that is beyond most presenters. After 20 minutes of talking, the presenter should do something else—ask the audience to talk in pairs, ask the audience to share their opinions of what has just been said, ask the audience a question, give the audience a 1-minute stretch break.

5. *Capturing the Ideas.* Many times in these conferences, the participants come up with some excellent ideas that aren't recorded or even taken seriously. In one situation, a person was designated to write down the ideas that the participants suggested. The notes, however, were not shared with the participants, who became concerned about what that person really wrote down. Was their idea captured correctly? What would happen with their idea? Would they get some credit? The correct way to handle this process is to have someone record the ideas on a flip chart.

When someone raises an issue or idea, the idea facilitator gets up and writes it on the flip chart and fills in the columns. That way, everyone knows that ideas and issues are taken seriously. And the person giving the idea can make sure it is written in the manner in which it was suggested.

Look at your companywide presentations and make sure they are varied, allow time for interaction, and engage your audience.

Issue/Idea (With name of person who suggested the idea if he or she wants this recognition)	Importance of Issue (High, Medium, Low)	Prime Mover (Person responsible to get issue/idea to right group)	Recipients of Information (People who need to hear what decisions were made about this issue/idea)

"To Take" Visual Checklist

Equipment

☐ LCD panel—know how to set it up.

☐ Computer.

☐ Remote mouse.

☐ Overhead projector and extra bulbs.

☐ Slide projector and extra bulbs.

☐ Long electrical cord and power supply box.

☐ Screen if needed.

☐ Microphone-wireless lavaliere.

The Presentation Itself

☐ Slides in order and numbered.

☐ Hard copy of the presentation, just in case.

☐ Overhead transparencies in order and numbered.

☐ The flip chart.

☐ The video.

☐ Disk for the computer even if already loaded.

☐ Handouts.

☐ Product literature.

☐ Props.

☐ Markers for the flip chart and overheads.

☐ Extra transparencies, in case of need.

☐ Pointer to use when showing a flow diagram.

☐ Masking tape, to hang up the flip chart pages.

☐ Name tags.

Handouts

☐ How many people are expected?

☐ Are there enough handouts (meaning more than anticipated need)?

☐ Will there be a place to make copies just in case?

☐ Are the handouts in order so they can be passed out easily?

☐ When should they be handed out?

☐ Have I written reminder notes to myself on when to distribute the handouts?

Other

☐ Business cards.

☐ Food, if I carry it.

☐ Personal needs: special food, hairspray, mouthwash, and so on.

"Call Ahead" Visual Checklist

General Logistics

☐ Confirm the date and number of people attending.

☐ Confirm the time and when I can set up.

☐ Get directions to the location.

☐ What is the last date to change the number of people attending?

☐ Confirm the refreshments with number of people attending.

☐ Who controls the room temperature?

Room Setup

☐ What time can I get in the room to set up?

☐ Is the room the right size for the group?

☐ Here's how I need it set up. I'll send you a diagram including all the tables I need set up around the room.

☐ Do you have screens? What size? This is the size I want.

☐ Will you put the screen on a table so everyone can see it?

☐ Is it a real room or will there be a divider and who will be in the room next to me?

☐ Here's the type of table I want set up in front for my equipment and materials.

☐ Will you get rid of the extra chairs?

☐ Will I be able to see everyone in the room?

☐ How high is the lectern? (You want to be seen over it!)

Lights

☐ Are the lights on a dimmer switch? Can I adjust them?

☐ Is the switch close to the front of the room?

☐ Is there a light on the lectern so I can read my notes?

Power Supply

☐ What type of power cords do you have? This is what I need.

☐ I want a remote control wireless for the slide projector.

☐ I want a wireless lavaliere mike.

AV Person

☐ Can I meet your AV person the morning of or the night before my presentation?

Walls

☐ Can I pin or tape things to the walls?

"To Do's" before the Presentation Begins

☐ Put a "Please do not touch" sign on the computer. Or drape the computer with a cloth. Some people love to play with computers!

☐ Know the location of the restrooms.

☐ Know the location of the phone.

☐ Know when breaks are scheduled, especially if food will be brought in.

☐ Go through, one last time, any equipment that could have broken in the last 5 minutes. Especially, if someone has come up to look at it.

☐ Set up a straight edge to align the overheads.

☐ Check the extra bulbs.

☐ Make sure cords are out of the way.

☐ Put something to drink where I can reach it when speaking.

☐ Know what to do when a slide gets stuck.

☐ Be sure I can operate all the equipment.

☐ Have the name and number of the AV person and assign someone the responsibility of calling that person if I need help.

☐ Sit in the back of the room so I have a feel for what it will be like for participants who sit there.

ENERGIZING YOURSELF

KEY POINTS

1 Practice out loud with appropriate pauses.

2 Before your presentation, go in the restroom and rub your neck and hands to energize yourself.

3 Remove noisy articles from your pockets.

4 Check your clothing to be sure everything is in order.

5 Have an opening statement that captures people's attention.

6 Don't read your opening statement.

7 Look directly at individuals in your audience, unless the culture dictates otherwise.

8 Gesture—you will look more interesting.

9 Walk deliberately, do not sway from side to side as you talk.

10 Pause at the end of your sentences.

> I think the first impression is more important than many
> people realize. There are lots of competent, dedicated
> people who do not make good first impressions.
>
> Dean Rusk

Before you walk into someone's office to share an idea or step in front of 30 peo-ple to discuss a new ad campaign, consider both the nonverbal signals and the verbal signals you are about to emit. Who wants to see someone who looks bedraggled, listen to someone who sounds emotionally defeated, or watch some-one who makes no attempt to establish eye contact? As soon as people see you—you are on. Take the time to prepare for that lasting first impression. During your first 30 to 60 seconds, people are assessing you and thinking, "Why should I lis-ten to this speaker?" Carry yourself in such a manner that they think, "I believe this person. I trust this person. I think this person sounds confident."

When you are in a meeting, you certainly are not going to have a chance to plan an opening in the same way you can for a planned presentation. Neverthe-less, you can still begin with style. The more you practice these nonverbal and verbal behaviors during planned presentations, the easier it will be for you to re-member to use them during a meeting or a phone call. Your ability to look and sound energetic could one day mean the difference between your receiving or not receiving support for a new venture. Patrick J. Sansonetti, Managing Partner of Advent International, a company that specializes in International Venture Capital and has over $1 billion in venture assets with 16 affiliate network members around the world, says this about the need for style and flair:

> We'd rather have a dynamic team marketing a marginal product than the
> other way around. There's a saying in the venture industry that we'd rather
> make money with an egotist than lose money with a wimp. After I've gone
> over a business plan, I have in-depth and intensive meetings with the man-
> agement team. I want to feel that they have the communicating style to con-
> vince others of their company's value. I've turned down business plans due
> to the management team's lack of presence.

Step 5 teaches you how to energize particular forms of nonverbals such as posture, facial expression, clothing, movement, and gestures; physical, mental, emotional, and spiritual condition; and eye contact. This step guides you through your verbals such as language, voice, anecdotes, and examples, then ends by hav-ing you consider and change your pace in order to keep communication going between you and your listeners.

CRITIQUES AND FEEDBACK

The following form, "Questions to a Colleague," which I use in my "Presentations Kit Seminar" can provide you with invaluable feedback. Request that your col-leagues fill this out. Ask four colleagues, or if you are not in a business situation, ask people who see you speak in such situations as committee meetings. You can

Questions to a Colleague

From your observations, please check any habits you have noticed that I frequently do. Your candid answers will enable me to enhance my communication style as a presenter. Thank you.

My Appearance

☐ Fidgeting with a pen, pencil, or magic marker
☐ Fidgeting with notes
☐ Juggling keys or coins in pocket
☐ Closing and opening the pointer
☐ Twirling hair
☐ Swiveling around in chair
☐ Standing in front of the screen instead of beside it

Dressing	☐ too much	☐ just right	☐ not enough
Moving	☐ too much	☐ just right	☐ too little
Expressions	☐ overly done	☐ just right	☐ too deadpan
Posture	☐ too stiff	☐ just right	☐ too loose

My Eye Contact

☐ Frequently looking up toward the ceiling
☐ Looking over people's heads, not into their eyes

My Language

☐ Using unnecessary *uhs* or *ums* or other filler words such as _____

Technical words	☐ too many	☐ just right	☐ too few

My Voice

Example	☐ too many	☐ just right	☐ too few
Speed	☐ too fast	☐ just right	☐ too slow
Sound	☐ overly solicitous	☐ convincing tone	☐ unconvincing tone
Emotion	☐ too emotional	☐ just right	☐ no emotion (monotone)

Other ineffective behaviors you have noticed: _____

_____

Please list two of my presentation habits or behaviors that you see as effective.

1. _____

_____

2. _____

_____

never learn too much about your presenting habits and how to enhance your skills. This critique will point out your effective and ineffective presenting habits.

YOUR NONVERBALS

Somewhere between 60 to 80 percent of your success is influenced by your nonverbals. Reflect on the times you have decided you would not listen to a person due to his or her dress, monotone voice, or perhaps unreadable or confusing

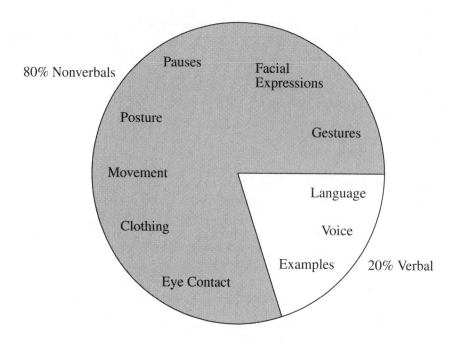

80% Nonverbals

Pauses
Facial Expressions
Posture
Gestures
Movement
Language
Clothing
Voice
Eye Contact
Examples   20% Verbal

visuals. Diane Gallagher, who has been a recruiter for 15 years, says about her first impression of a potential candidate for a job, "I make an evaluation in the first three to eight seconds. Is this person smiling? What is the person's body posture? Do I get a firm handshake? Does the person convey confidence and look me in the eyes? My initial impression is formed before the person says a word." Your listeners give you the same type of first look before you even open your mouth. (If they have met you before, that is another matter.)

Watch Your Posture

Many of us are victims of being told since childhood to stand up straight, yet we do not have the faintest idea of how to go about that task. Over the years, we have tried to satisfy that ideal. We hunched our shoulders, crooked our necks backward, and pulled in our stomach only to have a caved-in chest. First look at your posture on video or at least look at some of the photographs taken of you. If you decide you want to improve your posture, give yourself these directions so that they become second nature when you stand up to talk: "My feet are hip width apart, my arms are by my sides, my shoulders are over my hips, my neck is free, and my back is lengthening and widening." This is a good neutral stance. You can come back to it after you gesture, move around, or pick up materials.

What about sitting situations? When you are sitting, you want to be ready to move. You want to feel energized and have a look of confidence. The following sketches of three people show two with poor posture and one with effective posture. The person sitting back in the chair looks too comfortable and not in charge. The person with her legs all wrapped around will have trouble feeling grounded. The person sitting forward on the edge of the chair with a straight spine and feet flat on the floor has the best posture to sound enthused and stay enthused and to stay attuned to each person in the room.

The following general ideas will help you improve your standing and sitting postures:

- Learn the Alexander Technique (see References Exercise).
- Work with a physical therapist or an exercise coach.
- Do sit-ups and push-ups at least three times a week.
- Practice walking with a book on your head.
- Take an acting course for businesspeople. They do exist.

The preceding list could go on and on. Do only one of the suggestions, and over time you will notice a difference in your posture.

Control Your Facial Expressions

Your expression is the most important thing you can wear.

Sid Ascher

Cure yourself of those deadpan, artificial, and unfriendly facial expressions. To do so, you must first try making them. Stand in front of the mirror, and do all the things you need to create a closed face: frown, tighten your jaw, squint a little, scrunch your shoulders up toward your ears, and bring your lips close together.

Now talk. Say something like, "I want to begin by stating the four areas we will discuss in the next hour," or "This is an excellent ad I want to show you." What do you look like? If you were watching yourself, would you want to pay attention? Now, make an open face: relax your jaw, look around, open your mouth wide to talk, think positive thoughts, lengthen your neck, and feel your shoulders relax. Say those same sentences. See the difference in your face. Your face now looks animated, friendly, and genuine. That is all you have to do. The key is in practicing the open face habits.

Examine Your Clothing

Do you have any of the characteristics of the following four people?

- *The "Inappropriate for the Situation" Dresser.* The woman manager presented to the corporate officers once a month. Her nails were very long and painted a bright pink. Her hair was bleached blond and she rarely wore the "corporate blue suit." Top management wanted to promote her but felt she should learn to look more the part. She did not get the job, and unfortunately, she was never told why.

- *The "Just Dressed" Person.* A volunteer spoke at many of the organization's fund raisers. He usually wore casual corduroy pants, a striped shirt, and a pair of loafers. He gave one of the best talks of all the volunteers. Due to his appearance, however, he was never asked to talk with the corporate bank groups. Since he never *dressed* the part, he was not seen as someone who could *play* the part.

- *The "On-Again, Off-Again" Dresser.* A woman appeared at work, one day, dressed appropriately for the environment and, next day, dressed for a weekend excursion trip. Her boss wanted to promote her but was afraid she would be called into an impromptu meeting with the higher officers on a day when she looked as if she was headed for a vacation.

- *The "I Do Not Have to Impress You Anymore" Dresser.* A man was hired by the president of a consulting company to teach a series of two-day programs on benefit selling. He did an excellent job. On a warm spring day, a few months after that job, the trainer went to see the president about some other work and wore a bright flowered Hawaiian sport shirt. When he arrived, the president introduced him to the new director of training who was dressed in a navy blue suit. The trainer then went to wait in the president's office. He came in shortly and said, "I wish you had worn your power suit." The trainer was ready to become upset, but realized that the president had introduced him to the new training director who had never met him. The director's first impression was of a man in a flowered shirt coming in for a business meeting. The next time the trainer went, he wore his suit, and, much to his chagrin, the president said, "Oh good, you wore your power suit today." At that moment the trainer experienced the consequences of his past poor judgment and realized that, if he wanted to play the game, he needed to know when and where to follow the rules.

Feedback on Clothing.   If you are uncertain about your clothing, speak to a couple of colleagues. Ask them, "What do you suggest I continue, start, or stop doing to improve the way I dress?" If you ask them, "Do I dress OK?" they will probably answer with a "yes" and you will learn nothing.

Unfortunately, people do judge your appearance by their standards. In all the preceding examples, people were perhaps not judged fairly. In one of the examples, the corporate officers assumed that a woman with bright nail polish, obviously dyed hair, and a very short dress must not know the business. Do not let your style of dressing get in the way of the participants wanting to communicate with you. Dress appropriately for the group. You are the "package," and they want you to look well wrapped!

Key Clothing Points.   Keep the following factors in mind when you dress for a presentation:

1. Consider the dress of your audience. Always dress up to or above your audience, never below them. Dress so that you will have the best rapport with the group. If you are speaking to a group of college students about a volunteer wildlife program, you should dress accordingly and probably not wear a blue tailored suit.

2. Wear comfortable, immaculate clothing that makes you feel good about yourself. You need to have a couple of presentation outfits that make you feel and look confident.

3. Wear new clothing once before you present in it. This prevents any surprises about how your clothing fits and moves as you speak in it. Consider the woman who bought a gorgeous suit with a wraparound skirt. She wore it for a speech that she was giving, but found that when she sat down a certain way, the skirt opened up in front, showing her slip. While this was embarrassing, it was not half as bad as the experience of the woman at a fund raiser whose skirt started slipping over her hips as she got up to talk! It did not have a hook in the back, and the zipper had come unfastened. Women, in particular, should rehearse in the same clothes that they plan to wear for their presentation. Wear everything from shoes to earrings to scarf. This eliminates all surprises.

4. If you are young and want to look older, wear conservative clothing. Women around the age of 25 with very long hair may need to put it up at times to make themselves appear older and thus more credible for certain types of audiences. One salesperson bought herself glasses to wear to certain meetings. She said she feels that people perceive her as older; consequently she is taken more seriously.

5. Before you invest in clothes to present in, consider the colors that are most becoming to you and the looseness or tightness of the clothing. After you have decided what you need, then buy what you want, not what someone else tells you is stylish or looks good on you. You are the one who will wear this clothing day after day. Invest in those things that make you feel comfortable and attractive and that show the audience you care about your appearance.

6. If you will be traveling, read up on the best clothes to take. There are excellent books available on how to organize a travel wardrobe. Here are several hints travelers have told me:

   - "When I am going to be on my feet all day, I take two pairs of shoes and change them during lunch break. My feet never hurt at the end of the day."

   - "I pack my clothes in the plastic bags that come from my dry cleaning. The clothes don't get wrinkled."

   - "I carry food on the plane. That way I eat what is good for me and am not tempted to eat things I shouldn't be eating."

7. Don't forget to polish your shoes.

8. Be sure to remove any noisy articles from your pockets. When you are speaking in front of a group, the sound of jingling change is distracting. Some earrings can be noisy when you move your head. One woman noticed that her big, round, shiny gold earrings were not noisy but very distracting as they swung from side to side every time she moved.

9. Dress the part you want to play in the future. If you want to achieve a certain position in the organization, look at how those people dress, and dress that way *now*.

10. Dress appropriately. If you like to wear wild, outlandish clothes, do so only if that is appropriate for your situation. Sometimes a well-tailored suit does not set the right image either. (*Hint:* Have a couple of jackets with pockets—if your hands tend to get cold, shaky, or clammy, you can warm them, knead them, or dry them in your pockets before you shake someone's hand.)

Refine Your Movements and Gestures

The following list gives you some hints for movements and gestures.

1. Do *move around;* do not stand in one place.

2. Do *make eye contact;* do not talk to the visual, the floor, or the ceiling.

3. Do *use natural gestures;* do not force gestures, or fidget.

4. Do *keep your hands empty* (unless you are holding notes); do not play with objects.

5. Do *use your hands freely* for emphasis; do not use them rigidly.

6. Do *use a lavaliere wireless microphone;* do not use a stationary microphone.

7. Do *hold your hands at your sides* and/or gestures; do not take off and put on your glasses repeatedly, rub the same spot over and over; put your hands through your hair, or fool with an article of clothing.

8. Do *take two to three steps at a time;* do not take one step at a time (you look hesitant).

9. Do *make larger gestures than you would normally* if your audience is more than 50 people; do not make small gestures.

Your movement and gestures form a part of your audience's first nonverbal impression. This impression either encourages people to listen to you, or it discourages them. Take a moment and envision yourself watching a diving competition. How long would you stay interested if the person kept going to the edge and then backing off? How about if the person just peered over the edge of the diving board but was not decisive enough to take the dive? Quite probably you would start daydreaming or, if possible, leave. Some people present in the same manner as a hesitant diver. They never really jump into the talk. You must take the leap. Put your whole body and conviction behind your talk. Walk into a room looking ready to go, calm, and confident. Act confident even if you do not feel it. Have your notes in order so that you do not begin by shuffling through papers. Organize yourself so you can walk up to the table, put your papers down, and begin. Do the same when you walk into someone's office to discuss something. Remember the last time someone had something to discuss with you and you spent minutes waiting for the person to find the information in all the papers he or she was carrying? Have the information you need with you so you appear to be in charge.

Gestures reinforce your points, keep you looking natural, and focus any pent-up energy. They also give you a way to release any accumulated energy. Watch yourself on video, and see how you now gesture. If you want to practice some gestures, practice making them a bit larger and clearer. This is not necessary when you are talking to 5 or 20 people, but when your group gets bigger and people are further away from you, you want to make wider gestures just so your movements appear more decisive. A little movement does not give the same appearance of control as a larger movement. Be careful. It is better to do what you do naturally than to make movements that look as if you are just making movements.

Some people decide or have been told that they make too many gestures. They attempt to refrain from gesturing when talking. This is like asking a stallion to stand still. That is not what the stallion wants to do. If you are a "stallion presenter," then let yourself gesture. If you do not allow yourself to gesture, by the end of 10 minutes you are going to be exhausted from trying to hold yourself still.

Have you ever seen people who have attended presentation programs where they learned to gesture? They learned to say "Point 1," as they moved their right hand and "Point 2," as they moved their left hand. In fact, their whole department attended that program, and now they all look the same when presenting. Who wants to watch a whole department present when they all look like robots using the same gestures over and over again? If you truly want to change some of your gestures or add new gestures, you must look natural. A 2-day course on presentation skills will not give you enough practice. You need to take a course in theater or improvisational movement. It is possible to learn new gestures, but you must practice them so they become an integral part of you. If you don't normally gesture during your talks, try this: Use your hand to point toward your visual. That will get you moving a little. Even that simple gesture is better than nothing.

Another important thing to remember is to use a lavaliere microphone rather than a stationary microphone. Unless you are accustomed to speaking into a microphone, you probably do not have the skill to stand in one place and keep still while projecting your voice into the microphone. A speaker who uses her hands quite frequently was given a microphone to hold. She spoke, waving it all around, and consequently her voice faded in and out. She was not aware of waving the microphone. Her colleagues advised her to use a lavaliere microphone pinned onto her jacket. With the lavaliere microphone, she can use her hands and speak at the same time. A microphone that is pinned on demands the least amount of learning for you as a presenter. If it is cordless, you are even better off, since you do not have to worry about tripping over the cord. If it is not cordless, some people put the cord through their belt so they are less likely to trip on it. That means you must remind yourself to wear a belt that day. Before you present, call ahead to find out what type of microphone you will be given and request a cordless lavaliere microphone.

In a cross-cultural situation, you need to do some research to find out what gestures, movements, and postures are acceptable in that culture. You do not want to offend anyone by how you gesture, stand, or sit. In a situation with an interpreter, a mistake people make is to speak slowly, show little or no expression, and refrain from gesturing. This makes it very boring for the listeners. You will be much more interesting to look at when you become even slightly more animated than your normal style. Although people cannot understand your words, they can experience you as an expressive human being. Strangely enough, you will be surprised at what they do understand by watching you. Many of us remember when Nikita Khrushchev, then the leader of the Soviet Union and the Communist world, took off his shoe and banged it on the table at the United Nations to make a point. You need not go that far, but just remember that your nonverbals often communicate a lot more than your verbals.

Improve Your Physical Condition

What you are speaks so loudly that I cannot hear what you say.

Ralph Waldo Emerson

Today, much emphasis is placed on diet and exercise. You can read article after article and book after book, but until you create good habits for yourself, you are kidding yourself. Many people feel more energized and clearheaded when they consistently exercise. If you have a nervous constitution, you will do well to exercise the day of or the day before you speak. You will feel calmer inside. One woman was to present a proposal to only one other person. She felt very nervous. The day before, she took a 1½-hour dance class. The next day she felt calm, poised, and ready to make her 20-minute proposal. If you do many impromptu talks, you need to exercise consistently so you always feel ready and energized to speak.

Your diet is critical. Eat a well-balanced diet, including fresh vegetables and fruits. Learn about *your* dietary needs, and experiment until you feel that you have reached the level of energy you want. Several supplements can help you achieve that level of energy. Learn about nutrition and adjust your diet until you feel healthy and energetic.

If you have mucus in your throat, you may want to find out what foods are creating your problem. Dairy products can create this type of difficulty. People will find it unappealing to listen to you frequently clearing your throat during your presentation.

Be careful when you are the speaker after lunch or dinner. If you eat lots of fat and heavy carbohydrates, you will feel tired or look sluggish. Request a special meal so that you do not feel tired after eating.

Consider the following questions:

- Would you do a better job presenting if your body looked in better condition?

- How much exercise do you need to feel and appear poised?

- Do you need to do a few sit-ups and push-ups every day so you can sit and stand up straight?

- Do you feel calmer after exercising?

- Do you know whether any foods cause you problems? Should you avoid certain foods, particularly on the day of a presentation?

- Are there any supplements you may need?

Examine Your Mental, Emotional, and Spiritual Condition

What do you do for fun? How do you relax, unwind, and give yourself "space" to be? You can learn all the best presentation techniques and have the most interesting visuals, but if you do not feel centered and at peace, your communication will not be as clear as it should be. Effective presenters know how to take care of themselves. Remember the introvert and extrovert from Step 1? When you take care of yourself and your particular needs, you will feel more like presenting. Your response will probably be that you do not have time. Make time!

If the president of the United States, who is indeed a busy person, can make time to enjoy life, so can you.

What activities give you an experience of wholeness? Do you have a meditation practice? Do you dance? Do you garden? Do you belong to a religious group? Do you play sports, go fishing, or cook? Do what you enjoy doing, and you will find that, not only your presentations, but your entire life will improve.

YOUR EYE CONTACT

To make oneself understood to people, one must first speak to their eyes.

Napoleon

The eyes in this illustration look steady. They are not "searching eyes," which roam sporadically and jerkily around the room. When I see someone with searching eyes, I want to ask, "What are you looking for so frantically? Do you really see anyone as you dart from face to face? Why do you bombard yourself with a new face every half second?" Presenters who have scanning and darting eyes feel more nervous than presenters who *really look* at someone. Pause as you look at each person. People will genuinely appreciate it. Those who speak for a living—singers, television announcers, trial lawyers, and so on—are trained to talk to only one person at a time. When people feel that you really are looking at them, they are much more likely to trust you and give you the benefit of the doubt. The following list provides some hints on eye contact:

- Look at each person. Maintain eye contact until you finish your sentence or at least your train of thought.

- Know which side of the room you tend to look toward and look toward the other side as well.

- Do not upset yourself by concentrating on a person who seems to look disgruntled. That may be a characteristic facial expression having nothing to do with you.

- Be sure you spend time looking at the decision makers in the group.

- Maintain eye contact for at least three seconds. This is for those of you who need concise guidelines. When you begin this practice, look at each person and count silently to yourself, "1001 . . . 1002 . . . 1003 . . ."

- Do not keep your eyes away from the group for more than 10 to 15 seconds, or your rapport with the group will be broken.

- Ask a colleague to watch you speak to see whether you look up toward the ceiling when you talk. You may have occasionally noticed a person who looks up to the ceiling as if looking for information when conversing with you. In reality, that person is either trying to create a visual picture of your discussion or searching for a past picture that will help clarify the discussion. When this person makes or finds the picture, then he or she understands the discussion. As a presenter in front of many people, you cannot afford this luxury. You must train yourself to look at the group and at the same time create or find the pictures in your mind. You may also discover that you look up just for a break or to take a breath. Practice breathing and making eye contact with people at the same time.

- Remember to look at people; do not look over their heads.

- Do not talk to your notes or the screen.

In *Winning When It Really Counts* (New York: Simon & Schuster, 1988), Arch Lustberg says this about maintaining eye contact:

> I call it rhythm eye contact. Simply put, your mouth should never be moving while your eyes are looking down. Your mouth should never be moving when you're looking away from your audience. . . . To use the concept of the proper rhythm of eye contact, first consider the importance of the pause. No one can talk nonstop. We all have to pause. During the pause, we glance down at our notes. Then we make the mistake of beginning to talk again, still looking down at our notes.

Lustberg suggests that you pause, look at your notes, look up and into someone's eyes, and then start talking. For practice, find yourself a partner; if you are alone, use a spot in the room. Make some notes about something and practice this skill. Pause, look at your next note on the paper, and then look up and into someone's eyes or at the spot you have designated in the room. After a few minutes of practice, this will feel easier for you.

Even experienced speakers sometimes have lapses. For example, when Ted Kennedy was asked, "Why do you want to be president?" he looked at the ceiling, then at the floor, and, finally, after 15 seconds, he answered. His nonverbals gave the impression that he did not know why he wanted to be president. Do your best and plan so *all* your nonverbals enable you to reach your objective.

Beverly Robsham of Robsham Associates, an outplacement firm in Boston, gives this excellent advice to her clients. It can be taken to heart by every presenter:

> When you speak with the interviewer, put a smile in your eyes. Transmit that smile to whomever you're speaking. If you constantly smile with your mouth, you may feel foolish and appear insecure. Transmit your smile through your eyes. This develops a positive chemistry and gives the message that you can be trusted.

YOUR VERBALS

Before you read about ways to begin your presentation, eliminate any beginning "do not" behaviors from your presentation.

Beginning "Do Not" Rules

- Do not *ad lib* your beginning. When possible, plan your opening sentences. Practice saying them out loud over and over (5 to 10 times).

- Do not make your first sentence *too technically detailed.* The audience needs one sentence to get used to your voice; then they can begin to really listen.

- Do not use a *long first sentence,* since this makes it difficult for participants to follow your train of thought.

- Do not discuss all the *administrative details* in the beginning. This is not the way to capture people's interest.

- Do not have an *unspecified time deadline.* This is particularly true if you are in someone's office and want to present a new idea. During the entire time you are speaking, this person may be wondering, "How long will he go on? I have work to finish in the next half hour." Whether in person or on the phone, ask your listeners for a specified amount of time. Then listen to hear if they can give it to you.

- Do not *apologize* about such items as your ability, knowledge, or visuals.

- Do not *look at your notes* or the screen for the first two or three sentences. Look at your audience.

- Do not tell an *inappropriate joke* that is irrelevant to your subject or that has the potential to offend some people.

- Do not give participants 10 pages of *handouts* as you begin. The handouts will receive more immediate attention than you will.

- Do not *arrive late, start late, or start early.*

- Do not *make your first sentence a punch line.* Wait until your second or fourth sentence so people are tuned into you and your voice.

Begin Assertively

"Well-timed silence hath more eloquence than speech," says M. T. Tupper. Before you begin speaking, stand, organize your materials, silently count, "1001 . . . 1002 . . . 1003 . . . ," and then speak. What do you say after you counted? You may wish you could just keep counting to yourself, but you cannot. What can you say? Here are 10 ways you can open your presentation:

1. Arresting statements.
2. Facts.
3. Quotations.
4. Rhetorical questions.
5. Short, pointed anecdotes or examples.
6. Invitations.
7. Common bonds.
8. Statements of presentation's organization.
9. Positive comments.
10. Logistic statements.

Arresting Statements.   The following types of statement make people take notice:

Very few organizations have tried this approach. I believe we can.

Yes, you can save $20,000 this year when you follow the recommendations I will give you at the end of my talk.

Facts.   You can surprise people with facts such as those following:

This mountain is 15,000 feet high. Only four people have made it to the top.

We can save 10 hours a week of our people's time if we simply change two forms our customers are using.

Quotations.   Mention a quotation or two that relates to your subject. This works best if it is by someone well known to your participants.

Albert Einstein said, "My gift of fantasy has meant more to me than my talent for absorbing positive knowledge."

Robert Frost, in "The Road Not Taken," said, "Two roads diverged in a wood, and I— / I took the one less traveled by, / And that has made all the difference."

Rhetorical Questions.   This type of question can set the context for what is to follow:

When did you last have the satisfying feeling of having helped someone in need?

Raise your hand if you have ever used a computer.

Which of you is pleased about having invested your money in the most protected funds?

Are you a person who does not want to give because you believe that your contribution will not go to the people who need it?

Short, Pointed Anecdotes or Examples.

An appropriate anecdote or example can greatly enhance your presentation. It can be personal or more general than the following example, but be sure to clearly link it to your presentation:

I was born in California, close enough to enjoy the majestic Lake Tahoe/ Reno Nevada mountains. When I moved east and began skiing in Vermont, I was astonished at the difference in the size of the mountains from those at Lake Tahoe. The Vermont mountains seemed easy to me after having skied in the Sierras. I hope that today you will experience my recommendation as easy to follow, just as I experienced the paths on my first Vermont mountain.

Invitations.

An invitation can encourage listeners to take the journey with you:

I know that you are from different departments in the company; consequently, I have geared my explanations so that each of you will be able to use this information.

Thank you for coming to hear about our organization. The handout you have in front of you gives you room for writing notes, comments, and any questions you may have. So you can follow along, I will go through the items in order.

Common Bonds.

Emphasizing a common bond helps you feel a part of the group and helps the group feel connected to you. You create the atmosphere that "we are all in this together." If you have asked people, as you opened, to share their experiences or ideas, you can refer back to what they said during your talk:

Jim, I agree with what you just said, and I want to add to your last point.

I realize there are some people here who know as much about this system as I do. Please feel free to add your thoughts and opinions.

Sue and Bob, thank you for inviting me to speak at your committee meeting. Before we started, I had an opportunity to speak with several people. I am interested in hearing how my information will make their committees function more easily.

Statements of Presentation's Organization.

This type of statement gives the participants a broad overview of what they will hear in the next few minutes. Let them know the major points you plan to cover:

I have two goals today. I want to share my research and then present one recommendation.

I am here to teach you Computer 101 skills. At the end of our time together,
you will know how to do these two processes: editing and simple line graphics.

Positive Comments.   This type of comment makes people want to listen.
Your positive attitude is one of the major ingredients in the formula that makes
up the exciting chemistry you create with the group. Fuel people's positive attitudes by making statements such as the following:

I feel encouraged because we are discussing this new budget recommendation.

Congratulations. You, not I, deserve a hand for having sat here since 9:00 A.M.
I guarantee to make this as short as possible and as interesting and compre-
hensible as possible for each and every one of you. I will end by 3:45 P.M.

Logistic Statements.   Ideally, the logistics have already been taken care of
before you start, but if not, you must do that at the beginning of your talk. People
want to know when they can have a stretch break, how long your presentation will
be, when food and beverages are available, and any other details that will make
them feel more comfortable while listening to you:

Since this is the first time the overhead is being used, I want to walk around
and be sure everyone can see the screen.

I need about 20 minutes of your time. At the end of that time, let's take a
lunch break; then I will come back and answer any questions you may have.

You have been sitting here a long time. Let's take a 2-minute stretch break
before I start.

YOUR VOICE

The first task you have, before almost anything else, is to be enthusiastic. No matter how organized you are, you must also *sound* enthusiastic. You cannot convince
people of anything if your communication is dull and lifeless! Studies show that
people who speak well are perceived as more attractive, sexy, exciting, and intelligent. People who speak poorly are perceived as less attractive and intelligent.
Business graduates who had top oral communication skills earned a higher income and had better job offers than those with poor communication skills. Toast-
master International reports that psychologist Albert Mehrabian has shown we
are five times as likely to be influenced by voice than by spoken words as we
listen to a speaker. You need a vital voice; this is not a luxury—it is essential. A
cake does not rise without baking powder, and a talk does not "rise" without a
vital voice!

    What are you telling people by the way you sound? What do they infer from
your voice? If you have never heard yourself on tape, stop reading, make a phone
call to a friend, tape that call, and play it back. Do not tell your friend you are
taping yourself because you will not be as natural. To be even more daring, tape
yourself during a business phone call and you will learn much about your voice

vitality. There is nothing illegal about your taping *only yourself* during a phone call.

Make friends with your voice. The following are specific problems along with some exercises to help you overcome those problems. To change your voice habits easily and quickly, tape-record yourself doing the exercises. Find some interesting material to read when practicing the exercises.

Enunciate Clearly

> There is no index of character so sure as the voice.
>
> Benjamin Disraeli

Voice Exercises

Slurring words	→	Enunciate clearly; open mouth, elongate vowels.
Monotone voice	→	Vary voice range.
Talking too fast or too slow	→	Pause while speaking. Sip water to slow down; open mouth; elongate vowels; pause.
Speaking with a tense, closed voice	→	Relax mouth and jaw; push stomach in and out; make yourself yawn.
Speaking too loud; too soft	→	Project your voice; push stomach in and out; speak to the farthest corner of the room.
Using filler words and phrases: *Umm, er,* and so on	→	Be silent.
Speaking with emotional flatness	→	Speak with enthusiasm.
Speaking with lack of conviction and authority	→	Use appropriate voice inflection.
Speaking with an accent	→	Speak slowly at first.

Speak slowly. Do this by relaxing your jaw, opening your mouth, and speaking with an open, round sound. Pronounce and enunciate all vowels and consonants. Take time to give the vowels length. The longer you make them, the more slowly you will speak. You might think you are overarticulating a word, but you will not be. Listen to your voice.

Vary Your Voice Range

People can speak a monotone in a high or low voice. Women have a tendency to talk in a high monotone, which sounds childish and gives the impression that the speaker does not want to be taken seriously. For whatever kind of monotone you use, practice the following exercise. It will allow you to hear the voice ranges you can use when speaking, although you will probably never go as high or as low as you do while practicing the exercise:

1. *Medium.* Read in a medium-range voice for 1 minute.

2. *High.* Read in a high-range voice for 1 minute.

3. *Low.* Read in a low-range voice for 1 minute.

4. *Combine.* Vary your voice from high to low to medium range for 1 minute.

A more enjoyable practice in helping you enliven your voice is to imagine as you speak that your audience is full of children. (We are all a bunch of big kids anyway!) Tape yourself doing a talk, and hear the vocal variety you use. You can also try to change a monotone voice by telling an example. Examples and stories naturally lend themselves to more expressiveness in your voice. Finally, adding gestures invites a change in your voice range. It is hard to keep a monotone voice when you are gesturing. For experience, practice the following gestures:

- Say "Yes," and nod your head.

- Say "Look around," and move your hand from one side to the other.

- Say "I have three points to cover," then make a gesture as you say each point.

Pause While Speaking

When you pause you appear confident, you give people time to digest what you have said and you have a moment to breathe deeply. You must ask others if you are speaking too slowly or too quickly. You are probably not an accurate judge of the appropriateness of your speed. Also, find out if your speed is right for your audience. The right speed for a New York audience is not the right speed for a Texas audience.

People often think they speak too quickly when no one else agrees. Many people who say they speak too quickly just never pause. Lack of pauses is the problem—not speaking too quickly. When they pause, their speed is fine. Some people who do not pause say that they learned this skill at the family dinner table, which many times consisted of eight children and two adults. They learned to keep going so that they would not be interrupted while talking. These people now need to look around and see that they are *not* at the family dinner table! They need to take Oscar Wilde's advice, "He knew the precise psychological moment when to say nothing."

For those who like concise instructions, an ideal speed is about 120 words per minute. Speaking up to 160 words per minute is still fine. Time yourself. Use the following exercise to practice your speed:

1. *Slow.* Read in a slow voice for 1 minute.

2. *Fast.* Read in a fast voice for 1 minute.

3. *Combine.* Vary your pace: slow to fast, fast to slow, for 1 minute.

Here is an added hint for speakers who do not pause: Sipping a glass of water from time to time will slow you down. Do not forget to write, at different points in your talk, "Take a sip of water" or "Pause."

Relax Your Mouth and Jaw

People who have a tense, closed voice sound untrustworthy and unreliable. I recently attended a community meeting in which the main speaker kept his mouth much too closed when he talked. He kept saying, "You can trust our department. We do what we say." From the audience's response, I could tell that they were having trouble believing his words due to his closed voice. All he had to do was open his mouth more and relax his jaw. The meeting would have been so much more pleasant, and he would have been more believable.

If your voice sounds tense when you start presenting, try yawning or chewing before you go in front of people. Yawning opens your throat; chewing relaxes your jaw and tongue. Just before speaking, some people go to the restroom and yawn. Yawning is not that hard to do. Just open your jaw wide, and you will find yourself beginning to yawn. You can also massage the jawbone right next to your ear. Naturally these are things to do *before* you are in front of the group. While in front of the group, you can sip water from a glass and breathe, feeling your stomach move in and out.

Project Your Voice

Neither a whisperer nor a shouter be. When you whisper, you sound timid and self-conscious. People lose interest. They assume that you must be uncomfortable with what you are saying. For them, listening will be a struggle. If you shout, people will suspect your competency; after all, why else would you be yelling? Most people err on the side of speaking too softly. If you speak too softly, practice talking loudly in your car so you feel comfortable hearing yourself. Voice projection is an absolute must. The following technique, when practiced, will increase your voice projection. As you breathe in, note how your stomach expands. Then, when speaking, slowly move your stomach inward to support your talk. This type of breathing gives you the power to project your voice. It also reduces your anxiety level. Since voice projection is one of the most difficult problems to solve on your own, if the preceding breathing technique does not work for you, then consider taking a few voice lessons. Find a speech coach and take several lessons. Those may be all you need. If you do not learn to dynamically project, your presentations will lack the important ingredients of conviction, authority, and power.

One man practiced singing in his car with a full voice, but not so loudly as to become hoarse. The difference in his voice projection after only a week caused the whole class to applaud his determination and success. This person also practiced speaking to the furthest corner of the room, after he realized that the people in the front of the room could hear him easily. Rarely does a person who is practicing to speak louder overdo it. Frequently, the person practicing will ask, "Was I too loud?" Almost no one ever says, "Yes, you were too loud."

Be Silent to Eliminate Filler Words and Phrases

Frequent use of filler words and sounds detracts from your talk. They make you appear more nervous than you may actually feel. Some people use a comma or period as an opportunity to add an *er* or an *umm*. These words are not found in the dictionary, nor do they impress your audience. Weed out your filler words. Without them, you sound 10 times more powerful, knowledgeable, and sure of yourself. This encourages your listeners to relax and pay attention.

Weed Out Your Umms!

Practice the following exercise:

1. *Pause.* Read and pause at the end of each sentence, silently counting to two before you start the next sentence.

2. *Run-On.* Read all the sentences as if there were no periods. Add your usual filler words such as *er* and *uh*.

3. *Combine.* Read and pause at the end of some sentences; then run the sentences together or add the extra filler words between other sentences.

It may seem strange to encourage you to practice the habit that you are attempting to stop. Why? Once you start to hear all these added extras, you will stop yourself. Your awareness of hearing yourself will help you catch the word before you speak it.

Ask a friend to help you eliminate your filler words. When you use a filler, your friend can raise a hand or make some other gesture you can easily notice. If you are in a meeting situation, then a less noticeable gesture is more appropriate. A woman who wanted to practice saying less rather than more asked a friend in the back of the room to nod his head slightly when he felt she was about to say more than necessary. This immediate feedback helped check her tendency to speak too long.

Here is an effective technique to stop all those extra sounds, words, and phrases. Have a friend listen to you. Whenever you say *um* or another filler word, have your friend bang *very loudly* on the table. A soda can makes a loud, annoying sound. After about the fourth bang, you will begin to hear your *ums* before you speak. When you start to hear them before you speak, you are on your way to stopping the habit. This is a fun and painless way to cure yourself of *ums, OKs,* and other unnecessary expressions.

Some speakers have found that if they really concentrate on making eye contact with each person in the group, they use less *uhs.* If you do use many of these filler words, practice making eye contact with each person in your group for at least three full seconds. One person put a note on his phone that said, "No *ers.*" After a week, he had stopped his *ers.* Some people do not stop with *umms,* they fill in with whole phrases such as, "Do you know what I mean?" or "It is kinda like . . ." or "OK?" All these inclusions are unnecessary. They dilute your strength as a presenter.

Speak with Enthusiasm

> I like the person who bubbles over with enthusiasm. Better to be a geyser than a mud puddle.
>
> John G. Shedd

An emotional voice convinces people. To increase your ability to project emotion, practice the following exercises. Tape yourself as you practice.

Exercise 1

1. *Opinionated.* Read in a very opinionated, authoritarian voice for 1 minute.

2. *Factual.* Read in a factual voice for 1 minute.

3. *Enthusiastic.* Read in an enthusiastic voice for 1 minute.

4. *Combine.* Vary your voice from opinionated to factual to enthusiastic for 1 minute.

Exercise 2

1. Speak out loud about your ideal evening, vacation, or job.

2. Put some emotion into your voice.

When listening to the tape, you should be able to hear the differences in the readings. Sometimes you need to be able to sound authoritative and in charge of your data. Parts of presentations lend themselves to a clear, factual voice. For the participants' sake as well as your own, sound enthusiastic during your talk. Remember what Eleanor Roosevelt said, "You must do the things you think you cannot do." Yes, you *must* learn to put emotion into your voice if you want to convince others to take the actions you recommend.

If you practice the preceding suggestions and still want more help in using emotion when speaking, take an acting or assertiveness course. These courses are offered at colleges or through adult education programs. You will improve your voice projection and confidence. Two hours a night for 4 weeks is a worthy investment in learning to speak with interest and enthusiasm. Your career may depend on it.

Use Appropriate Voice Inflection

Have you ever listened to someone who ends sentences in a high voice tone, sounding somewhat questioning? After listening, you begin to wonder about the person's abilities and knowledge. The reason for this is that we are accustomed to hearing a tonal increase when a person asks a question. You perceive the person to be saying, "Did I say that right?" or "Am I OK?" These people have a bad habit that they need to change. They need to practice a downward inflection at the end of a phrase or sentence. Say the following sentence with both downward inflection and upward inflection:

> Here is more information. ↑ (upward inflection)
>
> Here is more information. ↓ (downward inflection)

Now take any sentence and practice lowering your tone at its conclusion. The more you practice consciously making your voice go up and down, the easier time you will have in sounding sure of yourself.

SPEAK A SECOND LANGUAGE

Presenters who must speak in a language other than their native tongue, make themselves nervous because they are afraid the audience doesn't understand them. They know that if they ask the audience, "Do you understand me?" the answer will be "Yes." Who wants to be the bearer of bad news and tell a speaker that only half of what he or she said was understandable? I have had people attend my presentations course who say that they had attended a presentations course several years ago, but their boss sent them to this one. After they begin to present, I can understand why. I know their boss hopes that they will improve their English in the seminar but has been reluctant to say it directly. We have a brief conversation, and I refer them to someone who helps people improve their English. No one, not even their boss, had told them that their presentations were barely understandable.

If you are the speaker and want some honest feedback, you have several options. Take a few people aside and ask them privately the questions that I have put on the following Language Questionnaire. Or hand out the Language Questionnaire to some colleagues and ask them to fill it out honestly. You will feel nervous if you aren't really sure how understandable you are to your audience.

The language questionnaire I have provided is short but will get you some excellent feedback. Give this questionnaire to people who have heard you speak only a few times since they won't have grown accustomed to your particular idiosyncrasies of speech. You owe it to your career to find out if your lack of clear pronunciation of words is hurting your career. Most bosses will not tell their employees to go take a class in pronunciation. Ask!

Hints for Speaking in a Second Language

1. When you start talking, say a couple of giveaway sentences so the audience gets used to hearing your voice and accent. They will need a few sentences to tune into you.

2. Speak slowly and pause. Why? Your audience may need a rest from trying to understand you as you talk. Give them a break.

3. If someone says they didn't understand what you just said, don't say it the same way again. You may have pronounced a word incorrectly, and if you say the same thing again, they still won't understand you.

4. Only put words on your visuals that you can pronounce.

5. If you get tired of speaking, have some visuals that you can show without saying much about each point. For example, you can say, "Here are the key areas we plan to address with our customers. Which areas do you have questions about?" You can then be quiet and wait to hear the questions. This gives you a break as well as your audience.

The Language Questionnaire

1. On a scale of 1 to 10, **how understandable** am I when presenting?

1	2	3	4	5	6	7	8	9	10
Barely				Halfway					Totally

2. Would you suggest that I receive some coaching on improving my language?

   _____ Yes _____ No _____ Maybe

3. If you think I need coaching, what type of coaching do you suggest?

   _____ Practice saying words—the pronunciation of words.

   _____ Practice learning where to put the emphasis in a sentence (e.g., where to raise or lower my voice).

   Other: _____

4. Do you think that by improving my speech patterns, my presentation recommendations and ideas might be more easily acceptable to my audience?

   _____ Yes _____ No _____ Maybe

5. Please comment on my voice mannerisms:

   The speed that I talk:

   _____ Just right _____ Too fast _____ Too slow

   Ending my sentences for clarity:

   _____ Easy to listen to. You end your sentences.

   _____ If you paused between thoughts, I could better follow what you say.

   _____ You pause too long between your thoughts and sentences.

   Voice modulation:

   _____ It's fine, it fits with the culture.

   _____ Needs to change.

   Change your modulation this way (e.g., lower your voice at the end of a sentence):

   _____

6. Please comment on any other things I could do (voice tone, gestures, eye contact, posture, walking around) that would help me be more effective when speaking:

   _____

7. Please tell me one thing I do well when speaking or gesturing that you suggest I continue doing:

   _____

Hints for Speaking When Your Language Is the Group's Second or Third Language

1. Be yourself as much as possible. People can feel that from you as you talk.

2. Don't expect people to ask many questions in front of the group. They may feel they don't speak the language well enough. It is better to have people form small groups and discuss any questions they have. Then a spokesperson from each group can ask the questions. Or you can circulate and answer the questions with each small group.

3. Speak slowly. Pause often.

4. Only use idioms that are understandable. Always explain idiomatic phrases to people from other cultures. A phrase like "Go to bat" can add interest to your talk when it is explained.

5. Use humor with caution. Avoid jokes when presenting to people from different cultures. Not only may they not understand the joke, they may also be insulted. If you want to use humor, first seek guidance about what is appropriate. Avoid sarcasm. It will be even less understood than humor.

6. Don't expect certain reactions from the group. If you get stares, don't interpret them as hostile or nonunderstanding. Many cultures aren't overly dramatic, nor are they encouraged to show how they truly feel in front of a group of strangers.

7. Never call on someone to read in front of the others. You don't know how well that person can read. In fact, you don't even know if he or she can read.

8. Know, ahead of time, about the people's culture. For example, Asians are not comfortable with long eye contact. Consequently, you don't want to approach an Asian in the seminar and talk to that person in a way that demands he or she keep looking at you. In some cultures, the American nod of the head for no, means yes. The fundamental rule here, as in every presentation, is to learn as much as you can about your audience before you present.

A Quick Voice Relaxation Exercise

When you have not recently practiced the other exercises in this section and you are on your way to speak to the vice-president, *stop:*

1. Go into the restroom.

2. Rub your hands over your face.

3. Knead your forehead and temples.

4. Open and close your jaw; relax it.

5. Squeeze and relax your eyes.

6. Roll your head slowly to the right and left.

7. Stand up and take two deep breaths.

Now your voice is at least more prepared than before.

YOUR LANGUAGE

> When one speaks too much, his words go unheeded.
>
> Konrad Adenauer

Your use of language can help or hinder your ability to establish and keep rapport with your listeners. Consider the following language hints the next time you speak:

- Suit words to participants.
- Avoid trite, unnecessary, and generalized expressions.
- Use active voice.
- Avoid loaded words.

Suit Words to Participants

A botanist is leading a group on a tour of a beautiful tree and flower garden. She knows all the Latin names for the flowers and trees that the group will see on the path. She starts by saying, "Now this is a *Betula papyrifera.*" One person in the group says, "She means, this is a white birch." This sets the pattern of the tour. The botanist says the Latin word and the knowledgeable person in the group translates. Specialists frequently lose their group as they "expound" with the special words of their profession.

If you are 24 years old presenting to people 64 years old, avoid slang expressions and words or phrases that refer to people's ages. If you are 55 years old talking to 23-year-old students, use language with which they can identify.

Avoid Trite, Unnecessary, and Generalized Expressions

The following types of words and expressions detract from a presentation's power:

- I want to take this opportunity to . . .
- It gives me a great deal of pleasure . . .

- Maybe, kind of, you know, I just, you guys.

- To make a long story short . . .

- Always, never, somewhat, quite, all.

- To be honest with you . . .

- Hopefully, awfully, okay.

- Great, fantastic, marvelous, the best in the world.

Superlatives can get you in trouble. You do not use a 10-quart pot if you only need a saucepan. You do not use a power mower when you have only two square feet of grass to mow. You do not send your car to the factory for an oil change. Match the action with the reality. Too many superlatives do not convince your listeners; quite to the contrary, they cause your listeners to be wary of you.

Use Active Voice

Talk to a group the way you talk to a person you enjoy being around. Sound conversational, not formal. If you talk *at* your listeners, they may respond by being distant and cool to your suggestions. Some people interpret the use of the passive voice as a means by which the speaker avoids responsibility. Take charge and accept responsibility for what you say. Use the active voice, as demonstrated in the following sentences:

- Say "I believe," rather than "It is believed."

- Say "Jim wrote the report," rather than "The report was written by Jim."

- Say "I recommend," rather than "From the facts, one could recommend."

- Say "Our team decided," rather than "It was decided."

Avoid Loaded Words

Some words can be quite "loaded" and may evoke a negative emotional response. You may not always know if a word is loaded for your listener. How do the following words strike you: *third world, old woman, developing countries,* and *disadvantaged people?* Some people would take offense at these words. Know your listeners. Avoid the loaded words.

Phrases, as well, can be loaded. What is your immediate response when you read this sentence: "Improving your language is a complicated, tedious process"? After hearing this, you may not feel as motivated to work at improving your language. Certain words or phrases are not the best to use: *complicated, tedious, long, drawn out, difficult to comprehend.* Which of the following phrases is more

---

Energy and Excitement

The day most wholly lost is the one on which one does not laugh.

Nicolas Chamfort

Nothing good or great can be done in the absence of enthusiasm.

Tom Peters

The greatest mistake you can make in life is to be continually fearing you will make one.

Elbert Hubbard

A person can succeed at almost anything for which he or she has limited enthusiasm.

Charles M. Schwab

The violence done us by others is often less painful than that which we do to ourselves.

François de La Rochefoucauld

I am persuaded that every time a person smiles—but much more so when laughing, it adds something to this fragment of life.

Laurence Sterne

For every minute you are angry, you lose sixty seconds of happiness.

Ralph Waldo Emerson

---

positive: "They are defective 20 percent of the time," or "They are correct eight out of 10 times"? Obviously, the second phrase is more positive, although you might want to use the first phrase if your focus is on the need for an improvement in quality control. Carefully choose your words and the manner in which you present ideas. For example, how do the following phrases affect you?

- I agree with all the experts who say . . .
- Everyone knows that the computer industry is . . .
- This fact goes without saying . . .

When you use such phrases, your listeners may think you are not open to discussion. Some might choose to disagree with you, due to your dogmatic statements, and some might choose to ignore you, as your statements sound overly emphatic and too generalized.

ANECDOTES, ANALOGIES, AND EXAMPLES

There are many good reasons for including anecdotes, analogies, and examples in every presentation:

- *They Interest You and Your Listeners.* People enjoy hearing stories. They always perk up. They remember stories longer than facts.

- *They Project Enthusiasm and Sincerity.* You can easily be enthusiastic when giving an example. This is the best way to modulate your voice. Spacing your examples throughout your talk rekindles the enthusiasm that may have died down.

- *They Change the Pace of Your Talk.* Examples add variety and spice and easily lend themselves to changing the speed of your sentences. You will find yourself naturally slowing down and speeding up for emphasis.

- *They Enhance Your Credibility.* People think you know what you are talking about when you give examples. If you have not yet had enough personal experience to use your own examples, borrow some examples from your colleagues.

- *They Show Respect for the Audience.* The audience will feel like royalty if you take the time to think of examples related to their life or work.

- *They Give You More Power.* Are you a storyteller in your environment? In *Corporate Cultures* (Reading, MA: Addison-Wesley, 1982), Terrence Deal and Allan Kennedy discuss the necessity of storytelling:

  > People tell stories to gain power and influence—and because they enjoy doing it. Storytellers are in a powerful position because they can change reality. Storytellers simply interpret what goes on in the company—but to suit their own perceptions. And what is power anyway but the ability to influence people's perceptions—without their realizing it, of course. . . . For the corporation, storytellers maintain cohesion and provide guidelines for everyone to follow. It's the most powerful way to convey information and shape behavior.

Your task, before your next presentation, whether to one or a hundred listeners, is to do the following. Whether or not you have slides, overheads, or a flip chart, go through your talk and pick several places, depending on the length of your talk, where you can insert an interesting example or anecdote relating to the point you wish to make.

Remember, your preparation time for a talk is not complete until you have inserted analogies and anecdotes. The analogies do not have to refer directly to the subject under discussion as long as you make the link between the analogy and your topic. I know a financial advisor who wanted to make the point that his company would do the research for the client. The advisor described his company as the limousine service of the financial services industry. He went on to say that riders who want to take a limousine tell the driver their destination, then let the driver take them there. The riders do not have to rent a car, find a map, or do the research to know which streets to take due to one-way or rush-hour traffic. They rely on the limousine service. At the end of this example, the advisor said, "Our company will be your limousine service. We will do the homework. You only need tell us your destination."

Before telling an anecdote or example, practice it out loud so you hear which phrases you want to emphasize. Be sure to explain how it relates to the point you are making. Some people will not understand your analogy and will need to hear how you link it to your subject.

The following "short" stories are effective analogies.

The Investment Manager's "Just Imagine" Scenario.   An investment manager was presenting on the broad spectrum of investment alternatives. He wanted a way to move into his topic, not just start right off discussing investments. The following is what he said:

> Just imagine it is Saturday and a beautiful, hot, sunny day. You are going outside, perhaps to the beach. What kind of shoes do you wear? Probably some nice open sandals to let your feet breathe. Two days later, you are on your way to work and the rain is pouring down. What shoes do you wear? Probably not sandals, unless you have a lifeguard job. Now it is winter— four feet of snow have piled up outside, and a wind chill factor is putting the temperature at -30 degrees. You find yourself some warm, high boots that you can use to trudge through the snow, dig your car out, and drive to work. Our economy has weather shifts as well. You need to consider the weather of the economy as you decide on your investments. Maybe it is sunny all over and you can invest in almost anything. Maybe now there are storm clouds, and you want to be sure the storm does not affect you. I can help you choose your investment objectives based on the weather conditions acceptable to you.

The Lawyer's Laugh about His Family.   A prosecution lawyer cleverly used his profession to honor his father at an awards ceremony. As you will see from this short summary, the son was exquisite at using his profession to make points and to point out some obvious issues while making light of them. In capsule form, he said the following:

> My occupation demands that I spend my time proving that someone is guilty. I am the prosecution for the state. I know it pleases you that there is one less member of the family to be involved in litigation. [This comment received much laughter since most of the people there had been sued by his father who was the guest of honor.] I am not here to build a case as to the verdict you should hand down. All of you have already made the decision

that my father is guilty of giving much to this community. This time I am fortunate to agree with the verdict. I am here to congratulate you on your excellent verdict. I shall now spend my time building the case which supports your verdict.

If you think you can get away with not using examples and anecdotes, tape yourself. Listen to or watch the tape. Ask yourself, "Am I interesting to listen to for a period of time?" If your answer is "no," add some examples. If your answer is "yes," please send me the tape!

YOUR CHANGING PACE

Your presentation needs to be like a dance with different phrasing and rhythms. Four qualities of dance—lyrical movement, sustained movement, percussive movement, and stillness—will help you understand how to change your pace. If you are alone now while reading this, move your arm and hand around in front of you. Demonstrate these different qualities. A lyrical movement has an even, average pace. A sustained movement is slow and even. A percussive quality shows quick, uneven, and surprising movements. Stillness is as it sounds, non-moving and quiet. Each of these rhythms has to be included in the flow of your presentation.

Inexperienced presenters forget to vary their pace. They start with one pace and continue it the whole time. You may have a soothing, lyrical voice, but if you do not stop or speed up on occasion, your audience will find their attention wandering. Telling an anecdote will get you out of the lyrical voice. A sustained voice done consistently lulls a group into a stupor. Short, to-the-point sentences get you out of the sustained voice. A percussive and choppy voice grates on people. Once in a while, quickness adds variety and spark to a talk. For a percussive voice, you must find a way to be quiet (for example, take a drink of water). Stillness focuses on the pauses in your talk. Pauses give you a chance to breathe and give your listeners an opportunity to digest what you have said.

Allow the time for a quiet moment. Isaac Stern, the violin virtuoso, said, "The important thing is not the notes, it's the intervals between the notes." For him, those intervals made the difference between sound and beautiful music. After a pause, people are more attentive to your voice. A pause is like the white space in an ad. You see the ad better because of the emptiness around it. If you pause too much, however, you will need to get your adrenalin moving (that is, get more exercise, sleep, or better food). As you listen to yourself, you will get a sense of the qualities you use and do not use. A general hint is to keep varying the length of your sentences. Your pace will change.

As you begin speaking, pay attention to the mood of the group. In dance terms, everyone may be enjoying a waltz; consequently, your group may not appreciate your sudden shift to music for a jitterbug. You could start with waltz music and move the dancers slowly into the jitterbug. People do not like to be startled. To begin, meet your group where they are.

Most of us will be presenting primarily to American audiences. Before you speak to other audiences, do your homework. While most people are generally more forgiving of errors in presentation etiquette involving nonnative speakers, you can score many points and gain respect if you are aware of particular problems and demonstrate your sensitivity to your audience. See the cross-cultural questionnaire in Step 6 along with hints of how to present in Japan, Saudi Arabia, and Mexico.

STEP 6 MOTIVATING YOUR LISTENERS

KEY POINTS

1 List three things you know will motivate your particular audience and include them in your talk.

2 If you are presenting to key decision makers, find out how they like information presented to them.

3 Intersperse your word slides with visual pictures.

4 Give people something to do (handouts, quizzes, discussion questions) if you are speaking longer than a half hour.

5 Provide food if it's early in the morning or late in the day.

6 Vary the pace of your talk with some visuals. Also talk without using visuals.

7 Call on the experts in the room in order to recognize their expertise.

8 Include something for the visual types, the auditory types, and the ones who like to be busy doing something.

9 Take frequent stretch breaks rather than one long break.

10 Give your audience members an opportunity to talk with each other and share their views on your presentation. You can do this after you discuss each major point.

A good talker is only a pitcher. Unless his audience catches
him with heart and mind, he's defeated.

                                                    Wilson Mizner

BASIC POINTS ON MOTIVATION

How does a speaker most effectively motivate all listeners? Step 6 gives you many
phrases, techniques, and exercises to capture and keep every person's attention.
Here are four excellent ways to begin: (1) know your listeners' names, (2) state at
which points you prefer people to ask questions, (3) determine the level of expertise of the people, and (4) share the type of participation you expect of them. You
must have rapport; without it, you will have a difficult time enjoying your talk and
so will your listeners.

Know Everyone's Name

Knowing people's names is a good way to begin. People like to be recognized, and
remembering someone's name is flattering. More importantly, people become favorably disposed to those who take the energy and time to recognize them. Are
you the type of person who, at the beginning of a meeting, can be introduced to
eight people and remember their names? If not, take along name cards and a felt-
tip marker so people can write down their names. Do a name card for yourself as
well. You will discover that the participants will not necessarily remember your
name just because you are standing in front of a group. This will be true even
though you may have been introduced. If you have trouble remembering people's
names, try the following exercise. Obtain a list of names ahead of time. Go over
the names. Repeat them *out loud.* When you meet each person, you will be somewhat familiar with each name. Say the person's name out loud when you are introduced, so the name has less of a tendency to go in one ear and out the other.

Give Question-and-Answer Guidelines

When you begin, let the participants know whether you prefer them to hold questions until the end of your talk or to ask questions as you speak. You can also ask
for questions after presenting each of the major points. You may feel more comfortable and connected to people if questions are asked at any time during the
talk. This is particularly true in sales, where you want the customer to ask questions. When you present to certain levels of management, those people will ask
questions whenever they wish. In fact, some of them will ask questions while you
do your opening statement, not even letting you begin your first point. These are
the kinesthetic types about whom you will learn in this step.
    The timing of questions depends on the situation. Ultimately, you must
judge if you would have better rapport with your group answering questions as

you speak or answering them at the end of your presentation. The most important criterion to consider at this stage is how you can best handle questions so that you achieve your objective in the most relaxed and pleasant way for all involved. Whatever you decide, let people know. Knowing in advance the appropriate way to behave puts people at ease. They like to know you have control of the situation.

Know the Group's Level of Expertise

It is helpful to know the level of expertise in the group. If you did not find out in advance, ask at the beginning of your talk. Some questions asked by different speakers are, "How many of you have ever traveled to a third world country?" or "How many of you have stocks?" or "How many of you have volunteered before?" Depending on your talk's content you can say something such as, "I see by the show of hands that some of you are familiar with this new system and some of you are not. I plan to go into as much detail as I feel that all of us need to have in common so we can make a decision as to the next step for the project." People appreciate your acknowledging their degree of experience and expertise.

You will know what to expect when you have an idea of the audience's knowledge and interest. With a show of hands, you will also have some people to reference during your talk. As you speak say, "Fred, given your five years of experience, I think this information would be particularly interesting to you," or "Joe, I saw by your raised arm that you have been in this business longer than I; please add anything I leave out."

State Your Expectations

People want to know what type of participation you expect and desire. There are five participation possibilities: decide, brainstorm, inform, discuss, and learn. Do you want people to make a decision today? Do you want people to brainstorm solutions to a situation you are presenting? Do you want to inform? Do you want a discussion that will lead to a decision at the end of your talk or that will be continued at a later date? Do you want people to learn a new skill? People respond more appropriately when they know what type of participation is expected of them.

MODALITIES

Visual   **Auditory**   **Kinesthetic**

Presentations need certain elements to satisfy the three modalities*—visual, auditory, and kinesthetic—that people use. A modality can be defined as a sensory way of processing information. Those of you who are visually inclined want to see some pictures here first or to have a broad overview of what you are about to learn. Those of you who are auditorily inclined would like all the details written down and backup facts and references provided as sources for this information. If you really had your way, you would like this book on tape so you could listen to it instead of read it! Those of you who are kinesthetically inclined would like to take a quiz or answer a questionnaire to discover what modality you most frequently use. It is difficult to know which modality to begin with and how to address each modality to satisfy every person. Although many of you may not consciously realize it, you use modalities every time you organize a presentation, be it for a few minutes or an hour. Naturally enough, your tendency will be to organize and present around your favorite modality.

Answering the following questionnaire will give you an idea about your modality choices. Some people do not have one preferred way of processing and organizing information; they may use several modalities. As you answer these questions, recognize that other people answer them differently; that they have different preferences. Remember, you do not present to convince or inform yourself; you present to communicate to and convince others. Use the questionnaire as a learning tool about the other modalities. The more you know about your audience's preferences, the greater will be your ability to adapt your talk to their needs.

Your Favorite Modality

Check off all the statements that best describe you.

Visual Types

☐ 1. I like to use a white board or flip chart when available.

☐ 2. I prefer to see the "big picture" before listening to the details or carrying out an action.

☐ 3. When given a choice, I like visuals.

☐ 4. I sometimes forget to share my internal picture of how I visualize a completed project.

☐ 5. I like to read and see something, rather than listen to someone explain the details.

* These modalities are taken from Neurolinguistic Programming (NLP). My purpose here is not to teach all about NLP, but to show how some of the model can be used very effectively to increase your rapport with your listeners (see References, for more information).

☐   6. If not given a picture, I will make up one in my head or on paper.

☐   7. I need visual order. I prefer to see things organized, neat, and tidy (for example, my work area).

☐   8. When getting directions, I want to see a commercial map or have one drawn for me. I am usually on the lookout for landmarks.

☐   9. I like to explain a situation by giving someone a picture of it. For example, if I was explaining how four roads entered a shopping mall, I would want to draw a picture of the mall's road patterns. Then I would feel comfortable explaining the situation.

☐ 10. I prefer to learn how to work on a computer by watching someone first.

Auditory Types

☐   1. I process information best by hearing details and statistics.

☐   2. I listen and remember the details of what was said.

☐   3. I think visuals are not as important as hearing a clear organized format.

☐   4. I want to hear how to work on a computer by listening to someone tell me the steps and "how-to's."

☐   5. I may repeat internally to myself or out loud what has just been said.

☐   6. While trying to listen to someone, I am distracted by background noise, such as the phone ringing.

☐   7. When getting directions, I prefer to hear how to get there. I want to know the street names and distances, and I sometimes plot out the distances on a map.

☐   8. I am a good organizer of facts and data.

☐   9. I retain information better by hearing myself say it out loud.

☐ 10. I can be easily irritated if the person talking does not have a pleasant sounding voice.

Kinesthetic Types

☐   1. I prefer to learn how to work on a computer by doing it, then when I get stuck, to ask questions or look up the answer.

☐   2. While listening, I like to do other things (for example, open my mail while someone is talking).

☐   3. I have a tendency to go off on tangents rather than stick to the main point.

☐   4. My role is to "massage" data and look at it in many different ways.

☐   5. I find that many times, as soon as a fact is stated, it has gone in one ear and out the other. I listen more for the feeling behind the words.

☐ 6. When asking directions, I want to be pointed in the right direction and will find the place sooner or later. I am frequently in trouble with a spouse or friend who does not want to drive around for an hour while I am getting a sense of where to go.

☐ 7. I may ask questions before a speaker even begins to present his or her major points and issues.

☐ 8. I am a doer.

☐ 9. I like to discuss a half-formed idea until it feels workable.

☐ 10. I enjoy asking questions.

Now add up how many you have for each modality:

_____ Visual   _____ Auditory   _____ Kinesthetic

Understand Individual Modalities

Which modality do you lean toward? Is it obvious to you? What does this mean? People have very different ways of receiving and processing information. Let us say you invite people over for a dinner buffet. Some are vegetarians, some only eat raw foods, and some like steak. Your buffet includes sautéed vegetables and steak; there is no salad. The raw foods people look at your offering, yet never pick up a plate. Nothing you have offered appeals to them. This same dynamic occurs with modalities. When speaking with one person, you need to know which of the three modalities he or she is most familiar with and adept at using. Offer your information in that modality first or as soon as possible.

When doing group presentations, you must be able to say and do things to interest all three modalities, or you will be like the dinner host whose "raw food" guests found nothing appetizing to eat. If you never offer the modality that the person uses, you will have limited rapport with that person. You may also have difficulty obtaining approval for your next steps. Stop and think about the people you really enjoy at work or at home. You probably work or play in the same modalities.

The following sections explore each modality.

The Visual Modality.   *"The mind is more slowly stirred by the ear than by the eye,"* said Homer. If you like visuals, then you probably agree with this quote by Homer. A large percentage of the population is visually inclined. If you are one of those people, you need to see the whole picture externally or in your mind. You see things in pictures, colors, and shapes. Until you see a picture, you have a hard time paying attention. You must know the overall outline before you discuss the details or you will feel slightly uncomfortable. When giving a talk, you would do better using the horizontal outline explained in Step 3. The famous artist, Georgia O'Keeffe, gives away her visual preference as she says, "The meaning of a word—to me—is not as exact as the meaning of a color." Albert Einstein visualized what it would look like to be riding on the end of a light beam. Mary Parker Follett, an organizational consultant, said, "The most successful leader of all is one who sees another picture not yet actualized. He sees the things which belong in his present picture but which are not yet there." James T. McCay says, "Remember, you can't act without a picture." An executive in a company commented, "You know, ever since I put up the white board in my office, my staff comes in and immediately starts diagramming out the problem. My meeting time with them has been significantly reduced."

The Auditory Modality.   In the days of radio, without television, more of the population was forced to process information auditorially. When operating from an auditory modality, you hear words, tones, and sounds. If a presenter does not have an agreeable voice tone to you, you have an almost impossible time listening to the content. You like to hear all the facts and logic. When you present, you need to believe that you have done your homework and have the statistics at your fingertips. You sometimes feel nervous because you are afraid you will be asked a question that you will be unable to answer. You tend to think you have to know everything and say it all. You do great background research. You do well with detailed overheads and index cards. You can give a systematically organized talk going from one point to another without taking detours. You *hear* in a way very few people take the time to hear.

David Brinkley describes his use of the auditory modality, "I've always liked a common sense approach to reporting. I was at Cape Canaveral for the Apollo moon landing. I tried to describe the takeoff, but the picture showed it better than my words. So I tried to see it in an ordinary way. I spoke about the noise of it, how the roar is so loud that you hear only a toned-down version of it on television. I said the noise was so loud that it rattled the coins in my pockets and vibrated the shirt buttons against my chest." People make comments about auditory people, such as "He chewed my ear off," or "She talked until I was blue in the face." Auditory people give off clues like cupping their ear and saying, "I just do not understand." This means they have not yet really heard what you are saying.

The Kinesthetic Modality.   If you do physical work and/or physical hobbies you process much of your information through this modality. You learn by doing and sometimes "wing" your talks. This can get you in trouble when your listeners wish you had put your presentation together before the talk, not during the talk. You wish to convey a feeling about your subject rather than list statistics or show pictures. You prefer to "muck around" in information. The image is you, rubbing your hands together and saying, "What can I do with this information?" You want a feel for the situation.

There are no value judgments attached to the modalities. They are simply ways people represent and process information. What makes a presentation effective or ineffective has to do with the inclusion or exclusion of one or more of the modalities.

The Kinesthetic Perspective

Think about the whole body.

Taisen Deshimaru

Learn your lines and do not trip over the furniture.

Spencer Tracy

The truth of a thing is the feel of it, not the think of it.

Stanley Kubrick

You think too much, Boss.

Anthony Quinn, in *Zorba the Greek*

Man, if you gotta ask, you'll never know.

Louis Armstrong, when asked to define jazz

Some people feel the rain; others just get wet.

Roger Miller

Use Every Modality

Visual Types **Like**	Auditory Types **Like**	Kinesthetic Types **Like**
• Overheads	• A varied and well-modulated voice	• Group or pair activities lasting from a minute to a couple of hours
• Pictures	• Statistics and facts	• Question time
• Analogies	• Detailed descriptions	• Objection time
• Metaphors	• Clear, loud voice	• Small quiz done in pairs
• Slides	• Calm and organized talk	• Hands-on activities
• Flip charts	• Audiotapes	• Pushing buttons
• Graphs	• To hear your enthusiasm	• To feel your enthusiasm
• Videotapes	• To talk out loud so they can process what you say	• Audience participation
• Demonstrations	• Voice with emotional intensity	• To touch things
• Broad overview stated		• To take stretch breaks
• To see your enthusiasm (e.g., by your gestures)		
• Stories and examples that create a picture		
• To see materials		

Use Modalities When Presenting

This section will expand your understanding of the modality choices available to you when organizing and doing a presentation. A group of people presenting for Oxfam America, a nonprofit organization working in the third world, wanted to learn ways to make their slide presentations more dynamic. The following sections describe how they changed their approach and choreographed a slide talk.

Opening with Questions.   The opening included questions in which people raised their hands in response to such questions as, "How many of you have been to a third world country?" and "How many of you have lived in a third world country for one month or more?" The next questions engaged the audience by soliciting information. "What third world countries would you like to visit?" "Let me hear some names," and "What attracts you to those countries?" (When you ask questions, be sure to tell the group how many hands went up, since some people may not be able to see everyone in the room.) In addition to involving the kinesthetic modality, the information gave the presenter an idea of his or her audience's experience with the third world and let the presenter take some breaths and relax before launching into the slide talk.

Stating the Objective of the Talk.   The presenter then stated the objective and listed the four areas to be discussed. The visual modality person needed to know the broad picture, and the auditory modality person needed to hear a structure.

Handing Out a Quiz.   People had 3 minutes to do the quiz about Cambodia with another person. The kinesthetic modality found satisfaction in doing the quiz and the auditory modality felt comfortable in having a paper of details, facts, and statistics. The visual person could "see" something.

Showing Slides.   The slides were pictures of Cambodia. The old saying, "A picture is worth a thousand words," is particularly appropriate for the visual modality. With some of the slides, the speaker told a human interest story, which captured more of the kinesthetic person's senses or the visual person's picture-making imagination.

Stating Statistics.   The quiz answers were written on a flip chart or board. The kinesthetic people wrote the correct answers on the quiz, the auditory people listened to make sure they guessed accurately, and the visual people saw something in front of them.

Concluding with a Story.   The speaker told a story about the Cambodian orphans in one town. The kinesthetic types responded to the story with emotional emphasis. The visual types pictured the scenes in their mind. The auditory types responded to a well-modulated voice.

Describing Next Steps.   The presenter handed out details about Oxfam (for the auditory people) and the monetary contribution or time commitment forms for all to fill out (for the kinesthetic and visual people).

Presenters returned and reported on their successes and their own abilities to relax and enjoy the fund-raising process. Also, they no longer turned off the lights as they spoke, so they experienced continued rapport with the audience while sharing information about Oxfam.

Apply Modalities to Skills Training

To help you put this all together, here are ways you can incorporate the modalities into your training, whether the training is for an hour or a week. Be sure you have this range of variety in your sessions, so you can satisfy all modalities. (*Caution:* Your training will not work as well if, one day, you do all visual things, the next day, you present facts, and, the following day, you let people do something. You will have more success if you vary your modalities during the *same* day.) The following approaches will be useful:

- Enthusiastically state a clear outline of what you plan to do (auditory).

- Show some visuals—not just those with numbers on them, but pictures or graphs (visual).

- Hand out a quiz and, in pairs or in small groups, let people guess the answers before you go over those points (kinesthetic).

- Give examples, anecdotes, and stories to add variety and spice (kinesthetic and visual, and auditory if you speak with a well-modulated voice).

- Vary the pace by letting people do things in pairs or small groups (kinesthetic).

- Have space on the handouts for people to write additional comments. Many computer programs will print audience notes that show the visual on half of the page with lines for taking notes on the second half of the page (kinesthetic and visual).

- Let participants speak to each other about the material. For example, ask them to share, in pairs, what they just learned (auditory).

- Speak in an inspiring and captivating voice (auditory and kinesthetic).

Modalities in a Classroom Training Situation

Visual Types	Auditory Types	Kinesthetic Types
They laugh at the pictures. They draw diagrams of whataever you say. They skip over the fine print.	They know the facts about everything. They listen to you and catch you if you make a mistake. They make sure that everything is organized.	They write notes but it may not be about the subject. They frequently leave the room. They keep themselves occupied with at least one other activity.
Strategies	**Strategies**	**Strategies**
• Use charts, slides, and props. • Give them outlines so they can see and follow along.	• Have people talk to one another about the information so they can hear themselves speaking. • Elicit questions. • Give out detailed notes.	• Encourage participation. • Create participatory exercises. • Set up time for breaks.

The Gillette Company knows the importance of training their executives and managers. Their Effective Management Program includes many case studies that use all the modalities. People speak to each other as they create solutions. Charts are used to organize the data. Involvement of every group member is necessary to solve the problem. Since all the modalities are employed, people are engaged through at least one modality.

Apply Modalities to Selling

Have you ever watched someone buy a car? Some people get all the facts—about the engine, the gas mileage, and the guarantee. Others look at the quality of construction, the paint, the interior upholstery, and the carpet. Finally, others run their hands over the upholstery, then sit in the car and drive it to get the feel of it. Some use all three modalities, but emphasize one over the others. Meanwhile, the salesperson is standing by, carefully observing the customer and ready to discuss the vehicle in whatever modality the customer is using to evaluate it.

This is the same type of attention you need to use when making a sales presentation. If your talk is to one person, use the most comfortable modality for that person. You will know which modality that is by the words the person uses and the ways the person wants the information presented. For example, the manger says, "Show me those reports that suggest you need more help," or "Tell me those statistics again and tell me what you recommend we do." Obviously, with large groups, you must use all modalities during your presentation. (*Hint:* When purchasing products for yourself, you would do well to use all three modalities in your final decision-making process. Many a person has bought something based on input from one modality, only to regret the decision later.)

ADAPTING TO THE MODALITY OF THE KEY PERSON

> The worst sin towards our fellow creatures is not to hate them,
> but to be indifferent to them; that's the essence of inhumanity.
>
> George Bernard Shaw, *The Devil's Disciple*

So far, we have talked about group presentations and the need to use all modalities. You have probably been thinking of certain people you know and the modality they most frequently use. Many people use one modality more than the others. Or at least they prefer to start in one modality, then move into the other ones. When presenting to these people, be flexible and adapt to their modalities. Read the following five examples of adapting to the modality of key persons:

1. *The Kinesthetic President.* One woman presented to the president of her company, who preferred the kinesthetic modality. That meant that he liked to "muck around" in the information and put his hands in it. He experienced every talk as an opportunity to delve into the information, ask questions, and have fun

playing with the data. The employee prepared her presentations using overheads. Usually, after a few minutes, the president would start asking questions, and the whole well-planned presentation never occurred. Realizing, on the one hand, that the president's favorite modality was kinesthetic and, on the other hand, that it was inappropriate to tell him to wait until her conclusion to ask questions, the presenter had to find a new way to approach this person. She solved the problem by opening with a quick (1 to 2 minutes) summary of her results and waiting for him to ask the inevitable questions. Then, when fitting, she would put up the appropriate overhead as she answered a certain question. After presenting this way a couple of times, she relaxed and felt more confident. The president even told her he liked her style of presenting. Sometimes she did not get to use all her meticulously designed overheads, which was a bit demoralizing, yet she reminded herself that communicating to convince the president was more important than showing off her overheads. Sara Jeannette Duncan's remark epitomizes the president's way of operating: "If you have anything to tell me of importance, for God's sake, begin at the end."

2. *The New Vice-President.* A new vice-president takes over the Research and Development Division of a major food company. He begins to think that his staff is incompetent. When walking into this vice-president's office, the staff sees that his desk is immaculate and that there is a white board on the wall and an easel in a corner. The staff is used to sniffing, tasting, and feeling all types of foods. Employees spend their day literally mucking around in food. The new vice-president did not come from a food company. In his past job, he measured people's competence by their clear visual presentations of their objectives and goals. His new employees had never worked like that. Finally, in order for them to work with him and have him believe in their competence, they began using visuals, keeping their desks neat, and writing on his white board. It was amazing to see how happy the new vice-president became with his staff due to their use of the visual modality.

3. *The Interviewer.* The manager interviewed and selected people for key jobs in his department. He admitted that he overemphasized the person's visual appearance in making a selection decision. After twice judging incorrectly, he now has a few detail-oriented people interview, to listen to how well the person knows the technical aspects of the work. He is even considering using some kinesthetic interviewing by having an applicant work on a project.

4. *Influencing Others.* James Rouse, the famous city planner and developer, was dissatisfied with the looks of some housing in his Columbia, Maryland, project, and he tried to influence the next decision by nagging and correcting his team of architects. He got nowhere. Then he decided to stop correcting them and tried to influence them by sending them to look at the world's best architecture. Inspired by Rouse's vision, the architects went on to create some of the most eye-catching and functional housing in the country (Warren Bennis and Burt Nanus, *Leaders: The Strategies for Taking Charge* [New York: Harper & Row, 1985]).

5. *The Family Business.* The husband and wife are both general partners in a partnership. The wife has responsibility for the finance and operations and

the husband, for sales and marketing. When they discuss the business, the wife presents charts, detailed projections, and, usually, a cost-benefit analysis. The husband fervently talks about doing more advertising and trade fairs. They frequently end up in a standoff because she says he does not have the information to spend that kind of money. She wants him to do more analysis. He tells her that he has a feel for this; he senses that these are the next steps. They either resolve their disagreement or have many days and evenings of antagonistic discussions.

This is not a content problem. It is a modality problem. The wife makes decisions in the auditory and visual modalities. The husband makes decisions by his kinesthetic gut feelings. They both need to respect each other's way of making decisions and to use other modalities as well. To meet his wife halfway, the husband could do some "due diligence" research to back up his gut feelings. The wife could recognize the value of his 30 years of experience in what he does and the high probability that he is correct. She could let go of her need for always having facts and data before making a decision. Instead of a compromise, they could agree to make the decision after including both his gut feelings and her research data. If the 14 million family-owned businesses in the United States (168 of the *Fortune* 500) knew how to present ideas to other family members and to accept the other's modality as a valid way of interpreting reality, decisions would probably be more thorough and they would certainly be more pleasant.

Use the modalities most understood by your listeners. They will enjoy your presentations and be more influenced into agreeing to your next steps.

PACING THE GROUP

When pacing one person or a group, be sure you do not get so far ahead that they cannot catch up. If you are unsure that your audience is with you, stop and ask, "Shall I speak a little more about the subject?" Do not ask, "Does everyone

Problem	Solution
Faces look blank; no question are asked.	<ul><li>Ask question.</li><li>Probe: What questions do you have? Shall I say more about this now?</li></ul>
There is lots of movement; people are looking at watches; there is almost no movement.	<ul><li>Take a stretch break.</li><li>End five minutes early and tell people.</li></ul>
You feel unconnected to people.	<ul><li>Establish and return eye contact.</li><li>Change your modality.</li></ul>
The room is too hot or too cold.	<ul><li>Have the temperature adjusted.</li><li>Take a break.</li></ul>
The day is very long.	<ul><li>Serve fruit in morning, nuts and raisins in the afternoon.</li><li>Ask questions in the middle of talk.</li><li>Include some "doing" types of activities.</li></ul>

understand?" Most people, even if they do not understand, will not admit to that in front of a group. People *will* admit, however, that they want you to tell them more about the subject. This does not make it sound as if they did not understand your point. It just sounds as if they are curious and want to have more information.

Vary the Pace

When you feel that there is no way to keep people's interests, let alone convince them of anything, do one of the following things. You will never know the results until you do it!

Stretch Breaks.   Take a stretch break by announcing, "Let's take a 2 minute stretch break." Then you stand there and stretch to give people permission to do so. People will follow your lead and appreciate your consideration.

Talking and Sharing.   Ask people to speak to the person sitting next to them and share something. The sharing you ask them to do should relate to your topic. The following examples might give you ideas. For an investments group, "Tell the person next to you about one of the best investments you have made and explain how you chose it." For selling a product, "Describe this product and share how it could help you or someone you know." To get people moving in the group, "Please talk to the person next to you about questions you may want to ask."

Brief Quizzes.   Give out a brief 5-minute quiz. Tell people that you will be giving the answers during the rest of your talk. Or, hand each person a piece of paper and ask them to check off the things they think your product can do. These types of handouts are excellent to use when you feel that your presentation needs a change of energy. This also gives you a chance to plan what you will do next.

Walking.   Walk and move around, and speak from a different part of the room.

Voice Variation.   Play with your voice. Pause longer. Be more enthusiastic. Speed up some, then slow down.

Pacing Issues

What do you do when someone talks too much during your presentation and slows the pace? Play amateur psychologist and figure out why the person is doing it. Is it a bid for attention or a desire to one-up your talk? Does this person just not know when to be quiet? Do yourself and the group a favor. Graciously stop the disrupter by saying such things as, "Thank you for your comment. I wish we had more time to hear everyone's viewpoint, but those will have to wait until after my conclusion." If the person starts again, interrupt and say, "I am sorry to interrupt you, but I must finish my presentation soon. I'll be glad to let you talk after I am done." Make these comments before you are angry, because you can still sound gracious. If you wait until you feel irritated, you will only sound that way. You win everyone's respect when you are gracious and polite to even the most obnoxious person.

How do you get people to talk during your presentation in order to moderate the pace? If you want to encourage audience participation, do not have a formal classroom seating arrangement or ask questions as, "What do you think?" or "Who knows the statistics on this?" or "Who knows the answer?" Many people feel intimated by these aggressive parent-to-child approaches. Group discussions work better. For example, ask participants to turn to the person sitting next to them and discuss their best guess as to the correct statistics. Then say, "OK, let's hear some of the group's guesses." This is much less threatening.

CONTROLLING THE ROOM

Theoretically, the presentation room is all arranged as a result of your request days before your talk. Realistically, rooms will rarely look like your requests. That is why you should arrive early enough to set up the room the way you want it. Before pilots fly, they double-check the equipment. Once up in the air, it might be too late. Do a test run of your equipment. Learn how to change a bulb and how to put slides correctly into the slide projector. Your "crash" may not be as obvious as a pilot's plane crash, yet it could occur and leave you with many problems you do not need. We are all too familiar with the overheated room leading to nodding heads and glazed eyes. The following sections give key points to consider with room control.

Obtain Appropriate Room Size and Shape

Be sure the room is large or small enough to accommodate the expected number of people. If the room is too big and you have to use it, set up only one part of the room and have your group sit in that part. Dismantle all the chairs and tables in the other part of the room, so it does not look as though you were expecting more people who just never showed up. If the room is too small, then at least organize the standing room. Ask people to stand around the edge of the room rather than three deep at the back. Sometimes the room has a pole in the center. If it does, try as much as possible to be sure everyone has a view that enables them to see the visuals.

Arrange Equipment for Easy Viewing

Set up your equipment in such a way that it does not block people's view of your visuals. If you are using an overhead projector, be sure it is the appropriate length from the screen to obtain as large a projection as possible. Do not be shy. Take the time to move the equipment around until you are satisfied. It is preferable to move the equipment than to have a frustrated vice-president who is unable to follow along with your overheads because the screen is positioned incorrectly.

Maintain a Comfortable Temperature

Better to have a room too cold than too hot. Do not forget to ask participants how the temperature is for them. Since you will be moving around, you might not tend to notice that the room has become very cold. If you are in a hotel, find out who can monitor the temperature and get to know this person. If you are in someone's office presenting your project, only to have the room get too hot, do not keep going. Consider some alternatives. When you keep going *as if* people are comfortable, their attention wanders. Keep in mind that a break to adjust the temperature may be exactly what people want and need at the time to regain their focus. By your handling of something as minor as adjusting the thermostat, the group will recognize that you are in control and can take charge of a situation. Their confidence in you will increase.

Request Proper Lighting

Lighting has become more critical with the increasing use of LCD panels, which need a certain light, not too much and not too little. Be sure when needed, you have control over the light. Most organizations' conference rooms have adequate light. Hotels are notorious for having dimly lit conference rooms. Be prepared to request more light, if only additional table lamps. Find out whether you can dim the lights, yet not turn them off. You rarely, if ever, want the room so dark you cannot see the facial expressions of your listeners.

Arrange Seating the Way You Requested It

Send, ahead of time, a picture of the appropriate seating. When you arrive, check to see if your picture matches the room's seating pattern. Be prepared to move chairs and tables. Find help, or you will get hot and sweaty moving the furniture by yourself. Be diplomatic with your host, but move the furniture. You are the one who is speaking, and you owe it to yourself to have the room arranged the best way possible for all to see and hear comfortably.

FOOD: EXTRA OR NECESSITY?

Never underestimate the power of healthy food to get people in a good mood!
    The difference between the sessions with and without food will be apparent to you even without the positive comments from participants. Every time you provide good food at a meeting, the atmosphere of the meeting will be improved.

Better to have a light lunch and snacks all day for people than to give them a big lunch and watch them sleep through your talk.

When you do training and send participants off in small groups to discuss or practice a skill, provide food such as nuts, raisins, or popcorn to take along. Not only will it energize the participants, but it will give them something to do with their hands. They will feel more at ease. Serving the right food is a wonderful way to invigorate a group. (*Caution:* If you give them peanuts to shell, be sure someone will be around to clean up the mess! Also remember that rich, sugary foods tend to put people to sleep.)

A speaker was worried about the receptiveness of his audience because his subject matter was complex and his talk was scheduled for 8:00 A.M. Before his presentation, he served the group coffee and delicious muffins. He later reported that his talk was a success, partially due to the good mood that he had helped create by serving refreshments. The importance of providing food cannot be overemphasized. Apart from the preceding practical reasons of providing good food, recognize that almost all people love to get something for free and really do appreciate the giver more when the time comes to agree to those proposed recommendations.

PRACTICING

> Practice what you know, and it will help make clear what
> you now do not know.
>
> Rembrandt

The subject of practice is included in this step on motivating your listeners because the more energized you sound, look, and feel, the more open and eager your listeners will be to consider your recommendations. You may never get people standing on their chairs applauding (which might not be an ambition of yours); but you owe it to your listeners to be coherent, credible, and interesting. Albert Camus said, "You cannot acquire experience by making experiments. You cannot create experience. You must undergo it." The experience you must undergo over and over is to practice *out loud* before your talk.

Practice in Front of a Mirror

Many people practice speaking by watching themselves in front of a mirror. They find this improves their self-confidence, can be done anywhere, and does not need anyone else. It is an effective way to become familiar with seeing yourself talk. The mirror gives you instant feedback so you can change a gesture right then and there. One shy person used to practice in front of her bathroom mirror. Finally, one of her roommates asked, "Who do you talk to in there?" The moral of this example is to tell anyone within earshot what you are doing.

Videotape Yourself

Lots of people have video cameras today. If you cannot borrow one from a friend or an organization, you can probably rent one. Video is a wonderful tool. If, on video, you see that you have a slumped posture, do 20 to 30 sit-ups a day and 5 to 10 push-ups. This will help your posture. When you view yourself on video, be sure to have someone watching with you. You need feedback. Both your strengths and your areas for improvement must be pointed out by an *unbiased observer*. Most people are too critical with themselves to be able to give themselves a positive critique. They need someone there telling them the strengths they exhibit while talking.

Generally, after seeing themselves on video, people think that they look better than they expected and, almost always, that they appear less nervous than they felt as they presented. The negative aspect of using the video camera is that you have to wait until you have completed your talk to see your behavior. You do not have an opportunity to adjust your gestures as you speak unless you turn the television toward you and watch yourself as you talk. Watch the video twice, because the first time you will be concentrating more on how you look than on what you say. The second time, see if your facial expressions and gestures are congruent with what you are saying.

Record Your Voice

Before video cameras became so popular, many people tape-recorded themselves presenting. This is an excellent idea, since you can hear exactly what you say during your talk. You can hear your voice modulation and the level of enthusiasm you put into your voice projection. Tape recorders are easier to carry around than most video cameras. Consequently, you can practice with the tape recorder in your car, in a hotel, or wherever you are. Listen to yourself twice, as you will hear more the second time.

Practice in the Car

When practicing for an impromptu talk, the car is a great place to be. You can speak out loud to your heart's content. If you speak too softly, practice increasing the volume of your voice.

Practice with Listeners

If you have the time, you may choose to ask two types of people to listen to you: those unfamiliar with your subject and those familiar with your subject. You want the people unfamiliar with your subject to give you feedback about the clarity of your talk. Believe it or not, one of the most common problems people have is planning to speak about a subject that they know well to people who know very little about the subject. The speaker assumes others have all the background detail, so they leave out critical aspects. Your sample listeners, unfamiliar with your area of expertise, can tell you if they do or do not understand what you are saying. Most people who are specialists talking about their specialty make the mistake of only rehearsing in front of colleagues who know the subject. These people cannot tell the speaker if the talk is too technical, since all the information is also familiar to them. They no longer have a feel for how foreign the material can be to others.

You also want feedback from people familiar with your subject who can tell you if your data is accurate. Receiving feedback from these people is especially important if your talk is to specialists in your field. You want to be sure you have every fact, technique, and skill correct. Pat Kirk, president of Phytobiodermie in Boston, had to prepare a presentation for spa owners on facial care and body cellulite treatments. She said, "I have been trained by the best in Europe to discuss what Phytobiodermie products can do for a person's skin and cellulite problems, but I do not know if they taught us enough about responding to the American market." After spending time with an expert in body and facial care products who quizzed her from an American viewpoint, Pat felt totally prepared for her 4-hour trainings to be done around the country.

Take a Presentations Course

If you want to improve your skills quickly, take a presentation skills course. During the course, you will have an opportunity to do many presentations in a short space of time. After this type of program, people say they feel more confident and now know the specific skills they must practice to communicate even more effectively and confidently.

Some people take a workshop, then say, "But I have no place to practice and now I am just beginning to feel confident." A good response to these people is, "Have you thought about Toastmasters, Dale Carnegie, volunteer work on the phone, taking a part-time sales job to learn how to do on-the-spot presentations, selling a product through multilevel marketing, attending evening courses at a college near you, doing volunteer work that involves giving presentations, or starting up a monthly presentations practice group?" There are many options for sharing with people.

MOTIVATING YOUR GROUP: HOW SOME PEOPLE DID IT!

- *Do the Unexpected.* Kay at Gillette gave a presentation to the operating committee about the new computer software program system installed in consumer service. Her goal was to tell them how the information was recorded during a consumer call. To add interest and life to her presentation, she recorded a real call from a consumer. Then during the presentation, she played excerpts from that call and described how the information from the consumer was put on the computer. Her presentation was a smashing success. She gave her audience all the details but in the context of an actual Gillette consumer's call.

- *Impress Them with Your Skill.* Linda, a consultant for Franklin Quest, calls her seminar participants' by name as she speaks. She can do this even when there are a hundred participants!

- *Customize the Presentation.* I recently was asked to do an hour-long talk on sales motivation to a group of people who had been in sales for 20 to 30 years. In advance, I called around and found out the names of the 30 attendees. By the time of my presentation, I had each person's name on one of the overheads. People were surprised, flattered, and appreciative that I had spent some time learning about them and then had figured out a way to tie each one of them into the presentation. For example, here's one overhead I used in the talk.

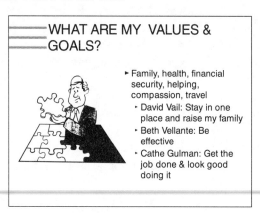

- *Play a Game.* Cindy of Polaroid plays a game when she does all-day Polaroid product training. She tells the participants to watch for the Polaroid logo, which will appear on some of her visuals. The first participant to see it and say something has a chance to answer a question about that particular product or feature and possibly win a small prize. She has found that it is a great way to keep her audience attentive and involved.

- *Speak to Their Experience.* Deborah, the Assistant Director for the Long Island Homeless Shelter in Boston, personalizes her talks on the homeless to create empathy for the homeless. She wants her audience to relate personally to the situation of a homeless person. She asks such questions as: "How many of you know someone who is addicted to alcohol? Drugs?" "How many of you know someone who has had to be hospitalized for mental illness?" "How close were some of those people to being homeless?" Using those questions, she is able to capture the audience's interest as they reflect on people they know and their experience with those people. When it comes time to ask for help, she has been successful in getting people to volunteer.

- *Use a Convincing Voice Tone and Follow the Habits of the Culture.* Randa, of the Millipore organization, grew up speaking Arabic, a language in which the voice is raised at the end of a sentence. Although the language sounds beautiful and there is a lyrical sound as the sentence goes up at the end, Americans assume that a speaker who knows the materials ends sentences with the voice tone going down. Randa was told by her boss and colleagues that she needed to sound more convincing in her talks. After taping herself and having a few people analyze her speech, she realized that she had to change the way she ended her sentences. After practice, Randa does this. Her boss told her she sounds much more sure of herself, which motivates her listeners to pay attention.

Questionnaire about Presenting in _____

Eye Contact

1. What is considered appropriate eye contact? Do I look at people? For how long do I look at them?

Gestures

2. Are there gestures that I should not do?

Audience Reaction

3. What signs, if any, will my audience give when they agree with what I am saying?

4. What signs, if any, will my audience give when they disagree with what I am saying?

5. Is the audience used to asking questions and interacting with the presenter or should I expect no one to ask me questions as I talk?

Visuals

6. What type of visual presentations is the audience used to hearing? Should I use slides, overheads, a flip chart, nothing?

Length

7. How long should I make my presentation?

Formal or Informal Style: Demeanor and Dress

8. Should I say the names of the people? First names? Last names? How do I greet them? Do I shake their hands before I start? How firmly do I shake? How do I relate to women if I am a male? How do I relate to men if I am a woman?

9. Am I expected to be formal and stand in the front of the room or can I walk around the room as I talk?

10. Do I hand out business cards? What is the appropriate manner for exchanging business cards with someone?

11. How do I dress?

(Questionnaire continued)

Language and Voice Tone

12. What words, concepts should I not say or use?

13. Will the people speak the language I will be speaking? Will there be an interpreter?

14. What are things I can say or do that will enable me to have excellent rapport with my audience?

Social

15. What am I expected to do socially?

Pace and Time

16. Will we start and end on time? How long will the breaks be?

17. Are people used to taking many notes? How do they learn best?

Customs and Traditions

18. What customs and traditions should I know about?

19. What do people do at the end of a presentation? Clap? Knock on the table? Get up and leave?

20. When do people start to work? When do they take breaks to eat? What type of schedule shall I plan on?

Materials

21. What equipment is available (overhead projectors, VCR equipment, electric power)?

22. What size paper do people use on copiers?

What Else?

PRESENTING IN OTHER COUNTRIES

If you are to present in another culture, the questionnaire on pages 187–188 will help you gather enough information so you can effectively present in that country. For more information on doing business in countries outside the U.S., see the newsletter *Worldwide Business Practices Report,* obtainable by calling 800-626-2772.

Japan

Eye Contact

Do not look directly into a person's eye. If you do, then do not linger long. Take just a glance and then look away. You may wish to look at the necktie instead. If you look too long, it could indicate aggression.

Gestures

You may gesture, *but* never touch anyone.

Shaking Hands and Touching

Wait for the person to hold out a hand; then reach out and shake it. If you are a woman, wait for the man to reach out to shake your hand. He may not, as it is improper to touch someone of the opposite sex.

> Some Japanese businessmen were visiting a U.S. company. A woman manager reached out to shake hands with one of them. The Japanese visitor rejected the handshake with a wave. This scene was uncomfortable for everyone. He was fine doing business with a woman as long as he didn't have to touch her.

People do not hug and kiss at work.

Audience Reaction

The audience will typically be quiet. You may see nods of agreement. You may sometimes receive applause at the end of the presentation. The audience may not ask any questions as they are not confident of speaking in English. They do not want to sound incorrect.

Interpreter

Get your own interpreter. Then with the interpreter, you decide how you want the translation done. Do you want straightforward translation or do you want the interpreter to modify what you say if what you have said is inappropriate and would cause problems?

> An interpreter modified what an American said because the speaker used a word that would have been so offensive to the Japanese businesspeople that the deal might not have gone through.

Preferably, find an interpreter who knows your industry. Spend some time with that person. Discuss how you will work together.

Dress

Wear a dark blue or gray suit. These are safe colors. Always wear a jacket (and, for men, a conservative tie) even if you know you will take off the jacket as soon as you start work. When you wear the jacket, you make a good first impression and show respect to the people you will be working with.

Words to Use and Not Use

Never swear. The Japanese like to hear and tell jokes, but your humor may not be easily understood if it is from a Western culture. You will feel foolish when people just look at you and do not laugh.

For Excellent Rapport

Be humble. Someone else can talk about your accomplishments, but don't you do it. Don't name-drop or boast. Do not stand too close to people. Speak slowly and clearly. Know how to exchange business cards. Be gracious and polite at all times. Disagree politely, yet not too directly. Never cause another person to lose face.

Listening

Be respectful and pay attention. Don't look out the window or up to the ceiling. You must always look interested in the topic even if you are not in charge of the matter being discussed. Don't lean back in your chair and put your hands behind your head. You give the impression of being too relaxed.

Social Situations

Accept dinner invitations. If it is a new relationship, it is not safe to say no to a dinner invitation. You must go. If it is an older relationship and you have spent time with the people, or you do not have very serious and sensitive issues currently with the company, you may excuse yourself as being tired with jet lag. Socializing is very important in Japan. Those of you who are introverts must learn how to socialize. Just take a little of the food that is offered you, if you are not sure you will like it.

Time and Length

The meetings start and end on time. Don't be late. The workday is about the same as, or somewhat longer than, the Western workday. Don't make your talk too lengthy. Have a break or change the topic after a half hour. The audience may be tired from the effort of attempting to understand the language. If it is being translated, you may need twice the time—a 1-hour talk could take 2 hours.

Handouts

Give your audience handouts, something in writing. Handouts are critically important. The Japanese want things written down. People attending the meeting will probably have to go back and write up a report about the meeting. The handouts will help attendees do that. Give out an agenda handout at the beginning of the meeting. The advantage of distributing your handouts at the start of presentation is that people can take notes under the key points as you talk. Many businesspeople have their visuals translated into Japanese. The audience reads the Japanese on the visual and the presenter speaks in English. You should practice this so that you will feel comfortable seeing your visuals in another language as you speak English. Show things visually with charts and tables, then use a verbal explanation.

Names

Do not call someone by his or her first name unless you are asked to do so. People do not call each other by their first names unless they are friends.

Equipment and Paper

You should be able to find the equipment you need to give a presentation. The standard paper size in Japan is not the same as U.S. paper size. The paper will be slightly longer and not quite as wide.

Business Cards

Have one side of your business card printed in English and the other printed in Japanese. Find out the equivalent Japanese title for your position and have that title put on your card. You can put "Dr.," or the like, on the card, but don't say your title out loud. You want to be humble about what you have done. Never throw or toss your business card or any paper. It is considered impolite. Get yourself a business card holder. Exchanging business cards is very important in Japan and you should practice with someone first. You present your card with the writing facing the person and accept that person's card graciously; either put it in front of you as you speak or place it in a nice business card holder. Never put it in your pocket or in your wallet in front of its owner. Also, don't write on the business card in front of the person, and don't keep your own business cards in your wallet.

Saudi Arabia

Eye Contact and Gestures

Eye contact is appreciated between the same genders, but not across genders. Gestures are acceptable, but placing the hands on the hips is a challenging gesture.

Audience Approval

The audience will shake their heads with approval or give a side nod of the head. They probably won't say or do anything to let you know at the moment that they disagree. Or you may see raising of the eyebrows or hear clicking of the tongue, which are negative responses.

Asking Questions

The audience will probably not ask you questions as you speak.

Using Visuals

Use visuals, the more the better when you are selling. Avoid having anything on your visuals that suggests idolatry. Better to get someone from Saudi Arabia to preview them first. You don't want to have high profile pictures of women or men. Use a visual to illustrate the points as you speak. This may help with any language problems.

Presentation Length

Speak no longer than 30 minutes.

Greeting People and Rapport

Do not shake hands across genders. If you do shake hands, make it light and brief. A proper greeting is *Sallaam Alikoum,* which means "Peace to you." Once you have established rapport, the Saudis will be very congenial and appreciative. Don't refer to women, especially family. Always acknowledge the most senior person first.

Business Cards

You give your card to the other person and say, "I would appreciate it if I may have your address and phone number." Then the person gives you his or her card. Do not accept anything or pass with your left hand; its use is reserved for private matters.

Social Issues

Expect breaks for public prayer. Ask ahead of time when those will be so you can plan your talk accordingly. Don't talk about religion or politics unless you really know what you are saying. Avoid any vulgar jokes about the Arab culture. The Saudi custom is for women to wear veils, national robes, and head covers. The national religion is Islam, which is very conservative. Read about the religion of Islam before you go; you will be glad you did. Ask the Saudis to explain their customs, then listen with interest and don't criticize. The Saudi weekend is half of Thursday and all day Friday. Always carry an extra photograph of yourself. You may need it to obtain an ID. When visiting in someone's home, don't say out loud that you like something you see. The host may feel obliged to give it to you. Never give alcohol as a gift. Flowers or candy are appropriate gifts when invited to a Saudi home. Once coffee is served at the end of a meal, it is the signal that the guests should leave.

The Language

The Saudis use English as a second language because so many people speak English. Ask your Saudi advisor to assess the audience's level of English comprehension. You might want to find an interpreter so you can be sure the people understand exactly what you are saying. As you speak, use short, clear sentences. Don't mumble or use English slang. Repeat what you are saying in different ways to ensure understanding. A dual-language presentation is very expensive and you may not need it. Your cover letter and thank-you letter, though, should be in both Arabic and English.

Dress

Dress neatly and formally in Western wear. Don't dress casually. Do not expose the sole of your shoe as it is offensive to Saudis.

Mexico

Eye Contact

Look directly at the person, but not for very long. Smile and be friendly and open as you look.

Gestures

Gesture freely. Do not show your nervousness with quick, anxious movements. Do not hurry. Do not laugh without reason.

Audience Reaction

Your audience will show agreement by nodding their heads, sitting forward, and looking attentive. They will stay in the room as you talk. People may ask questions to clarify, or they my interrupt to express disagreement. You can establish how you want your audience to act during your talk. For example, you can tell them when you will take questions—at any time, during the talk, after each major point you cover, or at the end when you have finished speaking.

Visuals

Visual presentations are preferred. Audiences like dynamic, innovative, and creative presentations.

Length

You can speak for at least an hour.

Greetings

If it is a first-time contact, use a formal approach by saying "Mr." or "Mrs." with the last name. Shake hands firmly, look at their eyes and smile. It is acceptable to shake hands with both men and women.

Business Cards

Exchange cards at the beginning of your presentation so that you can call the person by name during the meeting.

Dress

Find out ahead of time how you are expected to dress. Women should avoid wearing anything that will distract or offend, such as big rings, very long nails, and noisy bracelets.

Language

Many people in Mexico are able to understand English, but you should try to find out the level of comprehension for your audience and then decide if you want to request an interpreter.

Rapport

Search out information on the most recent news events in Mexico and figure out ways to bring them up. This will show that you are taking an interest in the country.

STEP 7 CONCLUDING WITH CONVICTION

KEY POINTS

1   Save time for your conclusion so you don't have to rush through it.

2   Let your audience know you are about to conclude.

3   Don't read your conclusion. End by looking at your audience.

4   Keep your voice confident and strong for the conclusion.

5   Make your conclusion brief and to the point, and then stop.

6   Summarize clearly the key areas you covered.

7   Recommend actions at your conclusion.

8   Find some convincing statistics to use as you conclude.

9   Show again a picture you want people to keep in their mind.

10   Reinforce the benefits of doing what you recommend.

What would you say about a concert if the last note was off key? Think back to a dance or concert you recently attended. How would you have felt if the performers had suddenly walked off the stage or just stopped playing or dancing right there in front of you? Imagine a whole group of runners doing a 10-kilometer race. They run and struggle to keep going and at the 9-kilometer mark, they all stop, leave the race, and walk off in different directions. Unfortunately, many presentations end, as T. S. Eliot describes, "not with a bang, but a whimper." Do not be one of those presenters. Ending your presentation dynamically and clearly takes both planning and energy.

Robert Levenson, Director of Marketing Communications at Boston Scientific Corporation, says this about conclusions: "What parts of every presentation are the most memorable? Certainly the conclusion is one. As the content of your talk builds the value of your ideas, the conclusion reinforces your status as an expert."

Some of the most superb conclusions can be seen at dance performances. At the conclusion of every 1½-hour ballet class, the teacher spends time having the class practice ending with style. Conclusions do not just occur naturally. They demand work. The conclusion gives you the opportunity to drive your point home; do not let down on your energy at this point. Your conclusion is one of the most crucial times in your presentation. Do not forfeit your presentation by ending hesitantly. Keep your voice loud and strong. Motivate yourself to sound enthusiastic. To conclude with style, know the final few sentences you plan to say. Many people tell you to memorize your concluding sentences. My experience is that this makes people nervous during their whole talk since they worry about forgetting their conclusion.

Know yourself. Know whether you need to write out a conclusion and whether you need to consciously save some of your energy for your conclusion. Before concluding, if all you can think about is ending and leaving, you may not reach your objective. The participants will feel your desire to get done as soon as possible. Your talk deserves an excellent conclusion. Participants will remember your style and organization much more from your ending than from your beginning. Keep in mind the last fireworks display you saw. Undoubtedly, the finale was beautiful!

CONCLUSION IDEAS

If you do not have much preparation time, at least plan your conclusion. There is absolutely no excuse for a flat closing. The following ideas can help you invigorate your closing:

- Present facts and statistics.
- Tell a "just imagine" scenario.
- Use quotations or citations.
- Refer to people in the group.

- Challenge the group.
- Present alternatives.
- Summarize major points.
- Ask for a decision.

Present Facts and Statistics

For the logical minded, present a reasonable number of facts and statistics. By doing this, you show that you have done the homework necessary to make the recommendation you have just explained. Even if you have mentioned these in detail during your talk, it does not hurt to reiterate a few key statistics during your conclusion.

Facts and statistics should tie your talk together, be easy to understand, and be carefully chosen. To maximize its impact on the audience; the conclusion should leave a burning image in the minds of your audience that lasts long after your talk is over. The following are a few examples of striking facts:

- Americans are currently getting 60 to 90 minutes less sleep a night than is necessary for optimum health and performance.

- A study found that those who kiss their spouse each morning miss less work because of illness than those who do not. They also have fewer auto accidents on the way to work and they earn 20 to 30 percent more money.

- Every 5 days, you get a new stomach lining. Every 6 weeks, you get a new liver. Every 3 months, you get a new skeleton.

- Case Reserve University reports that it is normal to be grumpy, grouchy, and generally down in the dumps on 3 of every 10 days. Only 2 percent of us are happy all the time, and 5 percent stay dreary and blue on 4 of every 5 days.

Tell a "Just Imagine" Scenario

End with a story about what will happen after your next steps are implemented. An ad agency painted this picture to the client: "Just imagine when this ad has been shown on four television stations. See your product sales doubling in three months. A talk show picks up an interest about your product. Hear your president speaking on the show. At the same time, your coverage in magazines triples. You will feel excited as many people learn about and use your product. Listen to your phones ringing day and night!"

When you describe a "just imagine" scenario, be sure you present the future in visual, auditory, and kinesthetic modalities. Once in a while, presenters make a negative prophecy such as, "If we continue to pollute our oceans, beaches will be dumps and no longer usable for recreation." Know the situation and use a negative prophecy with care. It may not provide the type of motivation you wish participants to experience.

Use Quotations or Citations

Use quotations and citations as long as they relate to your topic and major points. Do not include a quote just to put it in. Use quotes from recognized people in your area of expertise. If appropriate, find someone in your organization who will agree to let you quote him or her. Depending on the person, your ability to sell your suggestion could become much easier. Quotations establish your credibility as someone who has done research. If you used quotes during your talk, do not use them at the end as well. A few quotes go a long way. Short quotes are fine; long ones are tedious.

Refer to People in the Group

If there are people in the group to whom you can refer in a positive way, go ahead. For example, you might say that the marketing manager already looked over your summarizing statement and recommended some changes. Those changes are now included in your summary. When you are recruiting people to do volunteer work, you can say (if this is true), that at least half the people in the group present today already contribute their time and energy to your organization. Personal references are helpful as long as you do not say things that surprise or embarrass the person or persons you mention. Ask their permission first.

Challenge the Group

When you have presented a proposal that demands a change in the way things have been done, end with a challenging statement such as, "Do we have enough flexibility to make this happen?" or "Are we able to adjust to include this new product in our company?" or "Do you have the discipline to practice your presentations *out loud?*" These are all ways to hook those in your audience who like challenges. Sometimes you do not have to wait for an answer. Suggest boldly, "You bet we do!" or "You certainly can."

Present Alternatives

You will notice that certain formats lend themselves to this type of closing. You have presented alternatives. Now the group must choose which one they will act on. If you do not have an alternative you prefer, summarize the possible alternatives. If you do have a preference, emphasize that alternative. You may decide to exclude the others from your concluding statement.

Summarize Major Points

When you present in the information format, close by going over your major points. Say, "Next time you are stumped by a difficult customer service problem, remember to do one of these three things: Call me, send a message through the computer system, or have one of our two specialists paged. One of those actions will get you the speedy answer you need."

Ask for a Decision

Ask people to make a decision based on the information you gave during your presentation. Say, "You have heard all the facts and arguments. Now it is your responsibility to make a decision. Whatever that decision may be, I have confidence that it will be the best for our company." Decide whether you want to express your bias or not.

Some of the preceding conclusion ideas can be used in other places during your talk. If you do use them elsewhere, conclude with a different comment.

INTROVERTS AND EXTROVERTS—CONCLUSIONS

Think back to the brief questionnaire in Step 1. Are your preferences more extroverted or introverted? Apply that knowledge as you are about to conclude.

Introverts

Do not hesitate. Force yourself to speak up and sound convincing. *Executive Membership Alert* (vol. 39, no. 32, August 14, 1989) has this advice: "Let your conviction show. If your conclusion sounds hollow and shows lack of interest, your whole talk will not appear persuasive. Even if you're not the demonstrative type, display a little emotion during your closing statement through gestures (jabbing a finger into the air, thumping gently on the table or lectern) and a rising tone of voice." Do not hurry your ending. Stay around after your talk to discuss people's views on your recommendations. This could be the crucial time for you to obtain final agreement on a proposal. The following suggestions will be helpful:

- Practice concluding with flair and conviction.

- Stay around after your talk to speak with people.

- Be bold and state authoritatively what you think.

- Take some deep breaths before you conclude.

- Tell yourself that soon you can go off alone, but for now you need to listen to people's comments about your talk. In other words, do not bolt out the door as soon as you finish your last sentence.

Extroverts

Stop talking. More is not always better. Your summarizing *should not* be the same length as your talk. When you have finished your presentation and people come to talk with you, let them talk. You already gave your presentation; listen to their presentations. They gave you lots of air time; now they want some as well. Remember the following:

- Conclude sooner rather than later.

- Make your answers to questions brief.

- Prepare your conclusion. Do not count on "winging it" effectively.

FORMAT CONCLUSIONS

Just as the formats can assist you in organizing and structuring a more effective and convincing presentation, let those formats now guide you in putting together a most powerful conclusion. Each particular format has an impetus and a direction that leads to a certain type of conclusion. Listed are suggestions to use when concluding with each particular format.

Identify the Problem

1. Do a future story scenario and have people imagine the situation without this problem.

2. Challenge the group to commit themselves to solving this problem.

Present Strategy Recommendations

1. Paint a brief verbal picture of what will happen if each strategy is (or is not) implemented.

2. Emphasize one strategy you personally prefer, or recapitulate the available strategies.

3. Ask the group to decide which strategy or strategies they wish to carry out.

Sell a Product, Service, or Idea

1. Restate the benefits. Say these in slightly different words.

2. Give a "just imagine" scenario of the impact that buying the product, service, or idea will have on the buyer.

3. Make a personal reference to someone in the group (particularly a key person), if that person is in agreement with what you are suggesting.

Recommend Decision Alternatives

1. Give a personal reference of someone who believes in the alternative that you suggest.

2. State a positive quote made by someone who is using that alternative.

3. Personally suggest the alternative you believe is the best, giving reasons why.

4. Ask the group members to decide which alternative they want.

Identify Potential Problems

1. Describe a negative "just imagine" scenario.

2. Challenge the group.

3. Describe a positive "just imagine" scenario.

Teach Skills

1. Give a future scenario of people's delight in knowing new skills.

2. Tell about past participants and how they have used what they learned.

3. Summarize the major lessons of the session.

4. Challenge the group to use the skills.

Share Information

1. State a few key facts people need to remember.

2. Tell people whom to call for more information.

Communicate the Bad News

1. Summarize what you have said.

2. Present the alternatives.

3. If the situation becomes very emotional, set up another time to discuss the alternatives.

Report Progress

1. Summarize what you have said.

2. Make personal references to people in the group.

3. State what you hope to be able to relay at the next progress report.

The General Format

1. Suggest the next steps for your audience.

2. Recap your key points in different words.

3. Tell your audience what they heard and what they will hear at your next presentation. (This is useful if you are doing a series of presentations.)

Closing

A speaker talked loud and long, then asked brightly, "Are there any questions?" A hand shot up. The speaker nodded. "What time is it?" the listener inquired.

Kenny Nichols, *All About the Town*

Speaking without thinking is shooting without aiming.

W. G. Benham

The best impromptu remarks are well prepared in advance.

Ruth Gordon

Get up, speak up, shut up, and sit down.

Toastmasters International

CONCLUDING SENTENCES AND PICTURES

Observe Ways Not to Conclude

Do you conclude in any of these ways?

> Tony just left my office. He never stops talking. I thought he finally got to the point, but then he went on for another 10 minutes. I am not sure what he really wants me to do.

Sue gave a talk today. She made some vague points about our future direction, then ended with a funny story. I cannot remember her points but let me tell the story to you.

I never know what George really thinks is important. He has so many points and diagrams, yet he never summarizes which issue we should focus on. Nothing stands out.

The following phrases are the beginnings of some of the unacceptable closes you may have heard:

- If you want to try this . . . .
- I hope I have made my points.
- Maybe you could donate . . . .
- I guess that's all.
- I can't think of anything else.
- I am out of time.

Do Not Read Your Conclusion

You may be tempted to write out your conclusion word for word and then read it to your audience so you will not leave anything out. Unless you have phenomenal skills in reading speeches, resist that temptation.

The conclusion is one of the most important times to connect with your audience. It is difficult to read and maintain eye contact. Moreover, if your audience sees you reading, they will think that you lack conviction and be less likely to adopt your recommendations. Keep in mind also that your presentation success depends largely on your credibility. Your credibility, in turn, depends on your ability to convince your audience that you know what you are talking about. Many audiences will not give credibility to a person trying to read a conclusion verbatim.

Use Appropriate Closing Phrases

Closing phrases warn your listeners that you are about to end. Although some of you will think and feel that the following statements are stale or that they sound rote, they can be appropriate and useful in keeping everyone on track:

- In conclusion, what's most important is . . . .
- My one last point before I conclude is . . . .
- In summary, ...

- Let me take five minutes and wrap this up by saying . . . .
- Finally, ...
- Now that you have heard all the alternatives, I will conclude with my recommendation.

By using one of the preceding phrases, you alert the listeners that you are about to summarize. The foregoing phrases give your listeners a chance to perk up, pay attention again, and be prepared for your ending. Psychologically, the person may be thinking, "Yes, I can pay attention for another five minutes." Now that you have your audience primed, you need to show them the finale!

Conclude with a Closing Picture

Force yourself to conclude with a clear picture for all to see. Suppose that your job is to design cars. During your talk, you were forced to show the individual car parts rather than explain how the car would look when all the parts fit together. Your conclusion is your opportunity to give everyone a picture of the finished item—in this case, the car. You must be sure to show how all the pieces fit together; do not expect your listeners to do that on their own. This same process must happen for many projects or proposals. People are more apt to agree and support something when they can (1) *see* how it will work when completed, (2) get a *feel* for the results, and (3) *hear* the benefits to be derived from its implementation.

Adopt a Model

Observe the speakers who impress you, and try out their techniques. Consider the importance of a good defense attorney's closing argument in a trial. Think about how that attorney approaches the jury (an audience) and goes over the central parts of the case with the exhortation to find the defendant not guilty. That attorney must sound sincere, must demonstrate a thorough knowledge of the case, and must look each juror squarely in the face to acknowledge the person and make connection. There are models of fine speakers everywhere.

The Trainer's Conclusion

Whether you have presented a 2-hour session or a 2-week session, you had some major points that you wanted to get across to your participants. At the close of the whole training, you should go over those key points. Why? People forget and they need to be reminded of the areas you covered and why they are important. They also need to be reminded that their training was worthwhile.

Because trainers are so immersed in the information, they may forget that many people need an overview of the entire session along with a recap of a few important points about each area. Go back and put up your visual that lists the training objectives. Share with your group how you have met those objectives. This conclusion will get you excellent evaluations as well as force you to focus on meeting the objectives throughout your presentation.

STEP 8 MANAGING QUESTIONS AND OBJECTIONS

KEY POINTS

1 Anticipate potential questions before your talk and prepare your answers in advance. Practice saying those answers out loud.

2 Warn your audience that you are about done and will be taking questions soon.

3 Save enough energy so you feel like answering the questions.

4 Put people in groups to come up with questions if you think certain people are too shy to ask a question in front of the whole group (especially useful with cross-cultural groups).

5 Answer the question as briefly as possible and then say, "Shall I say some more about this?"

6 Rephrase the question if you need a moment to think before answering.

7 Be respectful to questioners even if their intent is to embarrass you.

8 Only answer questions related to your presentation and suggest that unrelated questions be discussed after the presentation.

9 Bring a backup visual of detailed facts that you might need during the question period. Only show this if you need it.

10 Have another enthusiastic, motivating conclusion to give after you answer all the questions.

You have concluded, and now you wait for the questions. Perhaps you are hoping that no one asks you a question. Remember when you were a youngster in school, how nervous you felt as you sat there at your desk, hearing the teacher ask you a question? You hoped to answer it correctly, with enough detail to satisfy the teacher. You knew the teacher hoped to hear a particular answer, and you felt concerned about being able to provide it.

Now that you are an adult, you would *not* expect those same feelings to manifest themselves when you are asked a question. The fact is, they do! You start to perspire, your voice shakes, and you may rattle on and on as if, the more you say, the clearer will be your answer. Then, after you answer, you grade yourself in your mind. However, there are no more grades on how well you answer each question. Grades are no longer the issue. You are being asked because the person genuinely wants to know the answer. Examine the present reality of your situation. You may be on automatic pilot, still worrying about being graded instead of recognizing that now *you* are the expert and that people are legitimately seeking guidance and clarification from you. What can you do?

There are several ways to eliminate your anxiety and to take control of the question-and-answer period. First, give your listeners notice before your conclusion. Say something like, "In a moment I will answer your questions." Consequently, some people will have thought of a question, and you will not have to wait for questions in a deafening silence. Second, you should have done your preparation and have answers ready for those anticipated questions and objections. The best way to control the process is by taking the reins; invite questions.

Welcome questions and objections with open arms. People will feel that you are confident and know your subject matter. Moreover, you will be able to hear and respond to the objections people have, thus increasing the chance of having them agree to your next steps. Make it easy for people to ask. Start with something like, "Who has the first question?" This tells your listener that you are open to questions. You can even start by using one of the following phrases:

- One of the questions that came into my mind as I talked is . . . .
- One of the questions that I frequently hear is . . . .
- What questions may I answer?
- The last group asked me this question for which I had to research the answer.
- I am often asked . . . .

Naturally, before you even present, make sure that you have prepared sufficiently to handle the questions that you anticipate. Even the best public speakers spend countless hours being briefed on how to handle questions that they are likely to be asked. If you prepare well, you will almost always have more relevant information about your topic than will your audience. Consequently, you will be able to use their questions and your answers to deftly move them toward acceptance of your recommendations. If you have control of your information, it will be very difficult for your audience to disagree with you!

One vice-president of the finance department presented her company's financial picture to the board of directors. This quarterly meeting felt very stressful until she began to list all the potential objections she would hear about her data. She realized that her stress was ultimately tied to her lack of proper preparation for the question-and-answer period.

One of the most satisfying experiences for a questioner is to receive a well thought out and responsive answer. To provide this kind of satisfaction, you must listen carefully to the question. You need the skill of paying attention, which comes with practice. People who do some type of meditation are usually better at focusing and paying attention. James T. McCay, in *The Management of Time* (New York: Prentice-Hall, 1959) says, "Preoccupation, or lack of alertness, is probably the greatest single factor that reduces your output. . . . It is in these moments of preoccupation that the incidents are born that can swallow up hours and days of your time to no avail." Focus closely on the question and give a succinct answer. This avoids any future misunderstandings.

If you suspect you need practice in learning to listen, take up a skill that demands your full attention, such as dancing, meditation, gardening, bird watching, painting, or playing an instrument. Your daily practice will give you the experience of being in command of yourself and being better able to listen to the real question being asked. You will be listening in the way Krishnamurti, the Indian philosopher, describes: "If you are listening to find out, then your mind is free, not committed to anything; it is very acute, sharp, alive, inquiring, curious, and therefore capable of discovery."

"DO'S" FOR MANAGING QUESTIONS

> He listened with the intensity one only uses when
> listening to oneself.
>
> Jane Wagner, *The Search for Signs of*
> *Intelligent Life in the Universe*

1. *Do* think of all the questions you may be asked. Practice your answers *out loud.*

2. *Do* ask participants (before your presentation) the types of questions and objections they might have to your recommendations.

3. *Do* treat every question as legitimate and well intentioned, even when you know it is not.

4. *Do* let the person finish the sentence even if he or she interrupted you.

5. *Do* restate the question if you believe people did not hear it or if you want to verify the exact question asked.

The Question Process

◗ In 5 minutes, I'll
conclude and take
questions . . .
◗ Before I take questions,
let me summarize . . .
◗ This will be my last
point before questions.

Transition to
question-and-
answer time

Who has the
first question?

◗ If silence say, "A fre-
quently asked question
is . . ."
◗ Or tell people: "Please
get in groups of 4 or 5 and
come up with a couple
questions you can ask."
This is good for the shy
people who want someone
else to ask their question.

Look at the person asking the
question. *Repeat* only if people
did not hear the question!

While answering the
question, look
around the room.

Don't look back at a hos-
tile questioner when you
finish answering the
question. Look to another
part of the room.

Proceed to the
next question,
and so on.

Wrap up questions.

◗ Let met take two more
questions and then I will
conclude.
◗ I'll just take one more
question but will stay
around for 15 minutes to
answer questions
privately.

Conclude again with style and
conviction. You must have
another conclusion planned
to use after the question period.

6. *Do* look directly at the person when listening to the question. Many people feel that if you do not look at them, you are not listening.

7. *Do* respond directly and stay on track.

8. *Do* admit if you do not know the answer.

9. *Do* show an appropriate visual when answering the question.

10. *Do* reorganize three questions asked at once in the way most helpful for you. Or choose to answer one and say, "Time does not permit me to answer all of your questions. I will be glad to answer your other questions after my talk."

11. *Do* answer questions from all parts of the room.

12. *Do* stop your internal dialogue so you can hear the question. "The quieter you become the more you can hear." Baba Ram Dass.

13. *Do* treat a "why" question like a "how" question. "Why" questions tend to make us defensive by thinking that we have to explain and justify. When you hear questions like, "Why do you think yours is the best solution?" or "Why should I contribute to your cause?" answer by listing facts, not by becoming opinionated. If you feel unable to stay logical and in control when answering a certain question, remember the cardinal rule learned and practiced by all politicians. There is no rule that says you must answer the question that is asked. Of course, you should always try to assist your listeners, but do not forget that this is *your* presentation and, whenever feasible, you decide the direction that it will take.

14. *Do* use every interpersonal skill you have.

15. *Do* look around the room as you answer the question.

"DON'TS" FOR MANAGING QUESTIONS

1. *Don't* bluff.

2. *Don't* browbeat a questioner even if it is warranted. You will lose the respect of your listeners.

3. *Don't* extract humor at the questioner's expense.

4. *Don't* indicate that you have covered the material.

5. *Don't* call on someone else to answer a question unless you give the person warning either by telling the person that you would like him or her to answer the question that is about to be asked (you do not want to embarrass someone if he or she has not been listening!); or by telling the person that you would like him or her to answer the question that was just asked, then state the question again.

6. *Don't* use expressions such as, "Frankly," or "To be honest with you." People will wonder what you have been until that moment.

7. *Don't* make your voice opinionated or patronizing.

8. *Don't* always end your question with your eyes back on the questioner, especially if it was a hostile question, or you may encourage him or her to ask another one.

9. *Don't* compliment a questioner by saying, "That is an excellent question." If you do not then compliment all questioners, people will think that their questions were not as appropriate.

10. *Don't* say one person's name unless you say everyone's name.

11. *Don't* say such unnecessary phrases as, "In my opinion," or "I think," or "It seems to me." Use them only when you want a moment to reflect on how you will answer a difficult question.

12. *Don't* give your questioners the "fire hose" approach, when all they asked for is a glass of water. Give them the information they need, not your accumulated knowledge.

13. *Don't* lose your temper. This may mean you must bite your tongue at times. You may feel relief when you speak angrily, yet the damage done may not be worth the instant relief you feel.

14. *Don't* judge the person while listening to the question.

15. *Don't* respond to an either/or question if you believe neither one is acceptable. Say, "I'd like to look at other possibilities before I say either of these options meets the needs I have outlined."

16. *Don't* respond to a hypothetical question if you do not wish to. Say, "I prefer not to answer that, since it is quite different from the situation we are in now."

17. *Don't* respond to innuendoes such as, "Listen sweetheart" or "For a woman you did not do a bad job." In most situations, ignore them, since they will lead you away from your objective.

Questions and Answers

Never answer certain questions until asked.
It is with a word as with an arrow—once let loose it does not return.

Adb-El-Kader

"Careful with fire" is good advice we know.
"Careful with words" is ten times doubly so.

Better to keep your mouth shut and have people think you're a fool than to open it and remove all doubt. Silence is the best answer to the stupid. The fool has his answer on the tip of his tongue.

Arabian folk saying

No one can make you feel inferior without your consent.

Eleanor Roosevelt

KEY PHRASES FOR ANSWERING QUESTIONS

Dean Rusk said that "before every presidential news conference, John Kennedy and a half-dozen of us would sit down and go over every possible question that he might be asked. When he went to a news conference, he had been briefed to the gills. So he almost never got a surprise question." Remember that people's questions sometimes reveal more about them than your answers reveal about you. Suppose you prepare thoroughly, yet you still hear a surprise question. Here are some possible ways to deal with questions for which you may not have a ready answer. Change these phrases to fit your situation, the person you are addressing, and your style.

- Please see me at the break, and we can discuss your question.

- I do not have that information now. I will make a note to get back to you.

- I will cover the answer to your question in the second part of my talk. Glad you are thinking about that point.

- Let me list that on the flip chart under issues for discussion, and, if we have time, we can go over it.

- Your question is beyond the scope of why we are all here. I prefer to deal with it later.

- To save time for some of you not involved in this issue, those of us who need to discuss this point can stay a few minutes after the meeting.

- I see why you are frustrated. However, if you listen to my recommendation, we may be able to resolve all your issues.

VISUAL, AUDITORY, AND KINESTHETIC ANSWERS

This section is for those of you who want to refine your question-answering ability. Decide which type of answer the person would prefer to hear: visual, auditory, or kinesthetic. Some questions are easy to figure out, and others are almost
impossible unless you know the person well enough to have a sense of the types of
responses he or she prefers. Sometimes the person gives you a clue. The clues can
be in the words used by the person asking the question or in the person's gestures.
The chart on the following page shows the comments each modality might ask.
Included are responses.

If you want to purposely upset people, try answering in a different modality
from the one used for the question. For example, someone who is auditory and
systematic might say, "Tell me what is going on with the project work I requested.
When can you sit down and discuss it with me?" You know that this person likes
to hear everything explained in a systematic fashion. She wants it step by step. But
being the obstinate person you are that day and considering that the person constantly gives you grief, you answer kinesthetically. You say, "I just am not sure. I
can only give you a feel. I have a few days before I will get to it, and then who
knows how long it will take." This type of response is bound to drive that person
up the wall. What is unfortunate is that many people do this to each other without
meaning to. Consider the advertising agency showing the finance department
their newest ad and asking, "What do you think?" The finance people respond by
asking the cost of running the ad in four magazines. They just work in such different modalities. Consequently, they find it hard to answer appropriately a question
addressed to them from a modality they seldom use.

Think a moment about where your eyes go when you are considering how to
answer a question. If you use the visual modality, your eyes go up and you lose
eye contact with the group. You are attempting to make a picture of your answer.
When in the auditory modality, you look straight ahead as you have an internal
dialogue with yourself. After this internal dialogue, you will know what to say.
People in the kinesthetic modality look down when trying to get a feel for an
answer. Watch yourself answer questions on video; see where your eyes move and
if you maintain enough rapport with your listeners. Train yourself to look at your
listeners as you answer.

OBJECTIONS

Know Why People Object

Why do some people object more than others? Why do some people ask such difficult or obtuse questions? Understanding the following reasons may help you respond empathetically rather than defensively.

VISUAL

COMMENT	RESPONSE
I do not get a picture of what you mean.	Let me show you a picture.
I can't see how we could do what you are suggesting.	I will create a picture of how we can go about this.
Don't you think you have incorrectly portrayed the facts?	If you look at those recent statistics, you'll see I have understated the facts.

AUDITORY

COMMENT	RESPONSE
I want to hear the information.	Let me say the key facts concisely and quickly.
I didn't hear you say how to handle the overcharging issue.	Let me rephrase what I stated.
It doesn't sound right.	What did you hear?

KINESTHETIC

COMMENT	RESPONSE
I do not get a feel for what you mean.	Let me try to give you a sense for how the system would work.
What will be going on?	Let's run through the process once again.
How are we going to get a handle on whether the idea will work?	We will do a survey to find out if our customers feel different about our service.

The Whole Picture.   You will be asked some irrelevant questions and given off-target objections. Why? People perceive the world from their own experience. Remember the story of the three blind men and the elephant? Each man felt only one part of the huge beast: the round trunk, a floppy ear, or the tough hide. Based on what each one felt, they all arrived at a different definition of the animal. You too may have a person who has only seen or heard part of what you are saying. Listen to the objection carefully, and if you have a listener who only heard part of your presentation, take time to fill in the gaps.

Responsibility Disagreements.   Differing perceptions often occur among people from various functions or departments. Each department has its own priorities, responsibilities, and biases. What is important to a marketing person is not necessarily as important to a systems person. Salespeople and customer service people frequently disagree, just given the nature of their priorities. If you anticipate having to present to people whose perceptions are dramatically different from yours, tailor your talk to them. Create a bridge between your views and theirs. One way to do this is to figure out what modality they prefer and present in that modality.

The Unexpected.   If you are presenting unexpected information to people, remember that the unexpected is, at first, many times not acknowledged or rejected as inaccurate. For example, new scientific information is frequently rejected. When possible, meet ahead of time with the key people and go over your "surprise" data.

Argument.   Edgar Watson Howe said, "You may easily play a joke on a man who likes to argue—agree with him." That is one piece of advice on handling the arguer. This sage advice, however, is not always appropriate. Instead, try saying that time does not permit you to discuss this anymore with the whole group, but you would be glad to discuss it after the meeting. Many times, these people have other plans after the meeting. Then say, "Please call me and we can discuss this further." You may find it tempting to argue back but do not! Even if you win the point, you risk missing your objective, particularly if the arguer is made to look foolish. You also waste the time of everyone who has to listen, which does not endear you to them.

Anger.   "Stamp collecting" and "cashing in" are concepts from transactional analysis, discussed in *Born to Win* by Dorothy Jongeward and Muriel James (Reading, MA: Addison-Wesley, 1971). This dynamic has to do with people collecting and cashing in their accumulated feelings the same way people collect and cash in trading stamps they have saved. For example, you receive a certain number of green stamps when you buy something at the grocery store. You paste those stamps into books and then, depending on how many books you have, you turn them in for a set of glasses, a television, and so on. In the same way, people sometimes save up their feelings, then cash them in. The cashing in lets them justify some behavior that they might not ordinarily do, such as screaming, sulking, or crying. Generally people collect the feelings they were used to feeling as a child. For example, if the copier breaks while John is copying materials, he gets angry and kicks the machine, whereas Joe feels sad and walks away looking as if he lost his best friend. Their responses are overreactions to the present situation, which is why these emotional outbursts of anger or sadness are called cashing in. You wonder what either person would do if something serious went wrong.

There are several ways to tell if someone is cashing in during your presentation. People's voice tones may give them away. The following kinds of remarks are good clues that someone is about to cash in his or her feelings:

- I have had it.

- This is the last time.

- It's always been like this.

If you experience the person as overreacting to the issue, he or she is probably cashing in. If you are a very kinesthetic person you are going to feel those emotions. That is your nature. As you feel the emotions, remind yourself that you do not have to take them personally!

You must do three things if someone is using your presentation to cash in their pent up feelings: (1) understand the person's issue, (2) stay detached enough to think clearly, and (3) give the most appropriate response, which is frequently one of empathy. If you do not respond to the person's feelings, the person's emotional behavior may escalate right there during your presentation. Think back to a situation where you were a little bit irritated, tried to tell someone something, and the person did not acknowledge your feelings. Chances are you got a little more irritated. If there was still no acknowledgment, before you realized it you probably were sounding very nasty. You may have even wondered how you ended up so angry. If the person had first said, "You sound irritated. I hear it," you might have calmed down and gone on with problem solving rather than with more complaining.

When you understand the dynamics of collecting and cashing in feelings, it is easier to remain objective. People who cash in their stamps are only trying to find a way to deal with their accumulated feelings. It is a very natural thing to do. As you reflect on how you collect and cash in your feelings, consider collecting only *gold stamps.* As Jongeward and James state in *Born to Win,* "The person who is in the process of becoming a winner will often decide to give up collecting negative stamps and consciously collect *gold stamps*—feelings of self-appreciation."

Take Two Attitudes toward Objections

It is important, first of all, to look forward to objections; and second, to take enough time in answering them.

Look Forward to Objections. Salespeople are taught to view objections as the beginning of the sale, since the prospect is showing interest in the product or service. Literally speaking, the fish is nibbling at the bait. Your first step in handling objections is to anticipate them and develop responses to them *before* you present! A good answer to a strong objection is an excellent hook. Remember, if you can convince those who object the hardest, you have come a long way toward convincing the rest of your audience. Invite and use those difficult-to-answer objections to your advantage.

Take Time to Answer. James Thurber said, "He who hesitates is sometimes saved." Frequently when speakers hear difficult objections, they hurry to answer them. Do not hurry. Slow down. Go through these steps in order:

1. Stop.
2. Breathe.

3. Think.

4. Speak.

These steps may occur in the space of a few seconds, but they must occur in the preceding sequence. Use these four steps when you feel a sense of panic. Sometimes, with a difficult objection, people will begin to say and do things that they later regret. They could have answered so much more effectively if only they had stopped first and taken a breath. Give yourself time, even if it is just 10 to 15 seconds, to take a deep breath and think about what you want to say before you say it.

Here are five techniques to use when catching your breath to give you time to think about how to respond:

1. *Repeat the Question.* Use precisely the same words as the person who asked the question.

2. *Rephrase the Question.* Use your own words and say, "Is that your question?"

3. *Say a Lead-In.* It will give your brain time to put together a response. Some lead-ins include, "That's a question others have been concerned about," or "Let me respond by saying," or "I want to answer you in the most appropriate way possible," or "That is a new question. Let me think about that for just a second." People use these lead-ins as ways to gain time to think. They also help you to say something besides *um* or *er*. You can also use these lead-ins when you are asked to give an on-the-spot talk. In fact, they are very useful when you have been caught off guard, since they give you a moment to compose yourself.

4. *Identify Feelings.* State the feeling you heard behind the words and voice tone the person used. For example, "I hear your frustration about this issue and hope my response alleviates it" or "I, too, understand the gravity of the strategy we are choosing."

5. *Take a Sip of Water.* This gives you a moment to compose yourself. Don't drink carbonated beverages unless you want to burp during your presentation.

After using one of these ways to catch your breath, go on to answer the objection. The following section gives you 15 ways to respond to an objection.

HANDLING OBJECTIONS

1. Include objections in your presentation.

2. Answer briefly.

3. Ask an open question.

   4. Ask a closed question.

   5. Clarify the benefits.

   6. Admit when you are wrong.

   7. Begin with a point of agreement.

   8. End eye contact.

   9. Ignore the objection.

  10. Postpone or table the objection.

  11. Defuse the objection.

  12. Ask for help.

  13. Tell a story or an analogy.

  14. Bite your tongue.

  15. Hiss when necessary.

Include Objections in Your Presentation

If you have meticulously planned your presentation, you will have covered many of the potential objections during your talk. During your talk, you can say, "An objection that some of you may have is . . . Here is how I suggest we handle that concern." Ideally, you want to answer the objections during your presentation so participants do not have to bring them up at the end of your talk. Sometimes bringing up one of the weakest points during your talk and discussing it works in your favor, particularly if it would have been the very issue in contention. However, it is unwise to raise a difficult issue that never would have been focused on otherwise. You will have to decide that for each specific presentation.

Scott Fraser at the Ballet Theater of Boston discusses how he includes responses to objections during his talks:

> Part of Ballet Theater's goal is to educate schoolchildren on the performing arts. When I visit a school system and talk about what the Ballet Theater can do for the children, I always hear the objection that the school does not have any money. Now I do not wait for that objection to come up. I bring it up within the first five minutes. I show them how other school systems made money with the community performances put on by the Ballet Theater of Boston. A portion of that money goes into supporting the arts in the school system. The superintendents show surprise and then interest when I show them the profit numbers.

Answer Briefly

You must be brief. The longer you take in handling an objection, the more chance you have of being unclear, not directly responding to the objection, or raising another objection in the person's mind. Many salespeople talk themselves in and out of a sale by going on too long in response to an objection.

Ask an Open Question

Open questions are important when you are not sure of the objection. Open questions invite the person to speak and to explain his or her views. They begin with words or phrases like, *What, Say more about,* and *How come.* The following are examples of open questions:

- What are several of your concerns about this project?

- How come you feel this budget amount is too much?

- Before I answer that, will you say more about your views on the next steps for this proposal?

Ask a Closed Question

Closed questions politely ask the person to take a stand. Prepare yourself if you anticipate the stand to be against your ideas. Closed questions can be answered with a yes, a no, or a short answer. They give you information that may prove there is no real disagreement. You may have heard the story of the two daughters who both told their mother they wanted an orange. The mother said she did not know what to do since she had only one orange. Finally, after much haggling and tears, the mother asked the daughters what they wanted to do with the orange. One daughter wanted the rind, and the other wanted the juice. So much for not asking specific questions. The following are examples of closed questions:

- Are you objecting to spending $10,000 now on the ad or to the thought of spending $50,000 later on a bigger ad?

- Do you object to the entire recommendation or only to the part of hiring a new person?

- Do you object to starting on the project next week or in a month?

- It sounds as if you are frustrated that we did not spot this problem earlier. I agree that we need a better way to examine potential problems and to create contingent and preventive plans. Do you want to implement some quality control as part of the installation of the system I am recommending?

Clarify the Benefits

A discussion of your recommendation's benefits helps people understand why the next steps are supportive of the organization or committee. Always be sure to cover the benefits in your talk. If you feel that you did an inadequate job of explaining the benefits during your talk, use the objection as an entry into reiterating those benefits. Focus on the benefits that will help your listener, not on those that will benefit you.

Admit When You Are Wrong

When you discover that you are wrong, do not be afraid to admit it. People recognize that it takes courage and self-assurance to say, "I am wrong." When done correctly, you win people on your side. Do not go on and on admitting your mistake. Stop after you acknowledge it. When you are shown to be wrong in either the information you presented or in your next steps recommendation, handle the situation as quickly as possible and with diplomacy:

- You are correct. I did not consider that.

- I will now add that information into my presentation.

- Your point is well taken.

Begin with a Point of Agreement

Before you directly answer the objection, state a point of agreement in common between you and the person, such as, "Before I get into that detail, it is true that we all believe something needs to be done about this situation." It helps you create distance from your disagreement and obtain a perspective on the issue. Both of you begin to realize that it will take many bricks to build your building. You only disagree about where the cornerstones should go. When you find something you can reach agreement about, say something like, "So the real issue before us is not whether to spend some money on a new system, but whether we can find an additional $10,000 in our budget to buy the better model. Am I correct in my assessment?" This "bridging" technique often results in eliminating objections, since people see how minor or inconsequential the objections really are. It puts the objection in perspective.

End Eye Contact

If feasible, after you answer an antagonistic question, end your eye contact by focusing on someone else. This discourages the person who asked that question from immediately asking another one. It also shows the audience that you are finished with the question and that it has been adequately answered. Of course, this depends on whose question you just answered.

Ignore the Objection

This is for the desperate situation in which you do not know the answer or you do not want to admit you are wrong about something you said previously. Answer anything you choose and act as if you answered the question. If any of you watch debates, especially the presidential debates in the United States, you will notice that, at times, the candidates do not answer the question asked. Believe it or not, many people are so intent on watching the candidate that they do not notice! Moreover, the candidates, as accomplished and trained speakers, know this is true. They are trained to use the questions as a way of bringing up one of their campaign issues. Here is an example closer to a situation in which you may find yourself.

> *Question:* Your department has hired five people in the last year. Do you really need all those people?

> *Answer:* We have just enough people to handle the customer calls and letters. We want to have a two-day turnaround on all letters and a same-day response time to customers.

Postpone or Table the Objection

If you decide it is not appropriate to deal with the objection in the group, table the objection and tell the person something to the effect, "I think your question might be better answered after our session."

Defuse the Objection

If it is a very negative objection, do not repeat it. Find some way to make the words the person said at least neutral, if not positive or beneficial to you. For example, "Why do you charge so much?" can be answered by saying, "Let me explain the value of our services to you."

Ask for Help

It is perfectly fine for you to say, "I am not sure of the exact response to your concern; can anyone here help me with that?" People love to help someone else and to show off that they know something. Your problem at that point may be to keep people from talking too long when responding to the objection. If you are with a team of people, one or all of those people should be ready to help you before you actually have to ask for help. You need to have a signal that you give one of your team members, and then he or she takes over. I call this second teaching. You are the first teacher, and a team member is the second teacher whose job is to back you up and support you.

Tell a Story or an Analogy

A financial advisor told me how he had learned to handle people who said in his seminar, "Well, I invested and lost half of my money. What do you think about that?" He would say something like this:

> I hear your disappointment. I have thought about some analogies to your experience, and here is one that may explain what happened with your stocks. When you go buy some fruit to eat, you have some choices. You can buy the fruit that is ready to eat right now or you can buy some fruit that needs to ripen in a few days. And sometimes you make mistakes and buy fruit that looks good, but when you get it home it is spoiled already or rotten inside. You have probably learned that it is hard to tell whether some fruits will ripen well. Unfortunately, due to a whole set of circumstances, the "fruit" you bought in the name of stocks was already spoiled. It should have been picked months before. On the other hand, unlike fruit, your stocks may ripen again over time. That is yet to be seen.

He found that telling this story calmed the person down and gave others in the room something to think about. It was also a great lead-in for him, since he was involved in selling long-term, blue chip financial packages.

Bite Your Tongue

Ben Franklin said, "Remember not only to say the right thing at the right place, but far more difficult still, to leave unsaid the wrong thing at a tempting moment." In the book *What They Don't Teach You at Harvard Business School* (New York: Bantam, 1984), Mark McCormack says:

> A learned—it's almost never instinctive—ability to bite your tongue has two incredibly important selling applications that are often overlooked. First, it allows you to collect your thoughts and therefore be more cautious or more circumspect in what you say. Second, it lessens your chance of saying a lot more than you need to, meant to, or want to.

Hiss When Necessary

If you suspect that an objection is not well intentioned, the following story may give you one way to respond:

> A certain swami was walking into the outskirts of a village one evening. As he entered the village, he saw a snake biting the villagers. The snake bit everyone who came within range, and, frequently, for no apparent reason, chased the villagers. The swami told the snake he felt the snake should stop biting the villagers and making their lives difficult. The snake agreed. A few months later, the swami passed through the village again and saw the once beautiful sleek snake covered with mud and lying in a ditch on the side of the road. The snake told the swami he was doing what the swami had

suggested. He had stopped biting the villagers. The swami looked at the snake and said, "Yes, but I didn't tell you not to hiss."

Handling difficult people and situations does not have to mean putting them down or letting them put you down. A certain amount of hissing on your part may be necessary to demonstrate your competence and to show others that you can handle those who would like to throw you into the ditch. The more politely you can hiss, the more you will appear in control of the situation.

Integrate Your Various Responses

Consider responding to certain objections by combining several of your answering techniques. Ultimately, that decision will be left to your judgment. The following are some examples:

Objection: I tried that and it did not work.

Responses:
State Facts. I know you had a problem. Here are two reasons why.
Postpone Objection. We can discuss that later. No need to take everyone's time on this.
Ask a Closed Question. What in particular did not work?
Ask an Open Question. Say more about . . .
Give Empathy and State Benefits. I hear your frustration. As soon as we clear up this one problem, you will experience the benefit of the fast service.
Defuse Objections. Sounds like I need to go over the process with you individually. I will be glad to do that at your convenience.

Objection: Are you aware that the latest statistics do not match the ones you have just listed?

Responses:
State Fact. No, I was not aware, and I will certainly incorporate those new facts into my conclusion.
Postpone Objection. No, let us talk at the break about how I can obtain your information.
Ask a Closed Question. Where did you find those latest statistics?

For those people who objected strongly to some points in your talk, but then agreed with your conclusion, do not say, "But just 10 minutes ago you said the opposite" or "You certainly change your mind quickly." Gracefully let the person off the hook.

CONCLUDING THE QUESTION-AND-ANSWER PERIOD

Every situation is different. Decide whether you need to wait and answer every question and objection before you conclude or whether you will stop even though you see that people still have questions. If you wait until there are no questions and the room is silent, do not say, "I guess I should stop now." Do not tell people that you only have time for one more question, since you may not want to conclude after that question. You can say, "I have time for a few more questions." If someone else is supposed to cut off the question-and-answer period, tell the person that you still want a few moments to conclude after the question-and-answer period. You must now delineate the next steps to be taken. These will be based on the concluding summary you gave and possibly what happened during your question-and-answer period.

STEP 9 RECOMMENDING NEXT STEPS

KEY POINTS

1 Determine what you want people to do as a result of your presentation.

2 Work on obtaining agreement about your next steps before you do the formal presentation.

3 Find a buddy who will speak in favor of your recommendations and help you out, if need be.

4 Suggest your next steps in a logical, systematic manner.

5 Explain what each step will entail.

6 Ask questions to find out why specifically someone is disagreeing with one of your recommendations.

7 Be prepared to negotiate about some of your recommendations. Have some alternate steps to recommend if you need to negotiate.

8 Make it easy for your audience to agree with you. Don't box them into a corner.

9 Take charge if two people in your audience are disagreeing.

10 Clarify and summarize who is to be responsible for carrying out each step.

> Effective executives know . . . that the most time-consuming step
> in the process is not making the decision but putting it into effect.
>
> Peter Drucker, *The Effective Executive*

After his presentation, a manager felt disappointed that nothing had happened
with his suggestion that some materials be purchased. When asked how he had
concluded, he said he presented all the reasons for the new materials, then sat
down. He did not recommend next steps. He needed to make a suggestion such as,
"I propose we purchase this equipment at a cost of $5,000. If everyone agrees, I
will request a purchase order today." By using this approach, he would have discovered the level of acceptance for his proposed purchase.

Prepare your presentation so it logically leads to next steps. Effective presentations include a recommendation concerning the next steps to be taken. When
learning tennis, the instructor emphasizes the importance of following through
after hitting the ball. This ability to follow through on a tennis stroke separates
the novice from the expert. The follow-through in a presentation is the delin-
eation of next steps. If you use any hesitant words, such as *maybe* or *sort of,* your
listeners will not be as inclined to take your proposed actions. They want to experience your confidence in the direction you are recommending.

People's acceptance is only a beginning. Execution is the key. Consider
IBM's philosophy: Nothing is sold until properly installed. This philosophy encourages the salespeople to make proposals that are possible to carry out. The implementation of the sale has to be feasible. Translate this into presentation skills,
and it means you have not reached your objective until people start taking the next
steps you have suggested.

How do you entice people to take those next steps? Make your next steps
understandable and present them in increments that people can agreeably accept.
"Inch by inch, life's a cinch. Yard by yard, life is hard." Give your next steps in
inches. When you tell your audience about the "yards," break them into inches so
people will feel that each "yard" is feasible. Do not overwhelm the group so that,
even though they may agree in principle with what you are saying, they experience you as proposing too much, too soon. Be cautious if you are an overdoer and
a perfectionist. For example, the division managers in a company said they
wanted to do a customer survey. An effective survey was created after much con-
sultation with outside sources and a lot of redrafting of the questions to fit the
different types of customers. This was definitely a "whole nine yards" survey. It
included all the pertinent information that the managers could conceivably wish
to hear from their customers. The Management Committee looked at the 10-page
survey and said no. The creators of the survey were surprised. The reason for the
managers' refusal is not really so mysterious. This next step was too much for
them. They wanted more of an "inches" survey. If a survey of 20 questions had
been presented to them, they probably would have agreed.

Your next steps recommendation is the punch line of your presentation. This
is where you have your listeners sign on the dotted line, commit to giving money,

or agree to implement a proposal. This part of your presentation is integral to your impromptu or planned talks. When you arrive here, slow down, be enthusiastic, and be clear.

CLARIFYING ROLES AND RESPONSIBILITIES

The "Clarifying Roles and Responsibilities" chart helps you organize for more complex situations. The chart provides a way to specify the responsibilities of each person involved in carrying out the total project. As the presenter, here are some ways to use the chart: Fill it out completely and obtain agreement from the group; fill out only the responsibilities and names and have the group designate the roles; have the group fill out the whole chart.

Clarifying Roles and Responsibilities
Goal: Create management development program

	Name				
Responsibilities	President	Vice-President Personnel	Vice-President Training	Training Manager	Management Committee
1. Call other companies for information	—	—	A	PM	—
2. List issues mentioned by board of directors	I	PM	I	I	I
3. Buy books	—	—	A	PM	—
4. See videos	—	—	A	PM	—
5. Growth issue questionnaire to managers	A	C	C	PM	C
6. Hire consultant for two days' help	—	A	PM	C	I
7. Develop curriculum outline	C	C	C	PM	C
8. Propose curriculum	A	I	I	PM	I
9. Do pilot test	I	I	I	PM	I
10. Make revisions	—	—	I	PM	I
11. Do program	I	I	I	PM	I
12. Make revisions	I	I	C	PM	C

Roles

A =   *Approver:* Only one approver; gives final go-ahead; sends back for reworking; can veto; specifies direction; allocates resources (money, people, materials, and machinery); usually highest ranking on the chart.

PM = *Prime Mover:* Only one prime mover; either does work or delegates it; follows up; held responsible if work not done; initiates and coordinates; makes sure everyone with a role on the chart is involved; makes sure people with an *I* on the chart are informed; has power delegated from approver.

C =   *Contributor:* Suggests ideas; understands part of job is to make time to contribute by adding information, pointing out problems, or concurring with the proposal.

E =   *Expert:* Appraises work or makes recommendations in terms of her or his expertise; contributes from expertise base.

I =   *Informed:* Needs to be kept up-to-date on the project; sends memos; meets periodically to update person.

All people on the chart are always involved in the process.
Anyone not on the chart can still be a contributor.

OBTAINING GROUP AGREEMENT

Chuang Tzu, an Eastern philosopher, tells the story of a zookeeper who said his monkeys were to have one banana in the morning and two at night. The monkeys, however, were dissatisfied with the arrangement, so the zookeeper said they could have two bananas in the morning and one in the evening. The arrangement pleased the monkeys greatly, and also pleased the zookeeper, since he did not need additional bananas. This funny story points out that you never know what arrangements might work to satisfy others. Your perceptions of what people will agree to may be not *at all* what they are thinking. There are several issues to consider when attempting to figure out what people will agree to and how you can obtain that agreement. How does your place in the hierarchy determine whether people will or will not agree with you? Do you have some alternative plans in case you need them? And do you have someone who will support you during the meeting? Consider these issues as you plan your next steps.

For those of you who commute, you probably have one or two alternate routes to drive, depending on the traffic. Thus, when you see a traffic jam, you veer off to a different road. This same flexibility applies to certain types of presentations. Plan those alternate routes. Have backup routes, materials, and people to support you, just in case you need them. A backup person can be especially helpful if you are asking for money, materials, new authority, or extra people. You may want to agree ahead of time that he or she will make a supporting remark after your next step recommendations. In scuba diving, this is called buddy breathing. If a diver's tank runs out of air or malfunctions in some way, that diver has a buddy who is designated to help out. Find a buddy ahead of time who will support your next steps and will speak up when someone disagrees with your recommendations. You can also have more than one buddy. Never turn down support. Before your presentation, discuss how you can discreetly signal for help.

Plan your major route, yet know one or two other paths that will also lead the group to the destination. Advise your buddy of those other paths. Consequently, you or your buddy will have the option of altering the route depending on the "weather" and "route conditions." The following is one example:

> Pat's presentation objective—to have flexible work hours—needed approval from her work team. Before the meeting, she discussed this idea with two team members. They were open to trying her plan. During the meeting, one person started saying, "This will never work. I do not even know why we are discussing it." Pat's colleague spoke up, "I want to at least discuss the advantages and disadvantages before we table the recommendation."
>
> This buddy support was essential to keep the presentation on track. Pat's next steps included a recommendation that all the team go on flexible work hours for the following month. This same person strongly objected. Nothing could be said to change her mind. Pat's buddy suggested a modification by which only certain members went to a flexible work-hour schedule and would report to the group after the month was over. The next steps were modified so that everyone agreed to experiment with flexible work hours.

NEGOTIATING

Aristotle said, "The fool tells me his reasons; the wise man persuades me with my own." Be prepared to negotiate your next steps. Save energy for that task. Since next steps call people to action, you can expect that you will find the most opposition—and consequently the most opportunity to negotiate—at this stage.

The best possible scenario is when everyone agrees with your presentation summary, works out their concerns during the question-and-answer period, then eagerly goes along with your next steps. But sometimes you may have to negotiate those next steps. The next several pages will give you a minicourse on negotiating. The References suggest several books on negotiation. It would be frustrating for you to present with organization and style only to see your next steps rejected due to your lack of negotiating skills.

Practice Negotiating Points

Consider the following points when you need to negotiate an issue:

1. Be prepared for negotiations.
   - What do I want to achieve through these negotiations?
   - What do the other people want to achieve?

2. Realize that everyone perceives the world differently.
   - Each side sees themselves as more reasonable and accommodating than the other.
   - Differences in perception cause escalation of hostility and damage negotiation.

3. Never box yourself or the other side into a corner.
   - Avoid ultimatums.
   - Avoid public positions with no escape route.

4. Use creativity and imagination.
   - Set aside time for brainstorming together, devoid of judgments.

5. Learn the power of silence.
   - Talk no more than 50 percent of the time.
   - You cannot give anything away if you keep your mouth closed.

6. Never give something for nothing.

7. Make it easy for the other side to agree.
   - They are not the enemy.
   - Do not sound locked into your view.

8. Understand there is never only one source of conflict.
   • If the person disagrees vehemently, what else might be going on?

9. Always be willing to do the paperwork.

10. Set a deadline.

11. Anticipate disagreement.
    • Be prepared to request another meeting to work out disagreements.

12. Regard none of the parties as wrong (whatever the conflict).

13. Speak in a language other people can understand, especially if you are a specialist.

Practice Negotiating Strategies

The following hints can help you negotiate your next steps:

1. Understand the other person's limits.
   • Never assume the other person will be reasonable.
   • Never assume the other person has the same values.
   • Do research.
   • Ask questions.
   • Use silence.
   • Mirror back tentative understandings.

2. Understand your own limits.
   • What is the minimum I can accept?
   • What is the maximum I can ask for?
   • What is the maximum I can give away?
   • What is the least I can offer?

3. Try to save face for both parties.
   • Make it easy for people to change their minds.
   • Do not become defensive with emotional outbursts. Say, "I hear how upset you are by this."
   • If things get heated, suggest a 5-minute break.
   • Acknowledge the person's concerns, "I hear your interests."

4. Deescalate conflict.
   • Do not polarize on a single issue.
   • Keep the same standard for all concerned.
   • Elaborate so everyone has the same interpretation of the situation.
   • Accept the other side's view.
   • "Cash in" your feelings before they take charge of you.

5. Behave assertively.
   - Stand up for your own rights, thoughts, and feelings.
   - Communicate: Give and expect respect.
   - Say what you want, and listen to what the other person wants.
   - Tell yourself, "I am confident and I respect my views."

6. Negotiate in the other person's modality.
   - (Visually) Let me show you how I see this next step occurring.
   - (Auditorily) I agree, we need to talk about this some more. Tell me again what you hear as the block to doing this recommendation.
   - (Kinesthetically) Give me a sense of why you feel this step needs to be revised.

7. Ask questions.
   - What information do you need that you do not now have?
   - What specifically is acceptable to you?
   - What would have to change so you could agree to these next steps?
   - Say, "Can we think about this together now?" if the other person just said, "I want to think about this."
   - "Do you agree we are of the same opinion on this next step?" This establishes some point of agreement. You want to find the bridge between your two views.

Practice patience when negotiating. Patience is absolutely essential. Gary Karrass in *Negotiate to Close* (St. Louis, MO: Fireside Books, 1985) tells the following story:

> Not long ago, a businessman from Japan attended one of our negotiation seminars. I had a drink with him the second night, at the end of the seminar, and he said this: "You know, Americans look upon negotiating as hunting. In Japan, we look upon it as farming. I figure there are only so many people out there I can sell to, only so many who will buy from me. So my goal is to take time and care with each negotiation. I want to get the best deal for me and I want the best deal for the customer. I want to farm the relationship. Americans want to get in there, get the deal, and get out—the hunting approach. I want to gather harvest from the customer relationship time and time again. And I want to do well each time. But I want the customer to also do well each time. I'm willing to spend the time and effort to achieve this."

This example encourages you to negotiate with a view toward the long term. If you expect to have ongoing relationships with many of the people with whom you are negotiating, tact and patience are particularly essential. As you listen to others' viewpoints, you may discover something Ralph Waldo Emerson said: "Our best thought comes from others."

Understanding and practicing the preceding negotiating hints will help you to get your next steps approved. You may learn, to your surprise, that by negotiating your next steps, you obtained more than you had originally planned.

Use Key Phrases to Negotiate Effectively

If you present frequently, you need to take a negotiation course. In my Negotiating Seminar, we cover the following considerations in the context of an actual negotiation.

Interests.   "Let's talk about what we need to achieve here and identify if there are any areas where we disagree."

- Note how the negotiation is characterized as a discussion seeking to mutually find points of agreement, even if it is agreeing to the existence of issues. Try to characterize the process as a discussion rather than as a "negotiation."

Clarify Interests.   "Let's focus on what is truly important not only to me but to you."

- This sets the framework for the goal of the negotiation and can be repeatedly referred to during the discussion so the parties do not lose sight of what they are trying to achieve.

Options.   "In what other ways can we approach this particular problem?"

- Seek to involve the other person in the brainstorming process. View an issue as a problem for both of you to solve.

Negotiables.   "I think that I can be a little more flexible in the cost (for example), if you can finish the project (for example) sooner."

- Proposing a tradeoff that makes logical and economic sense is a face-saving device that can often cut through tough problems. Giving in on a point without a trade can be viewed as a sign of weakness for further exploitation. Prepare for the negotiation by examining the negotiable elements and developing options that fit within your ultimate goals.

Consequences.   "Let's see what our agreements will mean for us in the future."

- This technique permits both parties to envision the consequences of arriving at a good and mutually beneficial agreement. Not only does it act as an incentive by making the future palpable, but it helps to clarify what points should be important to each party.

Objective Criteria.   "Let's agree on a few basics."

- For tough negotiations, it is always helpful to find areas where there is no dispute. Be on the constant lookout for points of agreement and let the other person know that you agree. The content of the process should not be confrontational. Where there are only a few points of disagreement among many points of agreement, issues are generally easier to resolve.

Visuals.   "Let's map out our discussion on this blackboard (flip chart or piece of paper)."

- You want to put as much down in writing as possible since it tends to firm up the points of agreement. In addition, some visually oriented persons may better be able to discuss issues that are depicted visually.

Facts.   "Those are the facts as I see them. Don't you agree?"

- As with objective criteria, you want to find as many factual points of agreement as possible. A discussion of facts may sometimes clear up a misunderstanding that was impeding the process.

Generalizations.   "That's interesting; none of our other suppliers has ever been concerned about that point before."

- Taking a particular point and turning it into a generalization places a strong burden on the other person to justify the point. In this example, a comparison with others who are similarly situated should also diminish a person's concern about a particular issue. Another way to generalize is to ask, for example, if the person has ever agreed to this point before or if a specific concern prevents the person from agreeing. The generalization tool is an information-gathering device that works to place the burden of explanation on the other party. It is only by collecting such information that a person will be a successful negotiator.

Anger.   "Let's take a 5-minute break" (in person) or "Let me call you back in 5 minutes" (on the phone).

- Unless you are using anger as a tactic (which is a topic in itself), don't let your feelings of anger infect the process. You may be very close to full agreement and not know that the underlying issue concerns an easily re-solved misunderstanding of fact. People respond to anger in unpredictable and personal ways that could complicate the process. Other cultures may view expression of anger as rude, uncouth, embarrassing or insulting, causing loss of respect and credibility.

Summary.   "Let me summarize what we have achieved together."

- A point-by-point summary prevents problems in the future, reaffirms points of agreement, and focuses on the result as having been a coopera-tive and successful effort.

Follow-Up.   "I will send you the agreement by tomorrow; can you sign it within 3 days so we can finalize our deal and move ahead with the project?"

- Show prompt action generated by the excitement of having structured the deal. Characterize the agreement as final and point out how getting the paperwork done quickly can help everyone.

MEDIATING CONFLICT

You have put together a superb presentation. You kept your listeners interested, and you have just proposed next steps to keep the project moving. Suddenly two

Negotiating

The only courage that matters is the kind that gets you from one minute to the next.

Mignon McLaughlin

It's not over until it's over.

Yogi Berra

Most people prefer to shelve unpleasant conflict. . . . It would be a good thing for them to show more endurance and courage during the negative than suffer the dissatisfaction of a poor agreement later.

Chester Karrass, *Give and Take*

Keep in mind the better you understand what you want and why you want it, the better your chances will be of acquiring it.

Fred Jandt, *Win-Win Negotiating*

people in your group disagree. Their talk gets heated, and you stand there in front of everyone wondering how to manage this argument. You thought that all you had to do was present the materials and people would just go along. Everyone is now looking to you to stop this battle between these two people. What do you do? Use the following process when you find yourself in this situation:

1. *State the issue and tell why it needs to be resolved.* Do this to clarify the issue and also to give everyone a moment to breathe and to obtain some distance from the conflict. Speak in a forceful voice (or else they will not stop talking) and say, "Let me ask you to stop for a moment while I state the concerns you both have."

2. *Ask people to share their view of the issue.* "Please state, in only a couple of sentences, what you see as the issue." The temptation for most mediators is to start talking about how they experience the conflict. The better approach is to be quiet as the mediator and hear how the people in conflict experience the issue.

3. *Ask the others in the room and the two people in conflict to suggest ways to resolve the conflict.* Write these suggestions on something for all to see. You need everyone to see the suggestions so that all of you stay focused on resolving the issue.

4. *Ask both people which suggestions are acceptable to them.* Other people in the group may also have to concur on the next steps.

5. *Summarize their agreement.* Summarize their agreement, and state how it affects your proposed next steps, if at all.

If these two people are in conflict over a point not directly related to your subject, say, "I hear both of your concerns about this. I want to finish working out these next steps and end on time. Then you will have time to do justice to your discussion. Thank you."

YOUR CONCLUDING SENTENCES

You have answered the questions and objections, stated your next steps, dealt with any conflicts, and perhaps had to negotiate some changes with your proposed next steps. It is now time for your last few sentences. The following tells you how to end:

- Reaffirm the final results! You may have just handled a heated negotiation. End with a positive, upbeat voice, no matter what happened just prior to this. Take a deep breath, and conclude with conviction. Do not speak those final sentences while picking up your notes. Say those last sentences while looking at everyone. Eye contact is important. Depending on your situation, you may want to give a thank-you such as "Thank you for listening to my proposal," or 'Thank you for taking the time to discuss which strategy we need to start implementing."

- After you say your last sentence, count silently to three like this, "1001 . . . 1002 . . . 1003." Do this while looking around the room at each of your listeners. Then sit down, walk off, or do whatever is appropriate. Have all your notes together so you do not have to organize them after your final sentences. You want to exit with style and not be remembered as the one fumbling with notes.

- Compliments may come your way. Do not justify your talk one way or the other by saying phrases such as, "Well, I could have used more time," or "The visuals were late getting to me." By telling the person who compliments you that your talk really was not that great, you are discounting his or her judgment. Just say thank you without shrugging your shoulders or grimacing.

STEP 10 TAKING THE LEAP! FROM EXCELLENCE TO ART

KEY POINTS

1 Personalize the presentation to the group. Use stories, visuals, people's names, their products, and so on.

2 Find ways to use appropriate humor in your presentation.

3 Ask several people to tell you your strengths as a presenter and then do them more as you present.

4 Stand straight, gesture, and feel animated inside.

5 Practice out loud and sound enthusiastic; forcefully project your voice.

6 Don't begin your presentation with a joke unless you are hired as the comedian.

7 Say people's names during your presentation.

8 Find ways to emotionally connect to each one of your listeners (e.g., eye contact, background, personalized comments).

9 Remember you are the message even when you use visuals.

10 Be yourself!

There is magic when a presenter is superb. You feel it, see it, and hear it. How do you identify the essence of that magic and then use it for yourself? At some time in your life, you have probably seen a magic show and felt amazed by the magician's skill. Did you then buy a book on magic to discover the inside tricks of the magic business? Probably not. If you had, you would have discovered all the steps necessary to perform a given trick. Up to now, this book has given you the essential steps to make an excellent presentation, whether it be for 1 minute or for 3 hours. The following flowchart summarizes the recommended structure of a presentation.

The Communicate to Convince Flowchart!

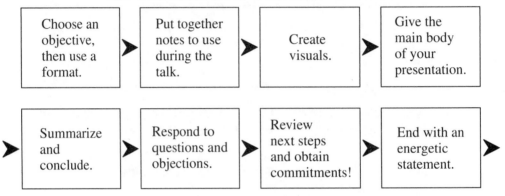

Step 10 will now teach you to make magic within that structured flow. It is not difficult. As with all skills, it takes practice and more practice, plus a belief that you can do whatever you set out to accomplish.

The essential differences between a superb presenter and a just fine presenter have to do with the way the superb presenter lives the following five "arts."

1. Use your humor.

2. Be yourself.

3. Persevere.

4. Personalize whenever possible.

5. Find your passion.

These five arts will lead you to discover the exquisite artist within you. It is by drawing on the power of your creative force that you can enthuse, motivate, and capture your listener's attention and willingness to take action. When you continually practice these five arts, people will begin to describe your presentation's organization and style with such words as, *superb, clear, effective, focused,* and *convincing.* They will feel that they can trust you because you exude a trust in yourself. Your technical skills will shine even brighter as you shine as a person. Your talks will become artistic expressions. You will communicate your

Humor

My method is to take the utmost trouble to find the right thing to say, and then say it with the utmost levity.

George Bernard Shaw

Good humor is a tonic for mind and body. It is the best antidote for anxiety and depression. It is a business asset.

Glenville Kleiser

There are three things which are real: God, Human Folly, and Laughter. The first two are beyond our comprehension. So we must do what we can with the third.

John F. Kennedy, from "The Ramayana" by Aubrey Mennen

My way of joking is to tell the truth. It's the funniest joke in the world.

George Bernard Shaw

What I want to do is make people laugh so that they'll see things seriously.

William K. Zinsser

A person without mirth is like a wagon without springs in which one is caused disagreeably to jolt by every pebble over which it runs.

Henry Ward Beecher

Do you bring other people up or down? This may be the most important question facing you in your career and your life.

Roger Ailes

Laughter is a tranquilizer with no side effects.

Arnold H. Glasow

enjoyment to your listeners, who, in turn, will communicate their enjoyment of you. Most of all, they will agree with your recommendations. Sounds too ideal? You will never know unless you practice these five arts.

USE YOUR HUMOR—THE FIRST ART

> Did you know throughout the cosmos they found intelligent
> life forms that play to play. We are the only ones that
> play to win.
>
> Jane Wagner, *The Search for Signs of*
> *Intelligent Life in the Universe*

If you are wondering why you should cultivate a sense of humor, consider these statistics. A study of 100 executives at the largest corporations in the United States disclosed that 84 percent thought employees with a sense of humor do a better job than those with little or no sense of humor. A survey of 737 chief executives of large corporations found that 98 percent said they would hire a person with a good sense of humor over one who lacks humor. These surveys are reported in Kushner's book *The Light Touch: How to Use Humor for Business Success* (New York: Simon & Schuster, 1990).

Humor in a presentation accomplishes three things: it relaxes you, puts your group at ease, and encourages people to be open to you and your recommendations. Reflect on how you best use humor. If you have a knack for making funny, on-the-spot, one-liner jokes, continue to do this. If you are not that type of person, do not try to be. At least, do not try the first few times in front of 40 people! Some people are great at telling jokes they have memorized. Other people become so nervous they forget the punch line. Experiment and learn how comfortable you are with humor. Think about how you now use humor in normal conversations and, if appropriate, do the same when speaking. (The References list books and resources on humor.)

Be Relevant

Be sure your humor is relevant to the topic. Never use anecdotes or humor that might offend your participants! If you are not certain whether your humorous comment will be appreciated, then do not make it. "When in doubt, cut it out!" After you tell a joke and people laugh, do not say, "But all joking aside," or "Seriously now." If you discount your joke, your participants will think they should not have laughed, since it was not relevant and thus a waste of their time. Let it stand on its own.

Be Spontaneous

Much humor is best if it is fresh and comes out of the moment. The problem with jokes is that, sometimes, if you use those you have read or heard, they are all too familiar to your listeners. It would be a major blunder to tell a joke in the afternoon that the audience has heard in the morning. The audience does not know what to do. Should they listen politely? Should someone say, "We heard that this morning." It is a touchy situation and very uncomfortable for your listeners. Try not to put them in that situation.

Dean Rusk was once asked this question in front of a group of 600 people, "Some of my colleagues and I are convinced that the second coming of Christ is imminent. What is your view?" He said, "I have to leave that to the good Lord, and he has not taken me into his confidence." Humor based on the reality at the moment can be funny if you can think fast enough to just say what is true right then and there.

Do Not Open with a Joke

Some people think they are *supposed* to tell a joke when they start talking. Do only what seems the best for you and *the most appropriate* for the situation. Unless you are really confident, do not start off with a joke. Why? You, as the speaker, are usually nervous enough in the beginning, and if the joke does not get people laughing, you will have a poor start. Also, people must become accustomed to your voice, particularly if you speak with an accent different from the majority of people listening. They may miss your one-line joke due to your accent.

Tie the Joke to the Topic

Even if your joke is tied closely to your topic, explain how it connects. Use a transition sentence from your joke to your content. Avoid telling a joke that is unrelated to your subject. Nothing seems more contrived than the person who stands up, tells a joke, and then says, "Now my topic is. . . ." Obviously, the person read somewhere that it is good to start or intersperse a long talk with a joke. What he or she did not read is that the joke should be appropriate for the audience and connected to the topic.

Use Appropriate Humor

There is a time and a place for humor. There are also situations in which humor is just not appropriate. Hopefully, you will figure that out before you present. The following scenario happened to one person who realized his humor and light-hearted style did not fit the situation:

> A man was representing his company, a restaurant, before a licensing board. He was asked if he had seen the restaurant that was being discussed. He said that he had seen it, but it was a while ago, and then he made some humorous comment about the restaurant being too expensive to visit these days. As soon as he said that, he knew he had made a mistake. This licensing board was in a serious mood and wanted no part of humor. He changed his voice tone and he answered the questions directly without any more side comments.

When you have been in a meeting for an hour and are asked to speak, if you think of a funny comment to start, say it. Do not say it if you are uncertain regarding the propriety of your humor. If your spontaneity gets the best of you, and you plunge in anyway, only to realize that you have offended someone, apologize before continuing. If you do not apologize, some people will not be listening to your content. They will still be irritated by your joke.

Again, be careful with your humor. A presenter lost a million-dollar contract because he made an inappropriate comment about his potential customer!

Cultivate Your Humor

Before we try to define what humor is, let us consider what humor is not and how some people have trouble feeling and being humorous:

> Lack of humor seems to come from the attitude of the "hard fact." Things are very hard and deadly honest, deadly serious, like, to use an analogy, a living corpse. He lives in pain, has a continual expression of pain on his face. . . . The rigidity of this living corpse expresses the opposite of a sense of humor. It is as though somebody is standing behind you with a sharp sword. . . . This is the self-consciousness of watching yourself, observing yourself unnecessarily. . . . Actually it is not Big Brother who is watching; it is Big Me! . . . There is no joy in this approach, no sense of humor at all. *Cutting Through Spiritual Materialism* by Chogyam Trungpa (Boston: Shambhala Publications, 1973).

What is humor and its effects? Steve Allen, a marvelous comedian, says the following:

> Some people want to be funny. There's no such thing as a person with no humor. Everyone has the physical capacity and musculature to laugh, to smile. Some people deny their silly centers. It probably goes back to childhood with the garbage a parent put in the computer we call a brain. A parent will say to a gleeful child, "Tommy, don't make a fool of yourself." That's too bad. Humor should be encouraged. I don't mean that your dentist should act like Jerry Lewis. I mean that people who have a sense of humor are more likable than those who don't. Even in something as serious as a presidential debate, the candidate who has the ability to amuse has a tremendous advantage. Comedy can defuse a difficult situation in a real-life argument. . . . There's a quicksilver element to comedy. You can't grab quicksilver. There's a hard-to-measure element to funniness. Humor is not a science. It's an art. You know you're being funny when people laugh at what you're saying. Laughter is, after all, a form of approval.

To cultivate your humor, it may be necessary to drop your rigidity for a moment and have a little fun. Try it! Humor adds that extra spark that electrifies or, at least, amuses your audience.

Ways to Begin

Following are three ways to use humor. There are many more.

Impromptu Humor.   Take those situations that upset you or that are not perfect for you. Make a funny comment. It does not have to get people rolling in the aisles. How about a smile or a chuckle from your listeners? For example, you are just informed that you only have 5 minutes instead of 15 minutes, since the room is booked for another meeting. So you say, "I have a dilemma. What shall I do? Stop and take questions, which means you may find out what I do not know, or keep talking, in which event you will not have time to ask questions and discover my ignorance. I prefer to answer your questions. Who wants to start?" If the bulb burns out on the projector, say, "Now wait, I asked for a total blackout of the building, not just the projector."

Anthony Robbins in *Unlimited Power* (New York: Ballantine, 1986) tells the story about a teacher in a classroom:

> All the kids—as a prank—arranged to drop their books at exactly 9:00 A.M. so as to throw the teacher off. Without missing a beat, she put down her chalk, picked up a book, and dropped it too. "Sorry I'm late," she said. After that, she had the kids eating out of her hand.

Rehearsed Humor.   People who read frequently find jokes in books or magazines. When you read outside your field of interest, you will pick up quotes, analogies, and all kinds of ideas to use. Keep a list of jokes, and use them at appropriate occasions. If you hear a good joke, write it down. You may be able to use it later on. The best jokes or one-liners are often those the speaker has obviously created. Dorothy Jongeward, coauthor of *Born to Win,* has been frequently told that she thinks just like a man. This comment is usually said by a man and meant as a compliment. Depending on the situation, she would respond with, "You said that with the tenderness of a woman." This is an excellent example of using a funny retort to make a point. When you use humor to defuse a touchy situation, people appreciate you.

Make Fun of Yourself.   Some of the best jokes are those in which the speakers personalize the situation by poking fun at themselves or making light of their weaknesses that cannot be changed. How can you make fun of yourself? Take a defect of yours and exaggerate it. One person told the group that he was so overweight he could not fit in his shower. So once a week he put soap flakes in his pocket and went through the car wash. You guessed it! The soap he used was the one he was selling to the audience! Another woman worked in a company where she was always told that she was too young to be doing what she did. She finally came up with, "You know, I'm young because I grew up with velcro tennis shoes. I never did learn how to tie my shoes. But I have learned how to tie these projects together to help all of us meet your, the customer's needs." This woman learned how to discuss her young age in a positive manner.

Your ability to use humor creates a lasting favorable impression. The following is a prescription for personalizing jokes from the book *The Laughter Prescription* by Dr. Laurence Peter and Bill Dana (New York: Ballantine, 1982):

1. Select a funny line or story that is appropriate for the situation.

2. Choose material that fits your personality.

3. Put yourself in the story.

4. Particularize it by naming specific places, people, and things.

5. Make it as brief as possible.

Show Pictures

You can also show pictures or cartoons. This way you get a chuckle and go on.

BE YOURSELF—THE SECOND ART

> You don't have to try, you just have to be.
>
> David Viscott

Many people have been told things about who they are and what they can do as individuals. Empty your mind of preconceived beliefs about yourself. Examine your inner self. You will find a person who can speak in front of people, who can be motivating, and who will be superb after giving up some personal limiting concepts and frameworks. Do not copy another person's behavior. "We all want to be famous people, and the moment we want to be something, we are no longer free" says Krishnamurti, an Indian philosopher. Be your own famous person. Do not develop a presentation personality separate from your normal way of being with people. So many people think that, once they get in front of people, they have to be stiff and serious, even when they are not generally like that in everyday conversation. They fail to see that they are still having a conversation with people; only more than one person is listening. Reading positive advice over and over will help you incorporate a healthy image of your presentation ability into your belief system. The following bits of advice are from famous and/or well-respected people:

Zig Ziglar: If I'm not excited about making a talk, there's not an audience alive that will be excited about hearing that talk. I make every talk as if it's going to be the last talk I will ever make in my life. I can honestly say that when I get off the platform that audience just got the very best I was capable of doing.

Bette Midler: Cherish forever what makes you unique, 'cuz you're really a yawn if it goes!

Nido Qubein: I think a speaker loses much when he or she stands there without any gestures, without any emotions, and delivers the presentation—versus the speaker who emotionally gets involved in what he or she is saying. I believe that gestures should definitely be used because God did not create us to be a rock. I want people to look at me and say, "He's feeling what he's doing."

Joseph Campbell: It's a wonderful moment when people can make the decision to be something quite astonishing and unexpected, rather than cookie-mold products!

John Venturella (vice president of Human Resources for Memorex Telex): One must be prepared, know the subject, do dry runs, and think about the audience's needs. The most crucial point, though, is to be yourself.

Faye Wattleton (president of Planned Parenthood of America): If there is anything that I want to leave with an audience . . . it is a sense that I have presented myself as honestly as I possibly can; that I am believable. I am not a fabrication of some image. I think the greatest trap that any woman can fall into is to try and form herself in a manner that is inconsistent with her own being. I suppose it takes a degree of comfort with yourself as a person, with who you are.

Peter London: My experience has been when I give myself permission to journey to the edges of the boundaries that I have set for myself, my senses become more acute. I become more perceptive. . . . Eventually I get a little frightened, disoriented, and retreat to safer more familiar domains. But to the extent that I did tarry at my permissible edge, to that same extent I carry back with me a greater appreciation of the actual infinity of the universe in contrast to the rather puny corner I have marked off as my own. And the exhilaration, the hybridization of being, which comes as another consequence of this, is vital stuff for me as an artist of things and of life. (*No More Second Hand Art: Awakening the Artist Within,* Boston: Shambhala Publications, 1989.)

Sandy Linver: I strongly believe that no speaker can be really effective unless he is being himself. (*Speak and Get Results,* New York: Summit, 1983.)

So your task is to *practice being you.* Let your personality come through. Sounds strange, doesn't it? Do not try to be like Joe or Susan. Be yourself. The best presenters let their quirks, personality, and style shine through. Who wants to listen to robots? Be you. The following are some examples:

- Joe has a great sense of humor. For years he was nervous as he gave presentations in which he tried to act serious. People saw him as artificial. He now uses his humor when he talks.

- Sue, the president of a company, spoke with great enthusiasm in company meetings. She moved around, looked animated, and felt connected to the people. At board meetings, however, she thought that she had to be serious and morose. After a few tense board meetings, she gave herself permission to be herself. The board, seeing this, recognized and affirmed her position as president. Everyone enjoyed those meetings after Sue brought her personality into the discussion.

- Bill loved to speak from notes. He did a great job, speaking clearly, enthusiastically, and full of feeling. The organization hired a public relations person who started writing out Bill's talks. His wonderful style deteriorated into a monotone voice with no eye contact with the listeners. After being candidly told about the poor quality of his speeches, he began to have the public relations person make notes for him to use. He wanted no more speeches written out. With clear notes, he was able to go back to being his real, lively self.

All these presenters used their personality traits to enhance themselves as presenters. Take an inventory of yourself and use yourself in your talk. Roger Ailes, Ronald Reagan's media coach, says, "The stakes are high. It's that important for you to accept that you (the whole you) are the message—and that message determines whether or not you'll get what you want out of this life. The secret of presentation training has always been *you are the message*. If you are uncomfortable with who you are, it will make others uncomfortable, too. But, if you can identify and use your good qualities as a person, others will want to be with you and cooperate with you."

Technique and skills are important, but in the end, you must be yourself and give of yourself to the group. Ultimately, the only thing you will ever have to sell is yourself. The best way to sell yourself is to be your natural self. *Being you* takes courage. First it takes courage to discover the unique you, as you unfold day after day, and second, it takes courage to share yourself with others. Do not play it safe. Life is short. Be courageous! Explore your possibilities as a presenter. (*Caution:* If part of you is arrogant and egotistical, do not be that part in front of people. Leave it at home—or better yet—at the garbage dump.)

PERSEVERE—THE THIRD ART

You organize a superb presentation. You are utterly convinced that your approach is correct, yet you do not receive approval for your next steps. Obtain that approval another way. There are many ways to reach your objective. Do not limit yourself. Milton Erickson, a world famous hypnotherapist, relates this story from *My Voice Will Go with You* (New York: Norton, 1982).

Going from Room to Room

I asked a student, "How do you get from this room into that room?"

He answered, "First you stand up. Then you take a step . . ."

I stopped him and said, "Name all the possible ways you can get from this room into that room."

He said, "You can go by running, by walking; you can go by jumping; you can go by hopping; by somersaulting. You can go out that door, go outside the house, come in another door and into the room. Or you could climb out a window if you want to."

I said, "You said you would be inclusive but you made an omission, which is a major omission. I usually illustrate, first, by saying, 'If I want to get into that room from this room, I would go out that door, take a taxi to the airport, buy a ticket to Chicago, New York, London, Rome, Athens, Hong Kong, Honolulu, San Francisco, Chicago, Dallas, Phoenix, come back by limousine and go in the backyard and then through the back gate into the back door and into that room.' And you thought only of forward movement! You didn't think of going in backwards, did you? And you didn't think of crawling in."

The student added, "Or of sliding on my stomach either."

We do limit ourselves so terribly in all of our thinking!

You have read the stories of people curing themselves of illnesses described as incurable by doctors, of people told that they would never walk again, but who did, of people being told their book would not sell, but who instead sold millions of copies, of people whose first presentation was so nerve-racking they threw up before and after, yet who went on to great success as speakers. All these people had the discipline to persevere. They followed their convictions.

Donna McKechnie, who, in 1989, became the lead dancer in *Chorus Line,* was told in 1978 that she would never dance again due to arthritis. With help from many people, she proved that first opinion wrong. She says, "You have to learn that there are no limits as a dancer. You have to learn that you can't have a doctor predict your destiny."

I had studied French for only two years at the University of California before going to spend a year at the French University in Bordeaux. Upon arriving, I took a crash course in French. One of my professors decided that I could not speak well enough and told the program chairman. The chairman called me in and suggested I go home, since it did not sound as if I would be able to take my classes in French. I refused to leave. At the end of the year, I received almost straight *A*'s. Not bad for someone who was told she could not speak French. I had my moments of tears and frustration; I just refused to quit!

If you have a good idea and no "expert" is yet paying attention, remember what some experts said in the past. Edison said, "The talking picture will not supplant the regular silent motion picture." *Business Week,* in 1968, said, "With over 50 foreign cars here, the Japanese auto industry isn't likely to carve out a big slice of the U.S. market for itself." In 1954, Dr. Heuper of the National Cancer Institute said, "If excessive smoking actually plays a role in the production of lung cancer, it seems to be a minor one."

Colonel Sanders went around presenting his idea for a business and was turned down many times before someone heard and accepted his idea. Who would have thought fried chicken would be so popular? So persevere; keep presenting that idea. Do not give up!

You may think you have done your best job, but you can always improve it and modify it. In that process, you will learn what is needed to obtain approval for your next steps. Aldous Huxley said, "There's only one corner of the universe you can be certain of improving, and that's your own self." So when people say no to your recommendation, your budget request, or your creative ideas, go back and think about how to improve your presentation's organization or style so that, next time, they will say yes. Before presenting again, go around and talk to some key individuals. You will learn about their objections, which you must find ways to overcome.

Persevering takes work and discipline. At times you will want to give up. You might get tired of practicing your talk, or you might put your talk on the computer only to have it purged into oblivion. Start over. No one knows what unforeseen circumstances will occur. Be assured that these circumstances will invariably occur, and at that precise moment, you must give yourself encouragement to continue. If you are a visual person, see your success at the end of the road. If you are an auditory person, talk to yourself or someone else about your objective. If you are a kinesthetic person, get up and walk around and do anything to get yourself literally "unstuck." If you quit, you will never reach your objective. Winners never quit, they just start up time and time again. And each time they start, they have a bit more information with which to move toward their objective. Learn from your mistakes and from those situations that did not turn out as you expected.

Sometimes you may feel like quitting, but someone else will still believe in you. They will know you well enough to know that you learn from your mistakes. This story from the book *Leaders The Strategies for Taking Charge* by Warren Bennis and Burt Nanus (New York: Harper & Row, 1985) underscores the value of learning from mistakes:

> Tom Watson, Sr., IBM's founder and its guiding inspiration for over 40 years, met with a promising junior executive of IBM who was involved in a risky venture for the company and managed to lose over $10 million in the gamble. It was a disaster. When Watson called the nervous executive into his office, the young man blurted out, "I guess you want my resignation?" Watson said, "You can't be serious. We've just spent $10 million educating you!"

PERSONALIZE—THE FOURTH ART

Facts, figures, and detailed analysis are important to your listeners; just as important are personal examples. Some people think that logic is enough, but rarely is that true. Consider this observation by Rabindranath Tagore, "A mind all logic is like a knife all blade. It makes the hand bleed that uses it." Personalize your presentation by talking to your group about them and by talking about yourself.

Persevere

You can do whatever you wish to do if you are capable of sustained concentration and take the time necessary to practice what you are learning.

Jack Valenti (President of the Motion Picture Association of America)

There is no failure except in no longer trying.

Elbert Hubbard

Such gardens are not made
By singing "Oh how beautiful!"
And sitting in the shade.

Rudyard Kipling, *The Glory of the Garden*

No steam or gas ever drives anything until it is confined. No Niagara is ever turned into light and power until it is tunneled. No life ever grows until it is focused, dedicated, disciplined.

Harry Emerson Fosdick

We can do anything we want if we stick to it long enough.

Helen Keller

It does not matter how slowly you go, so long as you do not stop.

Confucius

No candlemaker waits for the sacred hour of melting.

Trollope

If you think you can or you can't, you're always right.

Henry Ford I

Talk about Your Group

Think about the last talk you gave. If you had tape-recorded only the first 5 minutes, could someone listen to those 5 minutes and know something about your listeners? Let the audience hear you acknowledge their presence. Say something about them to them.

In transactional analysis, a target stroke is the type of recognition most appreciated by a particular person. The following are some examples to get your mind focusing on people's target strokes:

- Joe is a very visual manager. He is always asking his staff to show him how they plan to accomplish a task. Sam brings in a proposal done in a

flowchart format. Joe loves it. Sam knows that making up a flowchart
format is a target stroke for Joe.

- Susan loves to brainstorm and think up ideas. In a meeting, she suggests
  to the presenter that he consider a new way of approaching the issue.
  Rather than immediately telling Susan that it just will not work, the presenter asks her to say some more. As she talks, he asks her questions, and,
  at the end of 5 minutes, she decides that the idea is not feasible. The presenter's listening to Susan and encouraging her to talk is a target stroke
  for Susan.

- John is a no-nonsense person. He wants all the facts, and he wants them in
  abbreviated form. Martin calls him and says, "Here are the two choices
  we have. I suggest we go with this choice because of these three reasons."
  He states the reasons, then says, "So if you agree, I'll set up a meeting
  with the key people. Is 3:00 P.M. or 4:00 P.M. a better time for you?" He
  gets to the point, thus satisfying John's particular needs.

- Jeff did a lot of work on a project. During Tineke's presentation, she referred to Jeff's work and gave him credit. Jeff enjoys being recognized.

How does a presenter personalize? The answer is simple. You decide what is
important to your target person, and make references to these things during your
talk. Consider the following questions when personalizing your presentation:

1. What modality does the person or the group use most often?

2. What type of recognition does the person or the group appreciate? If the
   person is very introverted, he or she may not appreciate your asking for
   an impromptu presentation during a meeting.

3. How can you use the names of the people, their departments, or their
   cities in your talk? Depending on the situation, you can say, "Since I
   know some of you customers are from New Orleans, I want to let you
   know that there is a very good Cajun restaurant close by that visitors say
   is as close to Louisiana as you can get in California," or "The engineering division really put in some work to get this done," or "Sally and Joe,
   thanks for making my visit to your company so productive. Your sending
   materials ahead of time gave me a chance to tailor my proposal to your
   company's needs."

4. What is the common ground between you and your listeners? Some
   speakers see a river with themselves on one side and the listeners on the
   other. It is their job to get everyone on a bridge that connects the two
   sides. Others want their audience to walk across a bridge and join them.
   Find your own common ground with your listeners. What are the common meeting points? How can you talk about them? Speak about the
   points of agreement, common knowledge, and experiences shared with
   your listeners.

5. What would you be thinking if you were in the other person's shoes? Barbara, an importer of Indonesian clothing and jewelry, started her business by learning how to effectively personalize her dealings with store buyers. This is her strategy. First she visits the store, then she walks around and imagines herself in the shoes of the buyer. She asks herself what she as the buyer would buy if she bought for this particular store. Then she leaves. A few days later, after she has thought about the store and when she feels able to be enthusiastic, she calls the buyer and says, "I have been in your store and notice you have a line of silver jewelry. I have some merchandise that I think would fit in well. When can I stop by?"

6. Are there ways to encourage people to participate authentically? The more people feel that they have created and helped shape a proposal, the more they will be motivated to take part in carrying out those next steps. Do not be tempted to lock yourself away and do all the work by yourself, believing people will be excited to hear what you think they should do. Better to go around and talk to your listeners, hear their ideas, and have them contribute. This will be harder for those of you who have a tendency to be introverted, but you must do it if you want people to feel that they are an important part of the process.

7. What are you forgetting or ignoring to do socially that will make some people think you lack interpersonal skills? According to Carole Hyatt and Linda Gottlieb, in *When Smart People Fail* (New York: Penguin, 1987), the number one reason people fail is due to poor interpersonal skills. They suggest, "Another way to describe interpersonal skills is to call them 'social intelligence.' You can have great academic intelligence and still lack this crucial way of being smart. Social intelligence consists of being sensitive to others, listening to hear the subtext of what is said, giving and taking criticism well, being emotionally steady, and building team support."

Talk about Yourself

When you talk about yourself, you are more likely to put some of you into your talk. People want to know about you. Following are two examples:

> John, a past presentation skills workshop participant, reported this story: "I was asked to present three recommendations to the company outing committee. I narrowed the choices down to three locations. All three met the must criteria, but one picnic site had everything I wanted a company outing to offer. At the end of my talk, after I listed how each site met the musts but only one met all the wants, I almost received a standing ovation from the committee. I am certain that their enthusiasm was due to the fact that I had taken my family to the site of my choice. I shared with the committee several of my family's funny experiences of the day. I then said, 'Your next step

as committee members is to say yes to this location so I can reserve a day for our company. Here are three dates I can reserve. Which one of these meets with your approval?' The committee approved my recommendation in one minute. For days afterwards I felt excited about the talk I had given. My previous success helped me when I gave a brief project overview to my boss. Part of that overview included some comments about my struggle with other departments. I know she felt I had honestly acknowledged all that went into the project."

John injected something of himself and, in one of the examples, his family into his talk. People love this type of personalized presentation. They want you to be real, not to act pompous. It is an interesting and illuminating paradox that the warmer and more vulnerable you are, the more people perceive you as strong and in charge.

Your personalizing adds the spark to the mix. It is the fine-tuning a racecar receives just before and during the race to achieve the driver's objective. Personalizing gives you and your group that added energy. It also makes people comfortable.

FIND YOUR PASSION—THE FIFTH ART

You may have heard Rosabeth Kantor or Tom Peters speak. They speak eloquently and with passion about the need for innovation and excellence in American business. They are enthusiastic about their subject, talk with force, give examples, and walk around the stage with vigor and gusto. They put their hearts into their talk. Their passion comes from believing in what they are saying.

Part of your belief and commitment will be kindled by doing sufficient preparation. Preparation, as an initial step, will get you involved in your subject. It is hard to be genuinely passionate when you do not know the basic facts or when you lack organization.

When you are passionate, you are heading in one direction; there is no incongruity in you. In 1851, at a women's rights convention in Ohio, a black woman full of passion stood up and spoke. Sojourner Truth's short speech was not a technical masterpiece, but nevertheless, it became part of history:

> That man over there says women need to be helped into carriages and lifted over ditches, and to have the best place everywhere. Nobody ever helps me into carriages or over puddles, or gives me the best place—and ain't I a woman?
>
> Look at my arm! I have ploughed and planted and gathered into barns, and no man could head me—and ain't I a woman? I could work as much and eat as much as a man—when I could get it—and bear the lash as well! And ain't I a woman? I have borne thirteen children, and seen most of 'em sold into slavery, and when I cried out with my mother's grief, none but Jesus heard me—and ain't I a woman?
>
> If my cup won't hold but a pint, and yours holds a quart, wouldn't ye be mean not to let me have my little half measure full?"

Passion and Emotion

Computers are useless. They can only give you answers.

Pablo Picasso

Generally, audiences want to laugh, rally behind a cause, listen to stories, enjoy themselves—and feel something.

Roger Ailes (Speech consultant to President Bush)

A person under the influence of his feelings projects the real self, acting naturally and spontaneously. A speaker who is interested will usually be interesting.

Dale Carnegie

A word about being authentic. It means being willing to sacrifice "perfect" delivery for warmth.

Janet Stone and Jane Bachner, *Speaking Up*

Put your heart, mind, intellect, and soul even into your smallest acts. This is the secret of success.

Swami Sivananda

Do every act of your life as if it were your last.

Marcus Aurelius

All the arts we practice are apprenticeship. The big art is our life.

M. C. Richards

Passion comes from trusting yourself enough to use the skills in this book. A passionate speaker can change people's perceptions and instill in them a feeling of wanting to accomplish the next steps.

Passion also comes from training your body to give you the proper cues. Proper posture and voice control are critical. It is impossible to feel or convey passion in a talk that is given in a subdued, monotone voice by a speaker with hunched shoulders and downcast eyes. Standing straight, giving forceful gestures, and speaking out in an animated way are the tools you can use to generate passion in yourself. Try using these tools; they are always at your disposal. You will find that your mind and emotions generally follow the leads that your body gives you.

TAKING THE LEAP!

Until one is committed, there is hesitancy . . . always ineffectiveness. Concerning all acts of initiative and creation there is one elementary truth the ignorance of which kills countless ideas and splendid plans: that the moment one definitely commits oneself then providence moves too. All sorts of things occur to help one that would never otherwise have occurred. Whatever you can do or dream you can begin it; boldness has genius, power and magic in it. Begin it now!

Thomas Mann

You know how you want to be perceived by others. You know the actions you personally need to take. You know how to see and hear your listeners' responses. You have enough ideas of alternate routes to be flexible in achieving your next steps.

Create your next presentation right now. What do you see yourself doing? How do you sound? What do you feel? What are you telling yourself about how you feel? List the people, books, props, and resources you have with which to accomplish your next presentation exactly as you choose. There is nothing standing in your way. Only you can take the final leap to being the full you—the you that you were meant to be. Take that leap. You will discover in yourself an organized, dynamic, and convincing presenter!

REFERENCES

This list includes some of the references used in this book but is by no means an exhaustive list. These references are listed so you can continue to enhance all of your communication skills.

BUSINESS

Decision Making and Problem Solving. For an in-depth program, see the Kepner-Tregoe Program. Call *First Seminar Service,* 800-321-1990 for information.

How to Make the Transition from an Entrepreneurship to a Professionally Managed Firm by Eric Flamholtz (San Francisco: Jossey-Bass, 1986). Excellent book; covers how a company moves from one stage of growth to the next; gives organizational case studies, points out managerial tools needed, and discusses the tasks facing the president of an entrepreneurial organization.

EXERCISE AND POSTURE

The Alexander Technique by Wilfred Barlow (New York: Warner, 1973). Explains the Alexander Technique and then gives you practice exercises that eliminate fatigue and tension and realign your body for energy, control, and relaxation; considers the relationship between your head and neck to be the most important.

Awareness through Movement by Moshe Feldenkrais (New York: Harper & Row, 1972). Exercises, grouped into 12 lessons, consisting of simple, easy, slow movements that improve your posture, vision, imagination, and personal awareness. Author concentrates on the whole body.

POLAROID FILM RECORDERS

To learn about Polaroid's film recorders, call 800-225-1618 in the United States and 800-268-6970 in Canada. When you call, ask for their booklet, "A Guide to Effective Presentations," #780985 PP1319.

FLIP CHARTS

Flipcharts: How to Draw Them and How to Use Them by Richard C. Brandt. Order from Brandt Management, P.O. Box 29384, 8423 Freestone Avenue, Richmond, VA 23229, 804-747-0816. An 82-page resource book on everything you need to know about making and using flip charts.

FORMATS AND TRAINING IN SOME OF THE FORMATS

The New Rational Manager by Charles Kepner and Benjamin Tregoe (Princeton, NJ: Princeton Research Press, 1981). Explains some of the formats in detail.

HEALTH

Healthy Pleasures by Robert Ornstein and David Sobel (Reading, MA: Addison-Wesley, 1989). Provides sound, well-grounded advice on taking care of yourself; a wonderful book encouraging you to be healthy and enjoy life.

Minding the Body, Mending the Mind by Joan Borysenko (New York: Bantam, 1988). Required reading for anyone who presents; based on the author's work at New England Deaconess Hospital.

Deepak Chopra's Books: *Perfect Health, Quantum Physics.*

HUMOR

Current Comedy for Speakers, 700 Orange Street, Wilmington, DE 19801, 302-656-2209. A monthly flyer of current jokes you can use as a speaker, plus books you can order.

The Healing Power of Humor by Allen Klein (Los Angeles: Jeremy Tarcher, 1989). Thought-provoking book on using humor in everyday life.

The Laughter Prescription by Dr. Laurence Peter and Bill Dana (New York: Ballantine, 1982). How to add more humor to your life; funny, excellent anecdotes on everything from health to effective speaking.

Laughter Works. Publishes a newsletter, offers seminars during the year, and has a whole list of humor books and tapes. P.O. Box 1076, Fair Oaks, CA 95628-1078, 916-863-1592.

IMAGE

Your Public Best by Lillian Brown (New York: Newmarket Press, 1989). Creative suggestions for making successful television and public appearances; author was television makeup artist for five U.S. presidents, from John F. Kennedy through Jimmy Carter. Some presenters say Lillian Brown's advice made them look 10 years younger and 10 pounds thinner. Book covers everything from how to deal with a balding head on television to handling stage fright.

LCD PANELS

To learn about Poloroid's LCD panel, call 800-225-1618.

INTERNATIONAL BUSINESS

Worldwide Business Practices Report, International Cultural Enterprises, Inc., 1241 Dartmouth Lane, Deerfield, IL 60015, 800-626-2772. They publish a newsletter dedicated to helping people conduct business abroad. They also sell audio guides on doing business in over 20 countries.

MYERS BRIGGS: INTROVERT AND EXTROVERT

Center for Applications of Psychological Type. For information and a book list; write P.O. 13807, Gainesville, FL 32604.

Please Understand Me by David Keirsey and Marilyn Bates (Del Mar, CA: Prometheus Nemesis, 1984). Excellent overview of the MBTI preferences and people's behaviors in those preferences.

NEGOTIATION

Getting Past No by Urg (New York: Bantam, 1991). A five-step method for negotiating with anyone.

Getting Together by Fisher and Brown (New York: Penguin, 1988). Discusses how to create sustaining relationships when negotiating.

Getting to Yes by Fisher and Urg (New York: Penguin, 1981). Based on studies and negotiation conferences conducted by the Harvard Negotiation Project.

Negotiate to Close by Gary Karrass (St. Louis, MO: Fireside, 1985). Gives all kinds of good ideas on negotiation strategies. Full of clear and useful examples.

Negotiating Style Profile by Rollin and Christine Glasser. A 30-item questionnaire to rate yourself and to have your colleagues rate you on your negotiating style; a profile of five styles; very easy to use. Order from *Organization Design and Development, Inc.,* 101 Bryn Mawr Avenue, Suite 310, Bryn Mawr, PA 19010, 215-525-9505.

Winning When It Really Counts by Arch Lustberg (New York: Simon & Schuster, 1988). Excellent book giving ideas on how to think on your feet, project warmth when talking, and negotiate; full of lively examples.

You Can Negotiate Anything by Herb Cohen (New York: Bantam, 1980). Gives practical advice on negotiating with lots of examples. Fun and educational to read. Over nine months on the New York Bestseller List.

PRESENTATION PRODUCTS

Creative Training Techniques, 800-383-9210. Call to get their catalog. They have some fun presentation gadgets, plus an excellent Train-the-Trainer seminar, audiotape series, and newsletter.

Paper Direct, Inc., 800-272-7377. They sell gorgeous presentation folders and jackets, presentation display holders, portable presentation flip charts, and so on.

USI, 800-243-4565. They sell overhead projectors, laminating machines, and other presentation products.

NEUROLINGUISTIC PROGRAMMING (NLP): VISUAL, AUDITORY, AND KINESTHETIC

Instant Rapport by Michael Brooks (New York: Warner, 1989). Clear concise book on the use of NLP for establishing rapport with others.

Unlimited Power by Anthony Robbins (New York: Ballantine, 1986). Gives the reader ways to harness power; excellent book; points out ways to establish rapport with others. Much of the framework comes from Neurolinguistic Programming. Do yourself a favor and practice what he suggests.

PRESENTATION BOOKS

Get to the Point by Karen Berg and Andrew Gilman (New York: Bantam, 1989). Provides some practical, time-saving methods and gives interesting case studies.

How to Create High Impact Business Presentations by Joyce Kupsh and Pat Graves (Chicago, IL: NTC Publishing, 1992). Covers design of visuals, use diagrams and graphics, and color presentations.

How to Talk So People Listen by Sonya Hamlin (New York: Harper & Row, 1988). Points out the absolute necessity of realizing that you are only talking so others will listen.

Making Successful Presentations by Terry Smith (New York: John Wiley & Sons, 1984). Clear overview with many good ideas; chapter on visuals gives some excellent information.

Mastering the Business and Technical Presentation by Leonard Meuse, Jr. (Boston: CBI Publishing, 1980). Well done, clear and concise.

Never Be Nervous Again by Dorothy Sarnoff with Gaylen Moore (New York: Ivy, 1987). Filled with helpful anecdotes, quotes, and step-by-step advice.

The Persuasive Edge by Myles Martel (New York: Fawcett Columbine, 1984). Covers everything you would want to know about presenting; excellent chapters on dealing with the media and special situations; gives advice on typing an outline or a manuscript.

Presentations Plus by David Peoples (New York: John Wiley & Sons, 1988). Gives you great motivation to use visuals; good ideas about adding spice to your talks; has a section on 60 tips for 60 minutes.

Secrets of Successful Speakers by Lilly Walters (New York: McGraw-Hill, 1993). For people who are going to give motivational speeches. She quotes a lot of celebrity speakers.

Speak and Get Results by Sandy Linver (New York: Summit, 1983). First-rate overview of how to give a speech or do a presentation in any business situation.

Speak Up with Confidence by Jack Valenti (New York: Morrow, 1982). Concentrates on speech making; filled with wonderful, illustrative anecdotes by an exquisite presenter; provides hints on giving a written speech.

Speaking Up by Janet Stone and Jane Bachner (New York: McGraw, 1977). An excellent book focusing on women's particular issues and concerns when presenting; also gives a general overview of presenting.

You Are the Message by Roger Ailes (Homewood, IL: Dow Jones-Irwin, 1988). Discusses a crucial topic most presenters do not pay enough attention to. You, the presenter, are the message and that is what you need to concentrate on. Provides hints on giving a written speech.

You've Got to Be Believed to Be Heard by Bert Decker, with Jim Denney (New York: St. Martin's Press, 1992). Focuses on emotion versus fact: "People buy on emotion and justify with fact."

PROGRAM AND SEMINAR INFORMATION

First Seminar Service. Serves American organizations by helping their employees locate and identify the best available programs. For information, call 800-321-1990. Your company may already have an agreement with them. They operate like a travel agency for the seminar industry.

SELLING

Samurai Selling by Chuck Laughlin and Karen Sage with Marc Bockmon (New York: St. Martin's Press, 1993). Many great ideas on creative selling presentations.

Selling to a Group by Paul LeRoux (New York: Harper & Row, 1984). Section on why you should use pictorial visuals is very convincing; motivates you to become more creative; excellent resource for people who make many sales presentations.

SPEAKING CLUBS

Toastmasters International, P.O. Box 104001, Santa Ana, CA 92711, 714-542-6793. World's oldest and largest nonprofit educational organization. It has over 5,600 clubs teaching people how to present effectively. It also has a list of books you can buy.

VIDEOTAPES

Persuasive Presentations Guaranteed! by Wilder Management Services. Call 617-524-7172 to receive a flyer on the video.

VISUALS

To order free 3M sample flip frames, write: 3M Visual Systems Division, 3M Austin Center, Building A145-5N-01, Austin, TX 78769-2963.

VOICE EXERCISES

Professionally Speaking by Lilyan Wilder (New York: Simon & Schuster, 1986). Over 80 pages on working with your voice.

Voice Power by Joan Kenley, PhD (New York: Henry, 1988). A clear, entertaining book on improving your voice. Includes questionnaires and body voice exercises.

INDEX

PRESENTATION PRODUCTS

OVERTURE: A computer presentation software program. Now you can have the ten formats on line. Use the formats to organize and create your presentations. You can use this program in all the major presentation packages as well as the MAC. It also covers the ten presentation steps.

PERSUASIVE PRESENTATIONS GUARANTEED! A video. This 40 minute video entertains as well as teaches how to give results-oriented presentations.

THE PRESENTATIONS KIT TRAINER'S PACKAGE: This is the package so a trainer can teach the steps and formats. It includes colored overheads, trainer notes, and an audiotape covering what to say during the seminar.

AUDIOTAPE: This tape covers the ten steps in the book.

THE TEN STEPS PLANNER CARD: This laminated card summarizes the ten steps and ten formats from the book.

PRESENTATION SEMINARS

We have consultants in the United States and Asia who teach The Presentations Kit Seminar.

For information on these products and services phone or fax: 617-524-7172
Wilder Management Services
57A Robinwood Avenue
Boston, MA 02130-2157